NEMESIS

ONE MAN AND
THE BATTLE FOR RIO

MISHA GLENNY

THE BODLEY HEAD
LONDON

1 3 5 7 9 10 8 6 4 2

The Bodley Head, an imprint of Vintage,
20 Vauxhall Bridge Road,
London SW1V 2SA

The Bodley Head is part of the Penguin Random House
group of companies whose addresses can be found at
global.penguinrandomhouse.com.

Copyright © Misha Glenny 2015

Maps by Bill Donohoe

First published by The Bodley Head in 2015

www.vintage-books.co.uk

A CIP catalogue record for this book is available from the British Library

ISBN 9781847922663 (Hardback)
ISBN 9781847922670 (Trade Paperback)

Typeset by Palimpsest Book Production Limited,
Falkirk, Stirlingshire
Printed and bound by Clays Ltd, St Ives plc

Penguin Random House is committed to a sustainable future for
our business, our readers and our planet. This book is made from
Forest Stewardship Council® certified paper.

In Memoriam

Sasha Glenny
1992–2014

Brazil, this beautiful country, has the world's ugliest record. We are the number one champion in homicidal violence. One in every ten people killed around the world is a Brazilian. This translates into over 56,000 people dying violently each year. Most of them are young black boys, dying by guns. Brazil is also one of the world's largest consumers of drugs and the War on Drugs has been especially painful here. Around 50% of the homicides on the streets of Brazil are related to the War on Drugs.

Ilona Szabó de Carvalho, Igarapé Institute, TED Talk, October 2014, Rio de Janeiro

CONTENTS

III NEMESIS

IV CATHARSIS

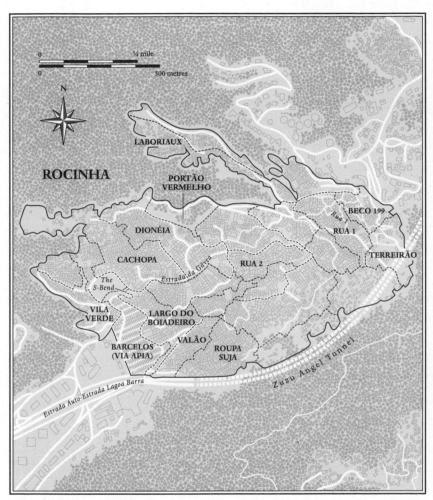

Rocinha

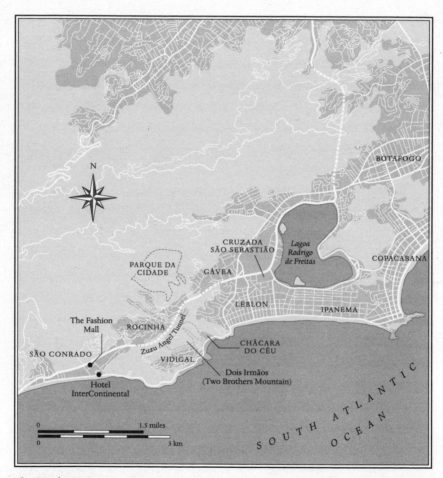

The South Zone

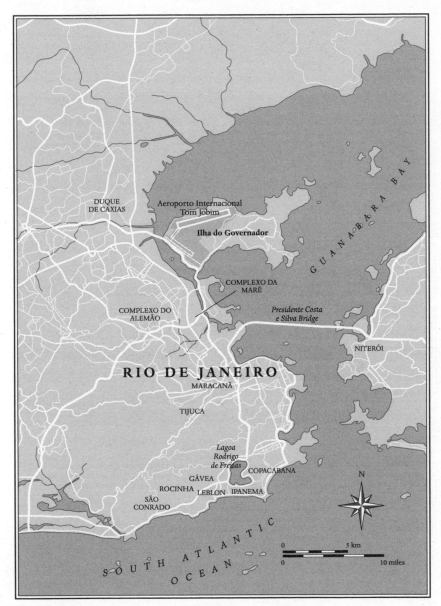

Rio de Janeiro

Brazil

PREFACE

Landing in Campo Grande for the first time was a strange experience. The capital of Mato Grosso do Sul is located some 250 miles east of the point where Brazil, Paraguay and Bolivia meet. It is also roughly the same distance south of the Pantanal, the world's largest tropical wetland. My first impression was that it barely felt like Brazil at all.

Only just over a century old, Campo Grande was built on a grid system, its wide boulevards and cross streets lined by plentiful trees. I was struck by the number of shops with large long windows. Butchers displayed literally dozens of lean cattle carcasses. A John Deere store boasted row upon row of tractors. It felt more like rural Texas in the 1960s than sensual Rio de Janeiro or industrious São Paulo.

At the starkly defined limits of the city, spacious buildings suddenly gave way to soil so vermilion it looked as though the ground had been painted. The contrast with the deep green of the vegetation turned the entire area into a cartoon landscape.

Just at the point where everything became red and green, I took an unsigned turn off the ring road. I had to dodge some oil barrels placed on a dirt track before reaching a wire-mesh gate. From here, most of the maximum security federal penitentiary was visible. I was immediately struck by the crisp and modern design of its walls and watchtowers. The buildings were finished in gentle pastel red and yellow.

After the first gate opened automatically, I had to negotiate one final obstacle – tank traps. Brazil has a rich tradition of prison breakouts, and Campo Grande was taking no chances. One of four special facilities dotted around this enormous country, the jail was built for those criminals deemed the most dangerous. Campo Grande does not resemble Brazil's more famous cities, and this jail is unlike most of its prisons.

Firstly, the prison guards were unfailingly friendly and polite. Some spoke quite good English, an uncommon skill in Brazil's interior. Within the constraints of their job, they all went out of their way to assist me.

There was no evidence of the squalor, overcrowding and latent violence associated with much of the prison system. The Campo Grande facility has an air of order and predictability. It is not an easy regime for the inmates, but there are no reports of human rights abuses and no complaints about arbitrary violence. Not a single prisoner in the four facilities has ever been the subject of a murderous attack by his fellow detainees, nor has there ever been a successful breakout. In most other Brazilian prisons these hazards are commonplace.

The notoriety of the prisoners is the chief reason for the jail's unusually efficient administration. In the past, the great bank robbers and drug cartel leaders would happily continue their work after incarceration from inside prison. In the provincial and municipal facilities it is standard practice to bribe the poorly remunerated guards to turn a blind eye to smuggled cell phones, to drugs, to video game consoles and televisions, or to women brought in for sex.

In Campo Grande, the only way the inmates can get messages to the outside world apart from letters, which are strictly monitored, is through their lawyers or those members of their family who have permission to visit. This represents a challenge even for the best-organised criminals.

After placing my personal effects in a locker, I was taken through a series of security screenings and biometric checks. I was allowed to keep my watch, my glasses and, by special permission of the courts, a digital voice recorder, but absolutely nothing else. These were checked and checked again before two federal officers led me into a rectangular room about 10 feet by 20.

To the left was a desk with a computer and a video camera on it. The wall to the right was covered by a backdrop with the words Federal Department of Prisons writ large. The room was used by prisoners appearing via video link to wherever their trial was being held – Rio de Janeiro, São Paulo, Manaus or Recife.

Opposite me sat the man I had come to visit – Antônio Francisco Bonfim Lopes. Until his arrest in November 2011, he had been the most wanted man in Rio de Janeiro, if not in all Brazil. The country knew him not by his birth name, but by his nickname, Nem, or, in its entire Brazilian Portuguese version, O Nem da Rocinha – Nem of Rocinha.

I had originally heard of Nem in 2007, when I took one of several tours offered of Rocinha, the largest slum in Brazil, possibly in all of South America. There are almost a thousand of these settlements dotted around Rio, but Rocinha is unique, as it lies slap bang in the middle of Rio's richest three districts. When I went there for the first time, it was already a popular tourist destination. You could travel in a people carrier up the main road, Estrada da Gávea, and stop off to look at the brightly coloured cramped boxes in which some of the 100,000 inhabitants live. A quick tour around an after-hours playgroup organised by a local NGO was followed by the purchase of a naïf painting to give something back to the slum's desperate economy.

One of my guides explained at the time that the man who ran Rocinha was called Nem. He told me in all sincerity that Nem, the head of the local drugs cartel, 'is the man who keeps the peace here in Rocinha'.

I was reminded of Nem four years later when he was arrested just after midnight a couple of miles from Rocinha. The circumstances were dramatic. I started to dig a little, and was surprised to find that before his arrest, he had given a few interviews to Brazilian journalists. The media had often portrayed him as a ruthless killer who had poisoned the lives of numerous young people by peddling drugs. The interviews hinted at a rather different story. Nem's answers were thoughtful, and suggested that he well understood the political and social significance of the role he played as the effective president, prime minister and most powerful businessman of a medium-sized city.

So in the Brazilian winter of 2012, I wrote to him in prison, introducing myself and requesting that he receive me. Now, eight months later, I was in Campo Grande: in front of me was Nem, Public Enemy No. 1. Of course, prison rules forbade me from engaging in any physical contact with him; even from shaking his hand. In the circumstances, our initial greetings were rather stiff.

He was wearing the penitentiary's regulation blue T-shirt and cotton trousers. When he stood to be led out of the room, I could see that he was tall and thin, maybe six foot two. He was brown-skinned, with a distinctive narrow face and a slight overbite. His hair was cut short, so the curls that were so familiar from the two most common images circulating around the Internet were not in evidence. Most arresting of all were his jet-black eyes, so dark that the irises and pupils appeared to merge. It was immediately obvious that these eyes were the primary source of his physical charisma: they could look into your soul but gave nothing back.

He always addressed me with the respectful *o senhor*, sir. Being sketchily acquainted at the start with the nuances of Portuguese, I would simply call him Antônio.

At one point during our meeting, I dropped my pen. Picking it up, I saw that his legs were shackled to the steel table that was itself bolted to the floor. He also refused a shot of coffee or glass of water, as he would have had to raise his hands above the table, revealing his handcuffs (in later meetings these were removed). He appeared to feel humiliated by his situation.

He was, however, perfectly willing to discuss his life, both personal and professional. Then, as now, he was on remand, so there were certain subjects on which he could not comment because they related to criminal proceedings still in progress.

Over the next two years, I would visit him ten times. On the first two occasions the meeting lasted for two hours and the others for three. Interviewing a prisoner inside a jail is always bizarre. But these encounters were especially odd. I developed an intense relationship with Antônio – always in the most abnormal circumstances, and perhaps partly because of them. Gradually we began to speak of profound and intimate matters, some of which he might not even have discussed with his family. We spoke about drugs, about violence, about leadership, about faith, about family and about survival in a hostile world.

What follows is Nem's story. Although his testimony is central to this account, I have not, of course, relied on his version alone. I spoke to his family, his friends, his enemies, the police who investigated him, the politicians who negotiated with him, the journalists who wrote about him and the lawyers who represented him. It is, I believe, a story that reflects much about the nature of contemporary Brazil – its positive and negative sides. But it also tells us about how men and women survive, and even prosper, in the most adverse conditions. How they negotiate the thin line separating life from death.

PROLOGUE
THE ARREST I
9–10 November 2011

From beneath the thick foliage of Rio's Atlantic forest, a large dark Toyota Corolla snaked slowly up the hill. The sleek luxury car was surely a government or corporate vehicle. This was a rare sight in the slum of Rocinha. Ageing vehicles ready to die – yes. Swarms of motorbike taxis – yes. Galumphing buses, which, defying the laws of physics, swung their backsides around hairpin bends – yes. But menacingly flash executive cars with low-slung bodies and fat tyres? They didn't belong. In Rocinha, a thousand eyes silently scrutinise the unfamiliar as a matter of course.

The car soon reached the high point of Estrada da Gávea, the road bisecting Rocinha from top to bottom. From here, the occupants could see the twinkling lights of the slum as they stretched down towards the Atlantic Ocean. It was night, and the three men could easily distinguish between the Hills, as the slums of Rio are known, and the Asphalt, shorthand for the middle-class residential zones. The slums are always less brightly illuminated. The dense mix of illegal and legal cabling that supplies power to these informal settlements delivers a lower voltage than the more ordered network serving the Asphalt.

After crossing the peak of the hill, the black car tilted down past Nine Nine, the last bus stop in the slum, just where the road twists sharply to the left. It was about 10.35 on the evening of 9 November 2011.

The three besuited men in the car drove slowly through the darkness. They were silent and apprehensive. The Driver was older than his passengers, perhaps in his late fifties. Next to him, another portly gentleman was repeatedly trying to get through to someone on the phone. In vain: there is rarely a signal at the top of Rocinha, and his provider had no coverage at this spot. A leather holdall lay on the back seat next to the third man, who was similarly stout. Like his two companions, he was a lawyer by profession.

After the tight corner, they travelled a further two hundred metres towards the brief stretch of no-man's-land that separates Rocinha from the elegant villas of Gávea, one of Rio's most expensive neighbourhoods. This point is marked by another hairpin bend, though this one turns to the right, just at the entrance to the American School in Rio de Janeiro. It is impossible to see, even during the day, but there is also a left turn on to a long, unlit road. At night, the trees and shrubs lining it add to the sinister atmosphere.

As the car approached this wealth barrier, a large man stepped out from the concealed road brandishing a semi-automatic weapon and waved it down. He was wearing the uniform of the Batalhão do Choque (combat battalion), the crowd control unit of the Military Police (PM).* Despite its name, the PM is in fact responsible for civilian policing in Rio.

The three men, pumped full of adrenalin, got out of the Toyota. Their body language was tense and there followed a sharp exchange with the officer. He demanded to search the boot of the car. The lawyers were very anxious that he should not.

At this point, two more senior PM officers rolled up. One, a Lieutenant, was clearly in charge. The Lawyer with the Bag showed

* See Appendix: Main Police Forces in Rio de Janeiro.

some personal documents: a passport and an official-looking ID. Although a Brazilian, he explained, he was also the honorary consul of the Democratic Republic of Congo, and since he was on official business, his car enjoyed diplomatic immunity and could not be searched.

Suddenly, the Man with the Phone realised he had at last got a signal and began dialling the same person he had been trying to get through to for the past three quarters of an hour. It was exactly 11.06 p.m.

At home in the neighbourhood of Tijuca, just beyond Rio's famous Maracanã football stadium, an inspector from a second police force, the Civil Police (PC), was reading his infant daughter a story when the phone rang. It made him jump. He had been expecting a call all evening and had begun to give up hope. The man on the other end was speaking quickly and incoherently. Even if his acquaintance down the line was not making complete sense, the Inspector knew there was no time to lose.

The Inspector rang his superior immediately. Within minutes he received the go-ahead to intervene in the unfolding events. The green light had come from the very top, from none other than the Secretary for Public Security, the boss of all police, not just in the city, but in the wider state of Rio de Janeiro. That such a senior figure had signed off on it indicated that something big was happening. All the more so given that the Secretary was not in Rio but in Berlin, where it was 2.15 in the morning. The Inspector kissed his daughter good night, grabbed his keys and ran for the car, talking on the phone all the time.

Back at the hairpin bend, the Lawyer with the Phone had walked off with the Lieutenant for a private word. During their intemperate exchange, he offered his phone to the policeman. The officer declined it angrily. Instead, he walked away and made his own phone call. He was now determined to bring in a third law enforcement agency: the powerful Federal Police (PF).

The Military Police officers were growing visibly frustrated until one of the Lieutenant's men walked over to his boss and whispered something in his ear. More discussions led to the three lawyers getting back into the car. It was agreed that everyone would go to the police station. The lawyers seemed happy to comply.

The convoy set off. A Military Police vehicle in front. In the middle, the Toyota with its three lawyers. Behind them two more vehicles with cops, including the Lieutenant. Altogether, eleven policemen were now accompanying the men, while several miles away, in the centre of Rio, the commander of the PF was busy mobilising a team of officers to intercept the convoy.

Suddenly the Toyota sandwiched between the police cars tried to break free, attempting an unexpected right turn. One quick-thinking police driver swerved and successfully blocked its progress. There was a pause as everyone stepped on to the street again. This time, the Driver of the Toyota took the Lieutenant aside for a private conversation.

The Lawyer with the Phone was barking into his mobile more aggressively than ever. He knew that if things went wrong, the consequences could be fatal.

Not too far away, the Civil Police's special forces unit, CORE, had been issued an order to mobilise. Weapons were taken out of lockers and the tarpaulin was removed from one of the unit's armoured vehicles. Elsewhere, two pilots from the Civil Police's helicopter division were also being scrambled.

Following the altercation on the street, the lawyers and the police set off once more in convoy. Before long the lawyers pulled off the main road again, this time into the car park of the old Naval Club, which abuts Lagoa, the big lagoon at the heart of Rio's South Zone. The vehicles stopped under the mighty statue of Christ the Redeemer, towering above them at the summit of Corcovado mountain.

For a third time, the lawyers and the Military Police officers embarked on an aggressive exchange. But just as it was all kicking off again, several cars screeched to a halt and a senior officer of the Civil Police jumped out of one of them to begin remonstrating with his PM colleagues. Soon after this, the Inspector from Tijuca arrived. At one point, the Driver threw his car keys to one of the PC cops and there was a scramble to ensure the Military Police officers didn't get their hands on them.

Next to arrive were the feds' squad cars, with their slick grey livery. A captain emerged to tell everyone that the PF were taking charge of the case. The senior PC officer advised him to get lost.

The three lawyers and the PC were insisting that the Toyota be removed to the 15th Precinct station, a mere five minutes' drive away. The Military Police and the feds were adamant that because the consul had claimed diplomatic immunity, the case now came under federal jurisdiction.

As the shouting and recriminations ratcheted up, one eyewitness insists that officers from the PC and the PM levelled their weapons at each other. Either way, under cover of this confusion, the Lieutenant crouched behind the rear of the Toyota and stuck a knife in the tyre to prevent the car from being removed to the 15th Precinct.

The heavily armed CORE then pitched up and simply parked its large vehicle in front of the Military Police cars to ensure they were going nowhere. At this point, the robotic thwack of blades came ever closer as the PC helicopter homed in on the scene, filming everything.

That footage would undoubtedly assist two onlookers: officers from the Secretary of State for Security's intelligence directorate, who would have a sobering story to tell their boss about how his new strategy for improving inter-agency cooperation was encountering some teething problems.

All this was taking place just a few minutes' walk from the

offices of Brazil's largest news corporation, Globo. Before long, TV cameras, flashing bulbs, microphones and shouting journalists joined the throng. It was a volatile cocktail of competing interests, chaos and weapons.

Now the Inspector felt he had to stop matters from getting further out of hand. He would have to talk it all through with his counterparts from the feds. For what the Inspector knew that the others didn't was that there was a fourth man hidden in the back of the Corolla.

After discussions with the senior federal officer, it is agreed that the Consul should open the car boot. He is surrounded by police officers from the various forces, most of them pointing a weapon at the car.

The boot opens to reveal a lanky man curled sideways with his knees drawn up to his chest, wearing a blue and white striped shirt and black trousers. He is hauled out of the car by his hands and feet.

As he emerges, the man is visibly disoriented by the crowds, the lights and the general mayhem. Journalists and police officers battle with one another to snap the best photographs of him. Lights flash in front of his eyes. One officer grabs the man's thick curly hair, yanking his head backwards to facilitate the digital gawping. Having spent the last two hours holed up in the boot, he is suddenly exposed to full-tilt hysteria, Brazilian style. He is surrounded by a great variety of uniforms, and shouts of 'He's my arrest!' 'No, he's ours! Get your hands off him!' He seems resigned – his face shows little emotion, like a tired rag doll being battered this way and that. He is probably experiencing a form of mild shock. But most of all, amid this frenetic activity, he looks very alone.

The Lieutenant triumphantly places handcuffs on him and, together with the chief federal officer, manhandles him into the back of the light blue Military Police vehicle that first encountered the Toyota Corolla at the entrance to the community of Rocinha. They then drive their prisoner off to the headquarters of the Federal Police.

The clock has just struck midnight when the captive, Antônio Francisco Bonfim Lopes, known to all Brazilians as Nem of Rocinha, is officially placed under arrest. Schedules are tossed aside and picture editors set about compiling the dramatic footage of the evening's events ready for the morning news shows.

The most wanted man in Rio, indeed the most wanted man in all Brazil, is finally under lock and key. It is a moment of triumph for José Mariano Beltrame, the Secretary for Public Security for the state of Rio de Janeiro. He can finally boast without fear of contradiction that his radical policy of pacifying Rio's lawless slums is working. His forces are clearing the city's favelas of drugs and guns and restoring the authority of the Brazilian state. The country can look forward, with even greater enthusiasm than hitherto, to the prospect of a safe football World Cup and Olympic Games.

At the time of his arrest, Nem is involved in a web of corruption, violence, drugs and political intrigue that has suffocated Rio de Janeiro – or as Brazilians like to call it, the Marvellous City – for almost a quarter of a century. He knows this sprawling web well. It implicates politicians, drug traffickers, lawyers, evangelical pastors and the police. One question remains, however. Is Nem the spider or the fly?

Part I
PROTAGONIST

1

EDUARDA
December 1999–June 2000

Vanessa dos Santos Benevides does not sleep. Her baby cries with an unprecedented vehemence.

Is it the weather? Late spring in Rio de Janeiro is hot and sticky, heralding the arrival of the Flying River. This determined pilgrimage of clouds, packed with precipitation, first gathers 2,000 miles north of Rio when incalculable tons of water rise from the Amazon river and its forests to travel south. Hemmed in to the west by the Andes, the Flying River swings round eastwards in a grand curve, to bear down on Brazil's central and southern interior and coastal lands.

In Rio, it unleashes a deluge that in seconds reduces visibility to two, maybe three yards. Every year these rains bring destruction and death in the form of floods and landslides. Newspapers and television programmes report terrible tales of families drowned under vast quantities of mud and rock: some in their cars, some in their homes, some in buses washed into ravines. The most vulnerable *cariocas*, as the people of Rio are known, live in the city's slums – the favelas.

The storms wreak the worst havoc on these communities. The favelas often sprang up on Rio's many hills and mountains. A landslide on this terrain can bury dozens of people within seconds. Primitive drainage systems, open sewers, hillocks of rotting garbage and flimsy construction techniques succumb quickly to the pressure of this immense volume of water. Ceilings crack, then crumble. Dense thickets of exposed electrical wiring short-circuit and flash briefly into flames before being extinguished by the flood. Paving stones and steps are loosened and washed downhill in the torrent.

When the clouds disperse, the moisture remains heavy in the air. The humidity levels are often barely tolerable. On the hills at night, the lack of air conditioning makes sleep difficult in a jungle of noise: screeching monkeys and yapping dogs; the deep bass vibrations from all-night funk parties; the occasional rat-a-tat of semi-automatic weapons; agitated men and women locked in vocal combat, perhaps drunk, perhaps just sick of each other.

It is on a night like this that Vanessa, the young mother, cannot sleep. Fatigue drains the exquisite light brown skin of her normally serene face. It is shortly before Christmas 1999. Her baby, Eduarda, looks smaller than her nine and a half months, and her wailing is incessant. Vanessa picks her up to comfort her and notices she is sweating more profusely than usual in this heat. The baby's neck is rigid, bent inflexibly at an angle so that her head is resting on her left shoulder. In the morning, Vanessa tells her husband, Antônio, that she is taking the child to the doctor.

The local health worker agrees with Vanessa that the baby probably slept in an awkward position, hence the badly cricked neck. She decides to fit her with a brace.

A week later, the neck is still completely stiff and the child screams with the pain. Eduarda's mother now takes her to the emergency room at one of the local hospitals.

Antônio leaves for work, agitated by an incipient sense of guilt. He fears that he might have something to do with his daughter's agonising condition. His office, like the hospital, is in Gávea, one of the three exceptionally wealthy districts surrounding Rocinha, where he was born and raised.

In the last few years, Antônio has worked his way up the company, Globus Express, to become a team leader in charge of the distribution of *Revista da NET*, the main TV listings magazine. He has responsibility for much of the South Zone, the area that includes most of Rio's famous landmarks, such as the giant sculpture of Jesus on Mount Corcovado and the beaches of Copacabana and Ipanema.

On his modest salary, Antônio and Vanessa have scraped together enough to move out of his mother's tiny apartment into a tiny apartment of their own. It isn't much, but it's a start, and the arrival of Eduarda – Duda – a happy, easy baby, has spread warmth around the little home. Both parents have been feeling blessed and are eyeing the future with hope.

But now the child stays for a month in the hospital and her condition worsens by the day. The doctors prescribe various remedies, none of which work. They suggest she may be suffering from tubercular osteomyelitis, a rare secondary condition when bacteria infect the bones of a TB sufferer. A lump appears on the right side of her neck and grows to the size of an egg.

Antônio wilts when he hears the news. He assumes, incorrectly but not unreasonably, that he has passed on TB to his daughter, as the disease is endemic in Rio's poorer districts. Signs posted prominently at the entrance to Rocinha read: *Coughing for three weeks or more? GO TO THE DOCTOR. You probably have TB.*

The airborne infection spreads quickest in densely populated areas, especially in slums, where family members and friends live tightly crammed together. Rocinha has the highest incidence of tuberculosis in all Rio state, and in some years the highest incidence in Brazil. At this time, some 55 Rocinhans contract the illness every month.

Only days before Duda's birth, Antônio's throat was getting sore. It worsened as he kept working in the alternating sun and rain. Nor did he eat properly. He preferred to save his luncheon vouchers, a second currency in the favela, to ensure that his mother and his pregnant wife were properly nourished. Despite a fever and a headache so intense it triggered hallucinations, he went on working until the day he collapsed – which was when he was diagnosed with TB.

His daughter was born while he was in hospital. He was forbidden to go near her for two weeks, and then was told he could not spend nights at home for fear of infecting her.

Now that Duda is ill, Antônio is convinced that she has caught the disease from him, despite having been told several months earlier that he was free of infection.

Duda starts a course of antibiotics, but her condition continues to worsen. She has lost her appetite, thereby further undermining her ability to beat whatever she is suffering from. For the first time, her parents realise that their little girl may be dying.

In despair, Vanessa plays her last card. Thanks to Antônio's modest health plan, sponsored by his employer, he is permitted to choose a GP from a supplied list. At random she picks out a name, an act she later ascribes to guidance from God.

Clutching her child, she follows the steep, winding descent of Rocinha's main thoroughfare, Estrada da Gávea. Below, the Atlantic Ocean meets the beach at fashionable São Conrado. Behind her, the drunken rows of houses painted in bright colours rise out of the mountainside's vivid green vegetation to form the distinctive panorama of the favela.

At the bottom of the hill, the road intersects with the highway leading west out of Rio. Every morning, tens of thousands of people pile on to buses here to go to work in the wealthy parts of town as maids, drivers, cleaners, gardeners, shop assistants, handymen and bartenders. Vanessa steps on to a bus choked with people. Most of their faces wear a look of numb resignation. The vehicle pulls away, bumping and crashing, and the baby's face contorts as her swollen neck is jolted up and down and from side to side. The experience is so obviously excruciating for the little girl that after the visit to the doctor, they can no longer bear to travel by bus and must instead spend considerable chunks of their dwindling funds on taxis.

The doctor's surgery is in Barra de Tijuca, a residential area often compared to Miami in style and size since its rapid growth during the 1980s and 90s. Ten minutes' drive through two long tunnels but a world away from the favela, Barra is home to broad boulevards lined with dozens of elegant villas and American-style mansion blocks in gated communities. These are occasionally punctuated by shopping malls framed with gaudy neon signs and oversized billboards. The dramatic rise in urban violence around Rio during the two decades of Barra's expansion explains the middle-class flight to this area. The mountains and lagoons that largely separate it from the rest of the city perhaps foster a greater sense of security.

Barra has an anodyne, artificial feel about it, but the services are good. The doctor examines Eduarda and says that she too suspects this may be TB. Fever, along with lumps and bumps, like Duda's little neck egg, can be signs of the disease. However, as the treatment is not working, she refers the child to the Instituto Fernando Figueira, Rio's specialist medical centre for children, adolescents and women.

Here the doctors surprise Antônio and Vanessa by informing them that their daughter does not have TB. 'We want to take a biopsy,' one of them says. The next sentence shocks both parents into tears: 'We think she may have cancer.'

Their routine changes. Vanessa stays by the child's bedside day and night. Antônio fashions his working hours so that he can relieve his wife as much as possible – both are getting tired. Duda will have to be put under general anaesthetic for the biopsy, which adds to the anxiety. Three days later, they take a tissue sample from the lump in her neck.

The results come through. The tests are negative: there is no sign of cancer.

With the new millennium, there is a new question: if not cancer, then what? The baby is still suffering great pain. Underneath her skin, lesions are growing on her skull and her spine.

More tests.

This time she attends the specialist children's unit at Lagoa hospital, situated by the great lagoon that acts as the hub of the South Zone. As Vanessa walks in with the baby, Dr Soraia Rouxinol and Dr Maria Celia Guerra take a quick look at the child. Once out of earshot, Dr Guerra nods to her colleague. 'Histiocytosis X.'

This is an impressive and, as it turns out, correct diagnosis. Impressive because histiocytosis X – or to give it its official name, Langerhans cell histiocytosis (LCH) – is most uncommon.

Doctors face two problems in diagnosing LCH. It is rare, affecting roughly one in 200,000 people. Some of the staff at Lagoa even believe that Eduarda might be the first recorded case in Brazil. In addition, absolute certainty with the diagnosis is virtually impossible: it is greatly complicated by the huge variation in how the illness manifests itself from patient to patient.

While not strictly cancer, LCH mimics certain processes associated with that disease – in particular the cloning of aberrant cells, which then come under relentless attack from the body's own immune system. Antônio describes it as having the effect of making Eduarda's bones crumble.

Only in the last few years have researchers been able to home in on the probable genetic cause of the condition. At the beginning of 2000, there is no such understanding, and specialist material on the subject is sparse.

As with TB, this disease is more dangerous for those under two than it is for older children. The powerful drugs used to combat it cure between 80 and 90 per cent of sufferers. If left untreated, it is fatal in some but not all cases. In others, it disappears as unpredictably as it comes.

Still weak, Eduarda is nonetheless prescribed a punishing course of chemotherapy and surgery. However, for the first time, her parents feel some relief; it seems to them that they can glimpse a path out of the nightmare they are living.

Vanessa has already been forced to stop working, and the reduction in household income leads to rent arrears. They have no choice but to return to the flat where Antônio's mother still lives with his half-brother, Carlos.

It is a typical slum dwelling. Space is perhaps the most valuable commodity in the favela. For many inhabitants, natural light in a home is regarded as a luxury. There is none in theirs. Even in a close-knit family, the absence of privacy means that disputes can break out at any time.

To reach the front door, you walk in single file down a long, narrow alley, which is quickly enveloped in darkness. During the rainy season, this is dank and smelly. The front door leads on to a tiny vestibule for shoes and then the communal room, measuring about 49 square feet. As children, Antônio and Carlos would sleep here. Along with a few mementoes, there are wooden devotional pictures of St George. These mix Christian iconography with that of African animist religions, Candomblé and Umbanda. The centre of all social activity is the small table in the middle of the room in front of a love seat and two stools. The walls are painted in peeling yellow and there are cracks visible in most corners.

The bathroom, when it is working, can squeeze in one person uncomfortably. Right now, it is not working and is a health hazard. The bedroom, just beyond the living area, is where Antônio's parents slept before his father died. It contains a bed and a single chest of drawers, which cannot decide whether it belongs in a doll's house or the real world. Henceforth Antônio, Vanessa and the baby will share this room.

Dwellings like these all over Rocinha will usually accommodate anything between four and ten people, frequently sleeping head to toe. Within this realm of poverty, there are still dramatic differences. The poorest live in what can best be described as wooden, concrete or tin shelters with no services and without toilet facilities. The provision of electricity and water is steadily expanding across the favela and up the hill, but the supply remains intermittent and subject to long, unexplained breakdowns.

In hospital, the doctors have encountered a problem. The needle in Duda's chest and arms through which the medicine is being administered has opened new wounds. The disease prevents these from healing. Furthermore, at any opportunity, the baby grabs the needle and tubes and tries to rip them from her skin. She is not taking in the medicine. The only way she can receive the treatment, the medics explain, is by using a specialist catheter inserted deep into her body.

The costs of Duda's illness are mounting. Both parents are exhausted. The family face very serious decisions. Something has to be done about the bathroom: it will pose a threat to the baby's health in the event that she returns alive but debilitated from hospital. The cost of the catheter and the refurbishment of the bathroom represents more than a year's salary, and Antônio has no savings left. Meanwhile, he has to take over the bedside vigil during the day to allow Vanessa some rest.

He approaches his boss, who he has always considered a decent man. Both of them know that if Antônio resigns from his post, he will not be entitled to receive the 90 Brazilian reals (R$) that the state would pay him for six months if he were sacked. So he pleads with his boss to fire him. The boss is reluctant. Turnover of personnel is high, and Antônio is the longest-serving employee and about the best man he has. Finally, the owner of the firm agrees to sack him but says he is welcome to return if ever he can.

Having to give up his job is a blow to Antônio. He has taken well to his role as supervisor. 'I had to divide up the team,' he remembers, 'write the individual schedules and decide who did what; as well, of course, as continuing to do my bit with the deliveries ... We had about two thousand magazines to distribute in a part of town where you couldn't really drive – everything was done on foot.' This proves to be a useful training in logistics, as well as experience of devolving responsibility to his more junior staff.

Things were about to improve further, as Antônio had invested his modest savings in learning to drive. He had just passed the test and could now take charge of the delivery van. He liked the work and until Eduarda's illness had been able to keep his head above water and fulfil his most important role, as a provider for his wife and child. 'I was happy,' he continues. 'We survived okay, paid our bills and saved a bit of money. I had nothing to complain about.' He seems not to dissemble when he remembers this. Rather, he looks wistful.

Antônio still needs about 20,000 reals. He is not a gambling man. He is not prepared to steal. It is still over a year before the first bank opens a branch in Rocinha, and in any event, an unemployed man with no assets, born and raised in the favela, would stand no chance of being granted a loan.

He knows just one man who is not only able to lend him the money but might actually be willing to do so. To most of the favela, and indeed the outside world, he is known as Lulu. For the last two years he has been the undisputed Don of Rocinha. He runs the drugs trade. This competes with the suppliers of gas and electricity as the most successful business in the favela. Lulu's is a cash-rich industry. He hands out loans, usually to residents who want to purchase their own apartment. This serves a dual purpose. The practice boosts the local economy, served either poorly or not at all by the state and more legitimate financial institutions. It also recycles the profits from the drugs trade, which are, of course, otherwise subject to legal constraints.

The roughest area of the favela is almost at the very top. This is Rua Um, Road One, and it is here that Lulu has his office. Above Rua Um lies the district of Laboriaux, which not only boasts the most spectacular view over Rio, but appears cleaner and more ordered than the rest of Rocinha – the favela's very own Mayfair. This is where Lulu actually lives.

Without funds, Antônio thinks long and hard about his next step. He has never engaged with drugs, never taken them, and has no intention of doing so. He is revolted by the associated violence, which has been a backdrop to his life. None of his childhood friends are in the business. They are all, like him, workers – taxi drivers, builders, waiters.

But he sees no way out of his financial predicament. He does not discuss his plan with anyone, not even with Vanessa. This is something he has decided to do alone.

Antônio asks a friend who is in touch with Lulu to arrange a meeting. It is two days before his twenty-fourth birthday when, with trepidation, he starts the long walk uphill on Estrada da Gávea. To his left is the area called Cachopa. Then comes another of Rocinha's sixteen districts, Dionéia. Up past the next bend Rua Dois, Road Two, leads off, and further on is Rua Um. From this perch, you can observe almost the entire South Zone – to the east Gávea, almost literally a stone's throw away; then the lagoon at the heart of everything, separating the valley of Botafogo from the high-rises of Ipanema and Leblon; there is even a glimpse of Copacabana; and when you turn around to face south, if you look hard enough, you can spot some of the sumptuous villas of São Conrado camouflaged by the Atlantic Forest.

This is Rocinha's ultimate lookout post. Here you can see everyone entering and everyone leaving. This is where Rocinha's most powerful man, boss of the favela's drugs trade, has his office.

Antônio begins his longest walk with his friend. Nervous but determined, he turns over in his head how to phrase his request and what to offer in return. He is Faust seeking out Mephistopheles. But Antônio craves neither unlimited knowledge nor worldly pleasures. He only wants his daughter to survive, grow and prosper. He senses that his life is about to change and that things may not end well. But in his mind, he challenges anyone who would point the finger of blame at him: 'And what would you do in my place?'

There is a sharp bend near the very top of Estrada da Gávea by a small marketplace. This is the start of Rua Um. Although a key thoroughfare, it can still only really accommodate people in single file, and a wheelbarrow can trigger a pedestrian traffic jam. Antônio walks down it, past the bars and the tiny grocery stores, then the fishmonger to the right and the butcher to the left, avoiding the dog shit, rotting fruit and sewers, until Rua Um forks.

Take a right and the path soon swings round towards the southwest along the sheer side of the Two Brothers mountain, eventually reaching the commercial district at the bottom – and normality.

Take a left and you cross into the traditional stronghold of the drugs trade. Men, women and children may appear to be dozing or chatting idly, but most are observing strangers heading towards Lulu's office. Word of their progress is being passed up the line so that Lulu's security is ready to receive them in whichever way they consider appropriate – either with resolute armed hostility or with apparent indifference. If you don't live or work at the top end of Rua Um, you usually need a good reason to be hanging out there.

Antônio turns left. But the security detail is not suspicious in his case, because his friend is familiar to them. By the time he gets to the top, he is slightly out of breath and still nervous. He has taken a long time to reach the decision to walk up Rua Um, but now he is set on going through with it.

Antônio comes to the end of his long walk up the steepest hill. Arriving at his destination, he enters by the front door. Never in his twenty-four years has he envisaged a change to his life so fundamental as this pilgrimage will trigger.

2

FAVELA

1960–1976

Antônio's mother, Dona Irene, hailed from Teresópolis, which lies between the states of Rio and Minas Gerais. The town is a way station in the mountains, 100 kilometres north-east of Rio de Janeiro. Her passage to Rocinha had been unusual. She lost her own mother, an indigenous Indian, when she was just three years old, the youngest of six children.

With a father unable to cope, she was introduced to an Italian family living in Rio but holidaying in Teresópolis. Charmed by the little girl, they took her back to Urca, one of Rio's most elegant areas, and raised her there. She left behind five siblings in Teresópolis with whom she would lose touch and whose names she now struggles to remember. Her peripatetic beginnings may not be typical of Brazilian children from humble backgrounds, but they are not uncommon.

Irene's relationship with the family she grew up in was ambiguous. She never went to school, but they taught her basic skills while expecting her to work for them as a domestic servant. Although semi-literate, she was self-willed and, to judge by her own description, a mischievous child with a sunny disposition. To this day she retains a cheeky smile that breaks out at any opportunity.

Like so many born into Brazil's lower depths, Dona Irene was forced at an early age to fashion survival tools for a life that always skirted close to homelessness, destitution and other misfortune. She was only twelve when she gave birth for the first time. The father, a casual acquaintance in his twenties, had no intention of assuming responsibility for the child, and so she had little alternative but to give her up for adoption. A year later, she found herself pregnant again by a much older man. She considered keeping the child but finally decided to hand over this one too. She buried the memory, deep enough to lessen the pain but sufficiently shallow so as not to repeat the experience.

By the time she reached her late teens, she had begun to live her youth to the full in the Rio de Janeiro of the early sixties, when the city's reputation as a centre of hedonism had broken national boundaries. Irene had friends who worked at the Glória hotel. There were few more glamorous institutions in Rio than this art deco masterpiece. Close to the presidential palace and the main financial institutions, it attracted a parade of movie stars, singers, dancers, politicians and wealthy businessmen.

One day, the 21-year-old Irene, petite, dark and pretty, had a row with a boyfriend at the Glória and stormed back to Copacabana, where she lived with her latest employers as a maid. But her occasional moods were rarely enough to smother her coquettish side, so when a bold handsome man smiled at her as she waited to cross the road, she couldn't resist smiling back.

His name was Fernando and he was in his thirties, or even a little older. Irene was immediately drawn to him, and to his spiffy clothes – white shoes, white trousers and a shirt the colour of wine. He was not Brazilian but Spanish, an airline pilot who flew the Rio route from Madrid.

Some months after they started seeing each other, he died in a car crash. The news of his death arrived circuitously and shocked Irene, not merely because she had lost her exotic lover but because she had been preparing to tell him that she was carrying his child. This was Antônio's elder brother, Carlos.[1] Unlike the previous two, born while she was in her early teens, she resolved not to let this one go.

Carlos inherited his father's build and, more importantly in Brazil, his skin colour. His mother was dark, with indigenous features, but Carlos looked European and white. Until he was seven, the middle-class family in Ipanema who at that time employed Irene as a maid treated him as one of their own. He ate with them, was schooled with their children and went on holiday with them. When Irene and he were out walking, everyone assumed that she was merely his nanny. Indeed, her employers wanted to adopt him, an offer she politely declined. Despite this refusal, Carlos's formative years were moulded by privilege, affluence, a clear sense of hierarchy and a strict moral code. This was his world and he felt at home in it.

When Irene's employers announced that they wanted her to move with them to France for three years, she decided that the boy should stay in Brazil. Carlos was sent, aged seven, to live with a family in Duque de Caxias, a city 20 miles to the north of Rio. Life was less sophisticated here, and his foster parents were strict. There was no proper health centre, and so illness and injury were treated by using traditional methods – rubbing coffee powder into wounds or drinking herbal tea.

Although no longer bathed in the comfort of Ipanema and its leafy boulevards and sandy beach, Carlos came to believe that the experience taught him order, tidiness and honesty, values that he insists have guided his life ever since. But their severe approach to child-rearing also taught him the meaning of fear and anger.

Irene finally returned from France in late 1973. It was not long before she started frequenting her old haunts, meeting up with her friends from the Glória hotel. One evening they went off to a *forró*, a very Brazilian dance party.

At this time, the outside world was beginning to discover Brazil through the smoky tunes of João Gilberto and Stan Getz, or through samba's promise of sweat and sex. Among Brazilians, however, the forró was the fastest-growing dance, music and party movement. There was a simple reason for this: internal migration was in full swing across the country. If Rio and the south represented the United States, then Brazil's north-east was Mexico. For three decades, a great river of north-easterners had been flowing towards South America's mighty industrial and agricultural engine houses, with the majority trying their luck in the cities of São Paulo and Rio.

The forró is rooted in the north-east. Once the most productive zone of the Portuguese empire, over the past two centuries the area has been noted for its underdevelopment, its poverty and its tough rural existence on or close to a semi-arid savannah. For a long time now, this has been Brazil's Wild West.

So when the country's industralisation accelerated after the establishment of President Getúlio Vargas's corporatist dictatorship in 1930, Brazil's business leaders looked to the north-east to provide a cheap labour force for the growing economic centres in the country's south. The *nordestinos* came in their tens of thousands, then in their hundreds of thousands, then in their millions, looking for work. Given the yawning disparity in education between the new arrivals and their hosts, many southerners suspected the nordestinos to be wastrels, lazy or criminally inclined. In reality, they were mostly just very poor and frequently illiterate.

Notwithstanding the grim life in the north-east from which they had escaped, the migrants often yearned for the places and communities they had left behind. Brazilians will sometimes argue that their word for nostalgic longing, *saudade*, suggests a complex intensity of attachment uncommon in other cultures. And among Brazilians, the saudade of the nordestinos appears the most potent of all, probably because they have uprooted themselves in much greater numbers in the past century than other Brazilians.

Not many migrants succeeded in returning home, except for the very occasional holiday. It was too expensive, too much of an upheaval, and employers did not look kindly on absenteeism beyond Sundays, when religious duties were to be observed. Instead, the labourers stayed in the favelas, environments that in some respects were as challenging as the savannah but where there was at least the prospect of work. Being a communal activity rooted in their original culture, and, equally, a great way to meet the opposite sex, the forró dances quickly became the centre of the immigrants' social life.

At the forró around the corner from the Glória, Irene was immediately drawn to the dapper, stick-thin Gerardo, who could swing his hips with style and verve. He was of medium height, with a thin, drawn face the intensity of which belied his easy-going character. From his accent she was able to guess that he was from the northeast, perhaps the state of Paraíba. In the early migration, Paraíba seemed to send more workers south than any other state, such that people from Rio's favelas are often simply called Paraíbanos, regardless of where they are actually from. New arrivals, of course, tended to cluster in favelas where their compatriots were to be found, and a majority of Rocinhans trace their heritage back to Paraíba. In fact, Gerardo Lopes was from another north-eastern state, Ceará, which has the second largest presence in Rocinha.

When Irene's employers found out about Gerardo, they warned her against the relationship. They were quite specific – Gerardo lived in Rocinha, which might as well have been Satan's earthly lair so far as Rio's middle classes were concerned. Never one to pay too much attention to advice, Irene decided to move in with her new lover in one of Rio's fastest-growing favelas.

* * *

The word favela, meaning slum or informal settlement, first evolved in Rio at the end of the nineteenth century. It was another import from the north-east. In 1897, soldiers returning from the province of Bahia after defeating the Canudos rebellion camped out on one of Rio's hills to demand that the government pay their outstanding wages. Rio was still Brazil's capital at the time.

The Canudos rebellion and the war that eventually crushed it were defining moments for the young republic (the monarchy had been abolished less than a decade earlier). Brazil's history has been studded with insurrections, some driven by separatism and regional competition, others by social inequality. Within five years of it being crushed, this uprising had been immortalised in Euclídes da Cunha's novel, Os Sertões or Backlands.[2] The campaign of the Brazilian army against a ragtag band of followers of a charismatic millenarian priest was a gruelling experience for the republic's unseasoned foot soldiers. With the rebellion defeated, the state apparently forgot its obligations to many thousands who had risked their lives on the savannah, and so these demobbed men travelled to Rio and settled on the hill that now hosts the favela called Providência.

They named it Favela Hill, after Mount Favela, which had been a strategic base for the rebels of Canudos, though the precise origin of the name is contested. Some claim that it actually came from the eponymous weed, poisonous and hardy, from which Mount Favela had originally derived its name. The story goes that these former troops, demanding their unpaid wages, were as unyielding as the favela plants in the hostile soil of the north-east. Once the soldiers had put down their roots, the government, try as it might, could not pull them up from their adopted home.

When first settled, Favela Hill was a bucolic mound overlooking the English cemetery, as it does today. It was also close to the then seat of government and the presidential palace.

The living space was available thanks to Rio's geography. The city's various districts are separated by countless hills and mountains, so cariocas are often as intensely wedded to their specific area as they are to Rio itself. A few tunnels were bored around the turn of the twentieth century, but it wasn't until the 1960s and 70s that the city was properly linked by tunnels running through the most forbidding mountains.

The geographical formations helped cariocas to orientate themselves: if the hills were behind them, the sea was probably in front. But otherwise they were regarded as a nuisance. Since the days of the earliest Portuguese settlement of the city, few European incomers had felt the desire to walk up steep inclines to construct their houses. Instead they built on the flat land by the beaches, the bay and the harbour, and then on reclaimed marshland. So when the migrant labourers started arriving in the decades after the soldiers who defeated the Canudos rebellion, they followed the soldiers' example and put up their shacks in the only remaining open spaces. The mountains made it difficult for maids and servants to travel in from the periphery of the city, and so they lived amidst their employers on the hills.

The generic name, favela, stuck. Towns and cities across Brazil adopted it. But in Rio, a second name, more prosaic, competed with the term before trumping it – *o morro*, or the hill. In other parts of Brazil, the larger favelas tend to be on the outskirts of the city – out of sight of the lush green districts where the wealthier residents enjoy standards of living comparable to their counterparts in New York and London. So it is uniquely in Rio that the favelas are known across the city as the Hill.

The emergence of the favelas on Rio's hills had two important consequences. First, in the South Zone they always existed cheek by jowl with the relative opulence of the neighbouring districts, Ipanema, Leblon, São Conrado and Gávea. The extreme squalor of the Hill and the unfathomable luxury of the surrounding areas are often hugger-mugger in Rio, sometimes no more than ten yards apart. O *asfalto* was the name given to the middle-class areas with asphalt roads, to contrast them with the rutted tracks of the favelas. In short, all cariocas live either *no asfalto* or *no morro*, on the Asphalt or on the Hill.

Many middle-class cariocas succeed in living their lives by erasing the favelas from their conscious minds, a psychological process that is usually only punctured by the recognition of their own maid or odd-job man (who live in favelas almost by definition) as a sentient being. But there is also an influential lobby, nurtured by property developers, which would like to see all favelas banished from the South Zone. In their eyes, the removal of unsightly settlements would boost tourism and increase security for the middle-class districts – both visions that involve a good deal of wishful thinking.

Second, the favelas emerged as islands separated by middle-class areas from those on the city's other hills. As a consequence, the identification of people from the favelas with their own particular community has always been more intense than is the case in other cities, most importantly São Paulo. In Rio, 'each ravine is a nation', as the novelist and singer Chico Buarque put it.[3] Each favela has a powerful and clear identity of its own. This would have a significant impact on the development of the social economy of the drugs trade, and was a fundamental cause of the high levels and peculiar nature of urban violence in Rio as compared with São Paulo.

The original immigrants from the north-east tended to build on the lower slopes of the hills. In the 1920s, a few small-time farmers began raising livestock on a modest patch of land next to São Conrado, selling their produce to local people. As Rocinha – literally 'little farm' – began to employ more people in the 1940s, the community edged its way steadily up the hill. It soon became feasible to take the produce over the pass at the back of the Two Brothers mountain towards the affluent neighbourhood of Gávea.

* * *

By the early 1970s, when Gerardo, Irene's boyfriend from the forró, established his home in Rocinha, the settlement had reached less than a third of its present size. But then the city built the Two Brothers Tunnel[4] under the eponymous mountain, so that Rocinha and São Conrado became linked directly with the rest of Rio for the first time. New dwellings appeared higher and higher up the hill, and as transport improved, it became ever easier to reach Leblon, Ipanema, Gávea and Jardim Botânico, the wealthy areas where employment was most plentiful.

Gerardo's 'house' was a modest shelter made of wood and corrugated tin, built on a small piece of land that he had purchased from another family. It was tiny, with an indoor bathroom separated from the kitchen by a simple wooden divide. It was, however, just two minutes' walk from the thick Atlantic rainforest, whose trees were heavy with an exotic display of mangoes, guavas, mulberries and jackfruits, literally there for the picking.

Today that same apartment is just under halfway up Rocinha, buried deep down an alley that runs off the main road intersecting the favela from top to bottom. The breathless expansion of the community in the 1980s and 90s first ate up any remaining green spaces before building vertically, with apartment upon apartment upon apartment. Without a guide to lead you through the maze of veins and capillaries that feed the complex body of this dense settlement, it would be impossible to find Gerardo and Irene's house now. The living area was long ago deprived of most windows and fresh air.

Despite the miserable conditions, Irene took to Rocinha straight away. She was quick to make friends in an environment where you have little choice but to get on with your neighbours.

Few if any houses had a reliable electricity supply. Some residents took the risk of siphoning off electrical current from the main power lines. This involved 'stepping down', a hazardous process of voltage reduction that could result in grisly electrocutions or dramatic fires. The lines in were managed by local middlemen in an ad hoc organisation called the Commission of Light, which was not beyond extorting the few cents that residents might have to spend in return for feebly flickering lights. For shopkeepers and bar owners, there was little choice but to pay up if the beers were to remain cold. But for most residents, when the sun set, it would be time to light their candles and oil lamps.

Toilets were buckets or holes in the ground. There was no running water into the homes, and so all thirty thousand or so inhabitants would fetch their supplies from a few standpipes. One resident remembers how during the summer, it 'was pure chaos. The queue of people with twenty-litre cans, plastic buckets and washing bowls would go on for kilometres.'[5] When things got out of hand, the 'sheriffs', strong women from the neighbourhood, would sort out all the fuss, even if that meant throwing the occasional recalcitrant into the open sewer that ran down the middle of the hill.

School attendance was patchy, and after primary education, the majority of kids had already started working, if indeed they had even been to school in the first place. But although all those who grew up in the sixties and seventies in Rocinha acknowledge the material poverty, they still have a rosier memory of their childhood than many people do. Living an often feral outdoors life, they played games and foraged for food as they explored the forest behind the houses.

One group, however, have a decidedly more jaundiced view of their early years than others – women. 'Believe me,' says Raquel Oliveira, 'it was no fun being a woman.' Raquel lived in dire poverty as a child but by comparison to some of her contemporaries considered herself lucky. 'In one brothel there were girls of thirteen and fourteen both with kids already. Then there were two nine-year-olds and a pregnant ten-year-old. This was run-of-the-mill stuff, but the worst was reserved for the girls forced to work in Copacabana. You worked and could easily end up getting knifed. Perdition, I tell you.'

Although the children of that generation remember the absence of guns, thieving and police intimidation were real problems. But most of this occurred *outside* the favela, as a consequence of the informal system of apartheid that left residents vulnerable when they ventured down from the Hill and on to the Asphalt.

Antônio Francisco Bonfim Lopes was born at his parents' home in Rocinha on 24 May 1976. He cried a lot as a baby but grew up an inquisitive and friendly little boy with a thick nest of cropped but curly hair, and the darkest eyes.

His was the last generation in Rocinha whose earliest memories are free from images of violence. He recalls endless games with his friends running unhindered around the favela. 'But it was dirt poor too,' he adds. 'Both my parents worked and so as a small child, I was given to a minder. They paid her – but only if they had enough money.'

At this time, there were still only a few motor vehicles trawling up and down Estrada da Gávea, and provided that Antônio and his cohort stayed within the boundaries of the community, they were in no danger from the other lurking threat – officers of the Military Police. 'There were actually two manned police boxes in Rocinha at the time,' Antônio says. 'They didn't do much, just making their presence felt. I can't remember any nice officers. But I suppose you could say there were some who were less bad. Whatever, even when we were kids they would chase us, and whack us over the head if they caught us.'

For the middle classes, the favela was uncharted land where dragons and demons might hide. The favela kids felt the same in reverse – parents warned their children not to misbehave lest they receive a visit from Lucinho, the local bogeyman, who, they said, would appear at night and snatch them while sleeping. Antônio believed that Lucinho would launch his raids from the Asphalt, and doubtless for some families he stalked the favela in the uniform of an officer of the infamous Military Police. It was safer for little Rocinha boys to avoid anything beyond the Hill.

Like most of his peers, Antônio's life was communal from the start. When going to work, mothers would pass children on to other women, sometimes for cash, sometimes for payment in kind. Fathers were often ghostly figures who hovered dimly in the recent past but were frequently long gone by the time a child was able to form memories.

Happily for Antônio, that was not so in his case – his father was in fact more present than his mother. Dona Irene had to spend six days and six nights skivvying for a family in Copacabana. She would only arrive home on Saturday before leaving for another week on Sunday evening. Gerardo worked too, as a barman in Ipanema and later in Copacabana. Even though he only ever got home from work in the early hours of the morning, at least he was there when Antônio awoke. The young boy adored his father, who he remembers as even-tempered and very affectionate.

Carlos has different memories of his stepfather. It was Gerardo who had dragged him to this unpleasant hole in the first place; now he was targeting Carlos's most prized possession. 'I was in my teens,' Carlos explains, 'and Gerardo would turn off my record player and throw the vinyl across the room. Sometimes he would even cook for Antônio and himself, leaving nothing for me and forcing me to fend for myself.'

Antônio's abiding memory is of alcohol-driven tension that often turned violent. 'My mother was an alcoholic,' he admits frankly. 'Well, they both drank. But she would come home and pick fights with Dad. I hated it. It used to upset me so much.' He implies that his mother often provoked the trouble. He appears to identify her and Carlos as being on one side of the family, with himself and his father on the other.

The parents fought hard. When Irene returned home on a Saturday, she would often, Antônio observes, already be blind drunk and looking for a fight. She would wake his father and start battering him. Gerardo, tanked up himself, would respond. Living in such a tiny space, the drama was played out in full view of Carlos and Antônio.

Although a victim of polio, Carlos was well built and very strong. He would often step in to defend his mother. Still a young child, Antônio watched in horror as his half-brother lunged at his father. On one occasion, Carlos admits he hit Gerardo so hard that he was hospitalised. 'I had succeeded in punching out almost an entire mouthful of his teeth in the fight,' he says sheepishly. 'He left my father's face deformed,' Antônio notes with bitterness. While the fights were happening, young Antônio cowered, too puny to do anything, but secretly aching to defend his father.

Some people share Carlos's antipathy towards Gerardo. One family friend says that in addition to being a chronic alcoholic, he was also a violent thief, and that he provoked as many arguments as his wife did. It is hard to get an objective sense of Gerardo's character. Beyond doubt, however, is that Antônio observed a great deal of nastiness at home while still very young. Witnessing the persistent abuse of mothers at the hands of their husbands or part-ners is the single most important factor in determining whether boys are likely to develop aggressive and violent tendencies as young adults. In Antônio's case, the issue was more complex – he perceived his father, rather than his mother, to be the victim of abuse.

'Food was beans and rice, or rice and beans,' Antônio remembers. Sometimes at the weekend a piece of chicken might be thrown into the mix, but when times were especially tough 'we were forced to eat lung with polenta'.[6] He shudders at the thought of this speciality from Bahia. Usually offal was reserved for dogs. The fruits of the forest provided some valuable vitamins, although as the seventies turned into the eighties, this source of nutrition started to dry up, pushed back by the tide of unplanned housing rising up the hill and seeping into the crevices of Rocinha to suffocate the vegetation. Although Antônio has some happy memories of the time, it was a life of unremitting poverty. He was 'a sad little scrap', remembers a family acquaintance. 'He was so thin. I would always see him waiting for the bus almost swallowed up by his tatty T-shirt.'

When he was about seven, Antônio's mother took him with her for the first time to her place of employment. She was now working for a family living in a grand apartment building, several storeys high, on a leafy street in Copacabana. But more than the architecture, more than the spacious rooms, Antônio was astonished by the food – its variety, its colour, and its careful arrangement in bowls and on plates. This was an undreamt-of realm.

From an early age, Antônio instinctively understood Rocinha to be his world. He would think of himself as one of its citizens. Notwithstanding the chaos, deprivation and violence, he has always been adamant in his conviction that this is the finest place on earth and that growing up there was a privilege, not a curse. Carlos, by contrast, thought it was appalling. He had been ripped from a comfortable middle-class existence and cast into this midden. He and his brother stood clearly on either side of Chico Buarque's ravine.

From his mother's workplace, Antônio would be taken three blocks down to the bar where his father worked. Here, for the first time, he would see kids his own age living on the streets. Dumbstruck, he watched as his father chatted with them affectionately – some in rags, some with missing limbs. 'I'll never forget this kid called Pirate,' he says. He only had one eye – nothing in its place, neither eyeglass nor patch. 'I thought it looked as though somebody had just bored a hole through his head.' Inside the bar, his father gave Antônio a few coins and told him to distribute them to the street kids like Pirate. He explained that their lives were much harder than their own; that they had no parents or guardians; that they had no choice but to beg and steal; and that they lived in constant fear of arbitrary violence, even death, usually at the hands of marauding police patrols. Anything his father had left over he would give to the street kids, and he reminded Antônio on many occasions that giving was good. Antônio worshipped his father, not only as his moral guide. He insisted that Gerardo was both his father and his mother.

3

COCAINE

1979–1989

In the late 1970s, adventurers and fortune-seekers from across the country made their way to the banks of two rivers in the remotest part of western Brazil. Within a couple of years, several makeshift towns had arisen close to the Madeira and the Mamoré at the very edge of the Amazonian province of Rondônia. Accommodating at their peak roughly 20,000 people (almost all men), these settlements were barely distinguishable from the towns of the American West that had grown up alongside the railroad a century earlier.

Noisy, chaotic, raucous and muddy, they were made up almost exclusively of small enterprises, selling anything the men would buy – beer and spirits, dry goods, wet goods, food and clothes. But the busiest establishments had only one purpose: to buy and sell gold.

These *currutelas* were lawless places. Improvised banking facilities jostled with peripatetic brothels whose women and pimps would move from one pop-up town to the next, depending on where business was best. Brawls, shootouts, theft and chicanery in various forms were daily hazards, as if working long hours on and around the rivers and their banks wasn't tough enough. The amount of money spent by these hard-bitten customers in their mud-soaked clothes would naturally depend on how much gold they had found that week as they spent their days trawling, dredging and diving.

For over a decade, this part of western Brazil was home to one of the biggest *garimpos* the country had ever seen.[7] These open-cast or alluvial mines had been a Brazilian tradition ever since the *bandeirantes*, the pioneers of the interior, had struck gold during the 1690s in what later became the prosaically named state of Minas Gerais, or General Mines. As explorers discovered more of the country, revealing wondrous mineral troves, the poor, the desperate, the chancers and the cunning, collectively the *garimpeiros*, would gather, convinced that this time they would emerge with fabulous riches. Some certainly did, but many risked death and terrible injury for little return.

The minerals of Minas Gerais were just a few days' march from Rio de Janeiro and São Paulo. For centuries the Amazon's riches, located in inhospitable or inaccessible terrain, weeks away from the coastal centres, were out of reach of the garimpeiros. But in 1966, Brazil's military rulers announced their plans for opening up the country's final frontier in a programme dubbed Operação Amazônia. With the fervour of the Castilian conquistadors who had set out to find El Dorado in the late fifteenth century, the generals launched an ambitious plan of road-building. Within a decade, tarmac would be criss-crossing the Amazonian jungle, covering thousands upon thousands of miles. The aim was to subject the Amazon to a period of intense economic development, unlocking the rainforest's astonishing stores of natural resources. The generals also hoped this would alleviate, if not solve, the problem of homelessness in the north-east and the south by 'taking the people without land to the land without people'.

The roads enabled men, machines and raw building materials to reach a stretch of the Madeira and Mamoré river system that ran for some 400 kilometres. The latter flows into the former. In any other country after this confluence, the giant Madeira would be the king of rivers. But in Brazil, it is a mere tributary feeding the mighty Amazon itself.

The sources of both the Madeira and the Mamoré are high in the Bolivian Andes. As the waters tumble down to Brazil, they drag with them rich deposits of minerals. In the summer, between November and March, the thawing Andean snow combines with the tropical rainfall to swell the rivers. Their banks burst and flood the jungle for many kilometres in both directions. The riparian settlements must disperse until the waters sink down again with the onset of winter. Over thousands of years, these natural processes have deposited large amounts of gold on the riverbed. For centuries it lay there unnoticed and untouched.

Once its presence was confirmed in the early seventies, the garimpo started to develop. It was a slow process at first, but by the turn of the eighties, it was already home to a couple of thousand men. The work was dangerous, especially for the divers who would scour the bed of the river for the alluvial deposits.

Once the divers spotted a rich trove, they would direct enormous hoses to that area. Like giant worms from some dystopian world, these hoses were attached to pumping machines sitting on large rafts known as *balsas*. The hoses would suck up everything from the riverbed. The aggregate would then be taken ashore and another set of garimpeiros would sift carefully through it to extract the precious metal.

During the garimpo's heyday in the late 1980s, there were some 6,000 balsas floating on the rivers. But the costs could be high. Accidents were common. 'On some days, I would see up to three bodies float past Porto Velho on the current,' remembers one of the workers.[8] The rivers were deep, and many of the divers were struck down by the bends, not to mention the assaults launched by everything from tiny bugs to giant prowling alligators.

But relief of sorts was at hand. A stretch of the two rivers formed Brazil's border with Bolivia. After a hard day's work, the garimpeiros were soon in contact with traders on the opposite bank. The

Bolivians sold them coca leaves, used for centuries by local peasants either to chew or to make a tea, producing a narcotic effect that would take the edge off their back-breaking work. In addition – and for the first time – the traders by the river were also selling the coca leaves in their processed form, either as a semi-refined paste, called *pasta base*, or as a powder, cocaine. Before long, many garimpeiros found that not only could they banish the cares of the day, but they could augment their wages by selling on the cocaine.

Van drivers who ferried garimpeiros from Porto Velho to the garimpo returned home with their cabs full of paste. They soon found plenty of take-up for the stuff among the loggers who were relentlessly ripping up the Amazonian jungle in Rondônia.

Opportunities for loggers had also proliferated dramatically since the advent of Operação Amazônia. Their economic function was twofold: they could sell timber, including precious hardwood like mahogany; and by doing so, they would prepare the ground for a steady invasion of farmers, who were mainly engaged in producing either beef or soya. Some of the loggers' activity was legal, sanctioned by the state, although not necessarily beneficial for the planet. But much too was illicit. The loggers became adept at using armed gangs to overcome resistance by indigenous peoples or environmentalists; at money-laundering; and at transporting goods of dubious provenance over long distances.

By the early 1980s, these new entrants into the trafficking business had struck up a direct relationship with two of the three major exporters of cocaine from Colombia. For many years, the most important of these were the FARC (the Revolutionary Armed Forces of Colombia), who controlled an area of the Amazonian forest the size of Switzerland and had extensive 'kitchen' facilities enabling the full processing of cocaine from leaf to powder. The other group was not the famed Medellin cartel of Pablo Escobar, but its more ingenious rival, the Cali cartel, from the south of the country, who bought up large tracts of land in neighbouring Peru and Bolivia to grow and refine cocaine.

Thus two quite distinct cocaine trades emerged in Brazil. One was the wholesale market, which concentrated on shifting many tons of the refined drug every year across the country via plane and truck, heading for two different destinations: Brazil's largest port, Santos, which services São Paulo and the south-east; and Paramaribo, the capital of neighbouring Suriname, the former Dutch colony, whose post-independence military rulers were among the most corrupt in the world. From these two points, the cocaine would be loaded on boats destined for Spain's Atlantic coast or Rotterdam. In the 1990s, the Irish coast, the Balkans and west Africa were added to the list of initial destinations before the cocaine was sent to its termini – the lucrative and growing markets of the European Union, above all Britain, Germany, France, Italy and Spain.

With one important exception,[9] the wholesale cocaine business in Brazil has always been dominated by businessmen who bear scant relation to the images of gun-toting gangs from the favelas. Rather they integrate their smuggling activity into legitimate businesses, particularly those associated with farming, notably of cattle, which has spread across the Amazonian region in the wake of illegal logging. They make much larger profits than those engaged in supplying the domestic Brazilian market. They are also far less likely to be arrested.

That is not to diminish the vibrancy of the domestic market once Brazil became established as the transit country of choice to feed Europe's rapidly growing cocaine habit. Wholesalers did have a role to play in supplying the favelas of Rio, São Paulo and other big cities. But this was also an opportunity for small-time entrepreneurs who could carry a significant amount of paste or powder in a backpack and simply take the bus to Rio, where they were guaranteed a handsome profit. These freelancers came to be called *matutos*, and they played an especially important role in supplying Rocinha.[10] Many matutos started off as garimpeiros on the rivers Madeira and Mamoré before discovering that trading in coca paste was more lucrative even than sifting for gold.

And so another Amazonian cascade joined the Flying River in flooding Rio. This one did not travel by air but across land. Yet it was every bit as persistent. By 1984, as one observer noted, 'it was snowing in Rio de Janeiro' – a semi-tropical city – all year round.

Antônio was not yet nine years old. Yet powerful forces were already stirring. Poverty, the trade in drugs and guns, political turmoil, urban violence and globalisation were in the process of aligning themselves in a specific constellation to shift the entire trajectory of his life some fifteen years later.

When snow started to fall in Rio in 1984, the most popular drug in Rocinha was still marijuana. Until this point, cocaine had been a rarity, the preserve of the most affluent, usually with some jet-setting connections. In the underground of the 1970s, cocaine was referred to simply as *branco*, white, and marijuana as *preto*, or black. This reflected the natural colours of the drugs as well as the racial and class profile of their respective consumers.

Marijuana, *maconha* in Portuguese, had been a feature of favela life for many years without ever generating much controversy. The trade in weed barely registered with the residents unless they were in the habit of buying the occasional smoke. Maconha was a mere sideline for the two men who controlled the Rocinha branches of Brazil's hugely lucrative illegal gambling operation, known as the Animal Lottery. One lived up at the top of the favela, one down at the bottom. This rivalry between Upper and Lower Rocinha would persist.

As cocaine became more fashionable, a new man with considerable entrepreneurial drive set up shop in the favela. Denir Leandro da Silva, known universally as Dênis da Rocinha, lived halfway between the smoke shop he established and Rua Dois. The favela's first drug lord began modestly. But he was ambitious, and he anticipated that cocaine was about to change everybody's lives.

As *pó*, powder, started to reach Rocinha from the Amazon, Dênis's business began to develop and prosper. As it did, he cultivated a strategic magnanimity in his relationship to the rest of Rocinha. He would 'distribute food parcels and medicines, finance expenses such as funerals for the poorest residents; hand out sweets on holidays'.[11] Before long, he had established links with the growing number of distributors who were bringing the stuff in from Brazil's neighbours. Inside Rocinha he set up a management structure and culture that exist to this day. Money, not violence, was at the heart of his business.

When Antônio attended judo classes as a tiny boy, he would always be excited to see Dênis, who lived nearby. It might just have been one of those days when Dênis was handing out sweets to the local kids. Magnanimous gestures like this had a profound impact on dirt-poor youngsters like Antônio and his friends. Spotting Dênis da Rocinha was like catching a glimpse of a prime minister or president.

Dênis was a member of Comando Vermelho, or Red Command, the largest and most influential of Rio's criminal fraternities. At the beginning of the 1980s, Red Command was not necessarily associated with the trade in marijuana. Still often referred to by one of its earlier names, Red Falange, its most prestigious members were armed robbers and kidnappers.

The origins of Red Command went back over a decade, a weird subplot of one of the Cold War's chilliest phases. For this now fabled criminal syndicate that flaunts its stocks of coke and semi-automatic weapons across Rio was one of many unintended consequences spawned by Brazil's military dictatorship after it seized power on 1 April 1964.

In 1969, members of Brazil's most daring guerrilla organisations, the MR-8 from Rio and the Aliança Liberatadora Nacional (ALN) with its main base in São Paulo, started arriving in one of the most beautiful settings in Brazil – Ilha Grande. A hundred kilometres south of Rio, this paradise island lies an hour's slow boat ride across the water from the former royal vacation spot, Angra dos Reis. The final destination of the underground fighters was a gorgeous sandy beach on a small bay lapped by the blue-green waters of the southern Atlantic.

But they had not come for recreation and a rest from their revolutionary activities. Set just back from the beach was a building that looked like a stunted offspring of Colditz, the Nazi prisoner of war camp. Successive Brazilian governments had contrived to make the penal institute Cândido Mendes appear ever less appealing since it was first opened at the turn of the twentieth century. By now the most notorious prison in the country, it proclaimed a grisly slogan as a warning to the incarcerated: *O preso foge, o tubarão come* – the prisoner flees, the shark eats.

'It had been the fate of this beautiful place for a long time to be associated with human suffering,' wrote William da Silva Lima, one of the prison's most celebrated inmates from the 1970s, as he entered the forbidding edifice for the first time. Slaves, cholera victims, mutineers and anti-fascists had all been dumped here to rot at one point or another. 'The atmosphere was dominated by fear and suspicion, not only fear of the guards' violence but also of the acts carried out by the gangs of prisoners to rob, rape and kill their companions.'[12]

The two revolutionary groups, the MR-8 and the ALN, derived their notoriety from their collaborative success in kidnapping the US ambassador to Brazil. They were also feted in the underground, and indeed by left-wing activists across the world, for their highly successful and lucrative bank robberies, which financed their armed resistance to the generals.

Notwithstanding the generals' wish to paint them as ordinary criminals, the governor of Cândido Mendes prison placed the politicos in a separate part of Unit B, where their new neighbours included a group of the most hardened armed robbers that Rio could muster. Among them was William da Silva Lima. Although from a favela, he was known as the Professor for his love of books. His own remarkable memoir, written in prison, details the organisational lessons the young intellectuals behind MR-8 and ALN offered to the criminals.

When the guerrillas robbed a bank, they left as little to chance as possible. The team undertaking the actual raid would be supported by a back-up brigade of comrades stationed in disguise around the bank. Should law enforcement turn up, the officers would effectively be walking into a heavily armed trap, enabling the escape of those looting the cash. The group always ensured that the getaway cars were stolen just a few hours before the event so that they hadn't yet been registered as missing. Safe houses were prepared to assist the team's flight and to store the cash. And they always had a doctor (usually a medical student) on standby to operate on anyone who might have picked up an injury during the raid.

Initially sceptical of their fellow inmates, who were keen to stress their political status, gradually the favela bank robbers came to admire the dedication and above all the organisation of the guerrillas.

For a man who made his living through robbery, the Professor was unusually politically aware. Even such renowned villains as he were impressed by this level of organisation, and soon the revolutionaries were passing around the works of Che Guevara and the young French Marxist Régis Debray among the thieves and armed robbers. In 1971, eight of them formed the Union Group, which they soon rebaptised Red Falange, before finally settling on Red Command – often identified simply by its initials in Portuguese, CV.[13]

When the criminals returned to the streets, they did so not only with an ideological motive for their activities – they were now thieving in the name of social justice – but also with a new hierarchical structure. Authority was derived primarily from prison experience: the longer a man's sentence and the more frequent his successful attempts at escape, the more influence he could claim in the organisation.

In the early seventies, there was one division inside the Cândido Mendes penitentiary – a second group of toughs that refused to recognise the authority of the original Red Command leadership. Known as the Alligators, they formed a new organisation, O Terceiro Comando – the Third Command – which during the 1990s would contest the power of Red Command in a series of fearful three-way internecine battles. To this day you can spot a Third Command favela by the graffiti depicting alligators armed to the teeth.

The birth of these gangs prefaced an enormous change in the life of favelas. Traditional structures of power and respect would be swept away by one of the most powerful social forces Brazil had ever witnessed – the traffickers.

4

BODIES

1980–1987

Optimism was spreading through many of Rio's favelas during Antônio's early years. The military dictatorship imposed in 1964 was running out of steam. The favelas were experimenting with democracy by invigorating their residents' associations. These were united around the need for inhabitants' property rights to be recognised, but they soon started making bolder demands. Above all, they sought an end to the harassment of Rio's poor by the Military Police. Likewise, they wanted to close down the extortionate practices associated with the Commission of Light in the supply of electricity. This formed part of the clamour for the regularisation of all public utilities to the slums, including water supplies and closed sewage systems. The latter were badly needed in order to replace the notoriously foul open sewers running through the narrow alleyways.

Very quickly the agitation in the favelas began to look less like a bunch of pesky individuals and more like the beginnings of a political movement. In Rio, the radicalisation matured into the vanguard both for middle-class residents' associations and, more importantly, for those aspiring to replace the ruling military. This in turn coincided with the growing militancy of the union movement in São Paulo, inspired by a youthful band of charismatic leaders including Luiz Ignácio Lula da Silva, the future president, known universally in Brazil as Lula. Under pressure from these and other forces, the military regime was weakening, and as the generals looked less certain of their mission, the prospect of great change began to excite the country at large.

The armed forces signalled their broader intention to relinquish the reins of government in 1982 when they agreed to allow cities and states around the country to hold elections in advance of any national polls.

The emergence of the grassroots movement in Rio was an important development, heralding a period of great optimism both in the city and across Brazil. The movement demanding the restoration of democracy grew ever stronger, encompassing very different constituencies and classes. Among many cariocas, the period is remembered fondly as the belle époque for their city, when the prevailing sentiment was hope.

As Rio prepared for the return of democracy at municipal and state level, politicians began to realise for the first time that the favelas represented a rich seam of potential votes. If anything, they were more valuable than the more dispersed middle-class districts. For if it was possible to exercise influence over the favelas' residents' associations, a mayoral or gubernatorial candidate might count on a packed bloc of ballot papers. They began to recognise that the association leaderships might be able to deliver votes in exchange for material benefits once their election victory was assured.

Favela economies were burgeoning, too. The north-eastern market in Lower Rocinha was one of the largest open-air bazaars in Rio, with some of its fresh produce brought in daily on gruelling coach journeys that took over 24 hours. Shops and restaurants were opening close to the bus stops from where people would commute to Leblon or Barra. And the physical expansion of Rocinha by about 2,000 people every year indicated how Rio's service sector was booming. Certainly Antônio's parents were never without employment, although the heavy flow of new immigrants always ensured that wages remained rock bottom.

In Rocinha there were two residents' associations, both claiming to be the authentic representative of the men and women who lived there. The two presidents were equally remarkable characters, but very different from one another. Perhaps the most charismatic figure in all Rocinha was Zé do Queijo, Joe Cheese. He was a northeasterner, an immigrant from Paraíba. Since his arrival in the 1960s, he had established a monopoly on the allocation of building plots in the central district of Cachopa during Rocinha's rapid growth in the 1970s and 80s. With his prominent mop of black curly hair and dark glasses, Joe Cheese would swagger around the favela with two pistols at his side. To this day he is referred to as Rocinha's Lampião, the Robin Hood of Brazil's north-east.

Lampião was a notorious cattle rustler, robber and extortionist, who would stage raids from his rural hideouts in the semi-arid *sertão* in the states of Rio Grande do Norte and Ceará during the first three decades of the twentieth century. Successive governments regarded him and his followers, the *cangaceiros*, as a criminal menace. But to this day many nordestinos admire his ability to cock a snook at authority.

Joe Cheese consciously cultivated the thousands of new arrivals into Rocinha from the north-east every year in order to strengthen his influence in the favela. He would greet them with cheap loans and assistance in finding accommodation and jobs. This generated a deep loyalty among the disoriented newcomers, who were comforted by Joe's familiar accent and were ready to attach themselves to the 'strong man' – in the Brazilian tradition of *coronelismo*,[14] especially influential in the north-east. Encouraged by an anthropologist from Rio's Catholic University who had fallen in love both with Rocinha and with him, Joe Cheese transformed his informal network into one of the two residents' associations. He was a large and frightening man. His claim to political authority had real substance to it, but it was neither democratic nor accountable.

His opponent was equally striking. Maria Helena Pereira, a vivacious 25-year-old teaching assistant, had been elected as the head of the original residents' association. Brazil is at heart a conservative society, where women must struggle to make their voices heard. Yet as the dictatorship started to wilt, the women of the favelas were among the first to take matters into their own hands by organising themselves and asserting their demands. In addition to bringing up the children, favela women are often the main or sole breadwinners as well. Lacking crèches and primary schools, they would make complex arrangements among themselves to ensure that one of them was always looking after the children of the immediate community. To this day, children of the favela are passed around various mothers, who take it in turn to watch over them. Until quite recently, the women also had to wash, cook and clean without running water, so rotas would be drawn up for the collection of water from the communal spigot. Most women around the world are perforce better organisers than men, and consummate multitaskers.

Maria Helena's bid for the leadership of the residents' association was sponsored by the favela's nascent feminist organisation. She became the first woman to break through the comprehensive male domination of the local political structures. Like Joe Cheese, she was keen on distributing the essentials of life to as many as she could. At the time, the governor of Rio state had instructed that milk be dispensed to the city's favelas. The job fell to the Military Police, and with friends in the nearby PM station, Maria Helena coordinated the distribution from a large tanker around the upper reaches of the favela. While Joe Cheese dominated the middle areas of Rocinha, Maria Helena's power base was at the very top, close to Rua Um, and down in the commercial district.

According to her friends, Maria Helena lived in fear of Joe Cheese, and tensions between their supporters would occasionally spill over into violence. By 1983, the clash between the two had reached such an intensity that it drew the attention of Leonel Brizola, the new democratically elected governor of Rio. Brizola had been the most influential figure of the old left before the military coup of 1964. He had a proud record of opposing the dictatorship and commanded unparalleled respect among Rio's poor. Thus when he appealed to Rocinha's two 'presidents' to take their dispute from the alleys of Rocinha to the ballot box, both sides agreed.

The election of 1983 was Rocinha's first experiment in democracy, and it generated a huge amount of excitement. The Secretary of Justice for Rio state himself came to supervise the counting of votes as small delegations from each district marched ceremoniously from the polling stations down to the hall in Barcelos to await the outcome. With 10,000 votes cast, Maria Helena won by a whisker. There were claims from both sides that the votes in districts where their opponent held sway had been rigged. By all accounts this was true, but both probably understood that the skulduggery cancelled itself out. Rocinha was celebrated as a model not only for the rest of the favelas but for other districts as well.

Although he lost the vote, Joe Cheese did not simply disappear. Cachopa remained his fiefdom, over which the residents' association with Maria Helena at its helm had little influence. But the two rivals had other, more dangerous enemies. Joe Cheese's particular animus was directed at the drugs trade. And this inevitably brought him into conflict with the local don, Dênis da Rocinha.

Halfway through the decade, signs of change were appearing. In 1984, Dênis revealed his ruthlessness by ordering the murder of a man who ran a rival smoke shop, in Cowboy Street. Dênis was not primarily a killer, but everyone knew what to do when he was wearing a particular pair of white shorts. 'If you saw him leave home with those white shorts on, that meant somebody was going to die that day,' remembers one favela resident of the time. 'It didn't happen very often, but when it did, everyone just scattered and kept out of his way. He would be pretty efficient about it – everything would be over in a matter of half an hour or so.'[15] After his victim was dispatched, Dênis would stroll back home and change his shorts as a signal to his fellow residents that the danger had passed and life could go back to normal.

As the first Dono do Morro, Don of the Hill, he anticipated, perhaps unconsciously, the model that many dons in Rio would follow thereafter – nurturing local support by distributing some of the profits from the drugs operation, but sending out a clear message to enemies and rivals that dissent would trigger a decisive use of force. 'The drugs trade was a necessary evil,' Antônio argues when looking back at Dênis's time. 'Believe me. If it hadn't been for the traffickers, everyone would have been stealing, everyone would have been killing. We would all have greeted the dawn as dead people. The drugs business occupied the vacuum left by the state. Otherwise this would have been a lawless territory.'

Later, the dons also constructed a third pillar to support their edifice of power – corruption of the police. Each boss placed different weight on these pillars, which meant that the atmosphere changed dramatically from favela to favela and from boss to boss. Antônio's observations about the traffickers providing some semblance of stability were true as long as the don in question didn't rely too heavily on the gun. In those favelas where he did, lawlessness quickly returned – and the fallout could be extremely brutal.

As the rivalry between Joe Cheese and Dênis grew, it was mirrored by another deteriorating relationship, between Joe's opponent, Maria Helena, and Luiz Costa Batista, Rocinha's Animal

Lottery king. (Joe and Batista's antipathy towards Maria Helena was fed by the knowledge that she was hopelessly in love with Dênis – she was by no means the only one). Devised in Rio by the founder of the zoological gardens at the end of the nineteenth century as a harmless marketing campaign, the Animal Lottery originally aimed to attract more visitors to the zoo, which had fallen on hard times. The idea proved so successful that within a matter of weeks, Rio's government had banned the game as a threat to public order. The zoo may have lost the benefits, but the game itself spread like a bush fire. Although illegal, it is a Brazilian institution that has spawned some of the most colourful characters in a culture known for its big personalities.

Millions of Brazilians gamble on the Animal Lottery, and despite the fact that it is run by various mafias, its popularity is stronger now than it was a hundred years ago. It is also one of the few activities that knows no class boundaries, although, rather like the lottery in other countries, it extracts a disproportionate amount of money from the poor. Until the introduction of cocaine in the favelas, the master of the Animal Lottery was also master of the underground.

Both Dênis, the drugs don, and Batista, the Animal Lottery king, understood that the residents' association was a capricious beast that needed to be first tamed and then caged. The struggle between Maria Helena and Joe Cheese, more or less democratic, developed into a proxy war for influence between the respective local representatives of the cocaine trade and the Animal Lottery. And Dênis was serious about this – he had political aspirations, having imbibed the socialist ideals transmitted from the prison in Ilha Grande by the founding members of Red Falange.

Yet until 1987, the gangsters from the Animal Lottery and from the drugs trade continued to cooperate to stage at least one regular event: Cosmas and Damian's Day, 27 September, when toys and sweets are distributed to the children of the poor in Brazil to commemorate these twin saints. In Rocinha, the two underground organisations would fund a huge lorry with a six-wheeled wagon attached to the back that would drive slowly down Estrada da Gávea towards Lower Rocinha, showering the favela's kids with goodies along the way. But that year, the banner across the top of the truck feted the Animal Lottery king alone – there was no recognition of Dênis's role. Maria Helena was furious at this betrayal of her lover and made her feelings known throughout the favela. Dênis's deputies were so insulted, it was enough to put them on a war footing. Tension spread across Rocinha.

One hot, humid morning in October 1987, Maria Helena answered her front door. Whoever was knocking knew what they were doing, because she would only open the door when she heard the correct signal: a rhythmic knock followed by the password. She took three bullets in the face and chest, killing her instantly.

Nobody overtly blamed Batista for Maria Helena's death – in part because no one was certain that he was responsible. It could have been her political arch-rival, Joe Cheese. Some even whispered that Dênis had ordered the killing. It seems unlikely, as he was thought to nurture a dream that the two of them would one day emigrate to the United States and have children.

Others have suggested that her death was the consequence of her bitter quarrel with the then Secretary of State for Social Affairs, and that somebody in the government had ordered it. The motives and identity of Maria Helena's killer remained a mystery. But what her death did make clear was that henceforth, engagement in favela politics would carry some very serious risks. Maria Helena was neither the first nor the last aspiring politician to be sunk on the jagged rocks of the underground or high-level political corruption.

After her death, silence fell over the favela. The same happened just three months later, when Joe Cheese was taken out. Privately, most people thought that this hit was carried out on the orders of Dênis. But if anyone had concrete proof, they weren't volunteering it.

Notwithstanding these dramatic events, Antônio, like most Rocinhans, remembers Dênis's era as a time of relative tranquillity. It was a period before Rocinha, like other favelas, was plunged into the murderous chaos of the 1990s. By comparison with the coming decade, Dênis was indeed a benign figure. As petty crime increased at a time of great social change, 'people would look to him to solve their problems', according to Antônio. 'Burglars, for example, got the message that they could no longer steal – so they stopped stealing. If somebody was in the habit of shooting others because of some argument at a party, they knew they wouldn't be able to do that any more' because Dênis wouldn't tolerate it.

In the absence of a functioning police force within the favela, Dênis and the drugs trade started to assume the role. There was, of course, no regime of incarceration for offences committed, and so Dênis's criminal justice system involved anything from verbal warnings to execution.

For personal reasons, Antônio wishes the sanctions imposed by Dênis's rule had come earlier. 'Who knows? If they had been in full force, maybe my brother might not have done what he did to my father. Maybe he would have shown more respect.'

Notwithstanding the stability he engendered, Dênis was one of those responsible for crushing the delicate bloom of Rocinhan democracy at a time when it had only just begun to flower. The rivalry between the drugs cartel and the Animal Lottery mafia would continue. It was a complex chess game. Well-entrenched characters like Luiz Batista wielded influence in political circles and in the police, some of whom were itching to get involved in the favela action and the revenue it promised. The growing brigade of drug pushers was becoming better resourced. Their cash would later produce an extraordinary flow of weapons into the favelas.

As he grew from an infant into a child, Antônio began to acquire a set of friends who all lived close to his home in Rua Quatro, Road Four.

The favela was expanding at such a rate that it was dividing rapidly into recognisable districts. For each district, there was a little gang. Neighbouring Cachopa's was made up of a rough and tumble band of immigrants from Paraíba. Then there was the group from Valão, named after the large open sewage canal that ran down the middle of its main street. Roupa Suja, literally Dirty Clothes, was probably the most run-down district – a claim for which there was stiff competition. It, too, had its own gang of youngsters.

Some of these graduated to become 'beach rats', Rio's equivalent of Fagin's boys in *Oliver Twist*, carefully planning raids on the hotels and beaches of São Conrado, nicking personal belongings before scarpering back to the meeting point near Rocinha's Church of Our Lady of Good Voyage. There they would distribute the spoils amongst the whole team. One of their most valued accomplices was Federal, an Alsatian dog, who was involved in 'an elaborate strategy: someone would go ahead whistling and throwing a mound of sand on the victim's belongings. That was the signal for the dog to come bounding towards the treasure before snapping it up and making off with it in his mouth.'[16]

The gang to avoid was the one from Rua Um. Rua Um was a main point of entry into the favela for new immigrants from the north-east. It was also a place people preferred to get away from as soon as the opportunity arose, so turnover there was fairly fast as inhabitants inched their way down the hill. The further they descended, the more respectable they became. The area developed a sense of desperation that nurtured a slightly chippy attitude. The attendant swagger would become particularly noticeable and aggressive among its young men.

Antônio's secondary school was in Gávea, and so from the age of eleven he would take the bus up the hill every day and then on through Rua Um, effectively the mountain pass. By now he was aware that Rua Um had become the focal point of Rocinha's narcotics trade, and so it was a district he preferred to avoid. Being at the top of Rocinha, just below the highest point of the favela, Rua Um was a handy lookout: you could monitor all the comings and goings in Gávea just over the peak of the hill, and view the entire panorama of the favela on the other side.

As the eighties turned into the nineties, the atmosphere in Rocinha began to change. And the older he became, the more Antônio noticed people dying. 'At a certain point, you'd wake up and find that somebody else had been killed overnight,' he says. The bodies started appearing a couple of years before he began secondary school. Soon he would hear rumours of a new cadaver – sometimes anonymous, sometimes a vague acquaintance – more or less every day.

On one occasion, when he was not yet ten years old, a friend ran into him breathless and, tugging at his shirt, exhorted him to follow. 'There's a body,' he whispered, 'there's a body you must see.' They entered an abandoned concrete building with a glassless window letting in the light. Lying on the floor was a body covered in a white shroud. Gingerly, the friend pulled it back. Instead of a face, there was just a mush of flesh and bones. Horrified, Antônio raised his eyes to see that most of the victim's head had been shot off and his brains were now plastered against the wall. The boys dropped the shroud and ran away in terror. It was an image Antônio would never forget.

*   *   *

In 1987, Antônio's father, Gerardo, had started working in a hole-in-the-wall bar on Bolívar Street, just up from Copacabana beach and a couple of doors down from the Roxy cinema, another impressive survivor of Rio's art deco period.

One afternoon in the spring of 1988, he was tending the bar when a young man walked in and ordered a beer. The man sat unobtrusively for an hour or so before heading for the bathroom. He came out wielding a pistol, which he swiftly turned on the bar's owner with a demand for the day's takings. In a desperate but courageous bid to save his boss's life, Gerardo sank his teeth into the assailant's arm. Screaming with pain, the young man lowered his gun and fired it into Gerardo's knee. As Gerardo fell to the ground, he took some of the gunman's flesh with him. All he could think at that moment, he later told his wife, was that he would never see his son again.

Fleeing from the chaos of the gunfire, Gerardo's boss ran straight into a police patrol car that happened to be parked outside the Roxy. Seconds after the shooting, the cops had pinned the assailant to the ground. He was arrested and taken away.

At half past midnight, twelve-year-old Antônio returned from the Hotel Intercontinental – a ten-minute walk away in the rich neighbourhood of São Conrado. He had given up school in order to work. One of his jobs was that of ball boy at the Intercontinental's exclusive courts. Every day he would work a six-hour shift from 6 p.m., chasing after the wayward shots of Rio's recreational tennis players. Running and fetching. Fetching and running. In eighteen months, the members of São Conrado's tennis elite had rarely engaged the boy in conversation except to demand that he pick up another ball. 'I felt like one of those machines that fires the balls automatically,' he says before shrugging off the thought as though it were entirely natural. The tennis players he was servicing belonged to Rio's upper middle class, but they might as well have come from a different planet as far as Antônio was concerned.

Antônio's father would not normally return from the bar until the small hours of the morning. His mother, of course, was expected to remain at her post in Copacabana. Without a phone in the favela, Antônio had no idea what had happened until the next morning, when paramedics brought his father home with his leg in plaster. This was a quick turnaround for a man whose kneecap had just been shattered, even by the standards of Brazil's overstretched public health service.

With her husband no longer in work, Dona Irene started a new job on a construction site in Barra – hard physical labour for a slight woman in her forties, but the wages were somewhat higher than those of a domestic servant. Antônio's earnings from the Intercontinental amounted to pocket money, while Carlos had yet to find a job. With a dependent invalid and a reduced income, the family sank below the poverty line, at times being forced to eat the skin of carcasses thrown out by the local butchers for the dogs.

Immobile and inactive, Gerardo, who had always been strong and a hard worker, was steadily claimed by depression and despair. Hitherto gregarious, he spoke less frequently and with an unaccustomed indifference. As he became ever more feeble, his young son assumed the role of nurse. The leg wound never cleared up. On the contrary, tiny bits of metal festered under his skin, threatening his cardiovascular system, while his lungs were already weak from a prolonged bout of tuberculosis. Just under a year after he was shot, and still only in his late thirties, he suffered a serious stroke. A week later, a massive heart attack followed by pulmonary collapse finished him off. He had, it is true, been granted his wish to see Antônio again, but only for his son to watch him waste and die.

Antônio could not bring himself to attend the funeral of the man he considered father and mother. Henceforth he vowed never to enter a cemetery until his own passing. Having just turned twelve, he felt bereft and alone. He rarely saw his mother. Nor could he turn to his brother for comfort, given their history, their very different personalities, and the bitterness that had existed between Carlos and Gerardo. With his father gone, who would Antônio look to for guidance?

5
MORAL COLLAPSE
1989–1999

In 1987, while enjoying the beaches and women in Florianópolis, a city where Brazil's beautiful people are rumoured to live, Dênis da Rocinha was arrested. When news of his detention hit Rocinha, the favela rebelled against its middle-class neighbours 'by mounting a spectacle of violence, dubbed by the media in a sensationalist fashion "a civil war"', as one observer put it. She was describing how Rocinhans took to the streets and blocked the entrance to the Zuzu Angel Tunnel, causing the mother of traffic jams across much of Rio's South Zone. The police, with their usual uncompromising approach, cleared the tunnel using tear gas and rubber bullets. But they could not stop Rocinhans from throwing rocks and stones on to the passing traffic. The protests only stopped when Dênis eventually gave a signal from prison for them to cease.

The solidarity with Dênis demonstrated how in half a decade, the head of a drugs cartel had become the figurehead of an increasingly frustrated community. Dênis was a killer, but he administered his arbitrary system of justice and consolidated his control of the favela without the help of large-calibre guns.

His arrest generated widespread fear in Rocinha. Carlos Santos, a security guard from Rua Um, shook his head when he heard about it. Rocinha, he worried, 'is about to get messy. The various groups are now going to start squabbling and ordinary people will find themselves caught in the middle as usual.'[17]

Despite being locked up in Rio's notorious Bangu jail, Dênis continued to run the drugs business from inside his prison cell. His authority went unquestioned in Rocinha, and for a few years he was able to ensure that no power struggle broke out in his absence.

But his subalterns were impetuous, above all because they were so young. Brasileirinho, the most junior of the quartet that had taken over the running of the drugs operation, was just eleven years old. A few months after Dênis's arrest, he took part in a brief but highly symbolic event that perhaps best signalled the darkness about to descend on Rio de Janeiro throughout the 1990s and beyond.

After the funeral of one of Dênis's four proxies, shot dead by police, the other leaders, including little Brasileirinho, dressed all in white, took to one of Rocinha's roofs. Here they raised their semi-automatic guns and fired off a salute to their dead comrade in a fashion reminiscent of paramilitary ceremonies around the world. It was a swaggering challenge to the police and to the authority of the government at a time when the Brazilian state was entering a period of profound crisis.

In 1989, Brazilians were preparing to take part in the first direct elections for the presidency in two and a half decades. It was a moment of immense importance and pride. Paradoxically, as the sun of democracy rose, shadows were lengthening over the country. Along with the dramatic increase in drug-related violence, hyper-inflation was back with a vengeance after the failure of economic plans implemented by the team of President Sarney, whose administration acted as a transition from military to democratic rule.

Two of the most likely presidential candidates were well-known leftists. One was Leonel Brizola, now a grand old stalwart of the opposition, who had won the governorship of Rio in 1982. The second was Luiz Inácio Lula da Silva, an energetic activist from the metalworkers' union in São Paulo. Now in his mid forties, Lula had made a name for himself mobilising his members against the dictatorship. Like Brizola, he put the fear of God into the right wing of Brazilian politics. The right's candidates, by contrast, were lacklustre. They were ageing, and tainted by past association with the military.

Throughout Brazil, resentment towards the upper class was growing, especially now that hyperinflation was shredding the ability of ordinary people to lead a normal life. Rio and São Paulo were subject to unpredictable outbreaks of mob anger at the misery inflicted by spiralling prices, especially as this economic curse appeared to have no impact on the rich.

Since colonial times, Brazil had been one of the most unequal societies in the world, and little had changed during the twentieth century. Much of the wealth enjoyed by the top 5 per cent of the country swilled around the state and federal capitals as a means of keeping politicians securely in their pockets. Sitting alongside this institutionalised corruption was the highly decentralised nature of political power from federal to state level. Furthermore, the legacy of civilian and military dictatorships was a political system populated by unusually weak parties, which were regarded as vehicles for personal advance and enrichment rather than clear expressions of ideological commitment.

Lula's personality and politics cut right through this. And it was not just the destitute from the favelas who appeared to back him. Large swathes of the middle class were fed up with the government's failure to stem economic decline. Prices were rising by the hour; shops were holding back goods so they could take advantage of higher prices; yet all the while banks and industrialists appeared able to manipulate the situation to enrich themselves further through currency speculation.

Both Lula and Brizola were anathema to Brazilian business

and finance and much of the wealthy elite. The prospect of a Lula victory in the forthcoming October election was seen as a particular threat because his programme included the renationalisation of key industries. The United States signalled its concern too. Having driven the demolition of communism in Eastern Europe, the last thing Washington wanted to see was a man they regarded as little more than a socialist firebrand take power in the Southern Cone's largest country.

In these circumstances, Brazil's vested interests started scrambling to find somebody who could match Lula's charisma and charm. Their chosen candidate was Fernando Collor de Mello, then governor of the north-eastern state of Alagoas. Before the largest media conglomerate in the country stumbled across him, Collor enjoyed the support of just 2 per cent of Brazilians in his bid to become president. Apart from the people of Alagoas and a few nerdy political observers, he was totally unknown in the country at large.

Revolution was under way in Eastern Europe. Seizing the baton of change, Brazil too was now ready to embrace the outside world. Rather than risk experimenting with a leftist like Lula, whose policies increasingly seemed to belong to a system that was breathing its last in Prague, Berlin and Bucharest, the middle classes were persuaded to opt for somebody who promised to make their dreams come true. Tens and then hundreds of millions of dollars flowed into the Collor campaign accounts as big business became convinced it had found a man who would promote its interests in the federal government. Most media, too, needed little persuasion to place their support behind the handsome and persuasive young politician. In the election run-off against Lula, Fernando Collor won just over 50 per cent of the votes, making him the first fully democratically elected president in three decades.

It did not take long for the dream to reveal itself as a nightmare.

By the time of Collor's inauguration in early 1990, prices were rising at the breathtaking rate of 100 per cent per month. With his woefully inexperienced team installed in the presidential palace, Planalto, Collor announced that he would freeze all savings, both personal and commercial. The result was little short of catastrophic. Businesses across the country went bust, while individuals were forced to file for bankruptcy, some never to recover.

Collor also lifted tariff controls at a stroke, rendering countless Brazilian businesses uncompetitive against foreign imports. He did this largely through the use of presidential decrees, a tactic devised in order to avoid the moderating power of Congress, which he succeeded in transforming into a bitter enemy. Inflation fizzed out of control, eventually reaching an eye-watering 2,708 per cent.[18] Far from being a new start for Brazil, at times it seemed like a return to the worst form of despotism.

By 1992, it was clear to the outside world that Brazil had suffered a complete moral collapse at the heart of its government, a grave complement to the wave of violence that had crept across the cities. Collor's rule ended in impeachment, with political and financial scandals on a vast scale.

The dangerous fragility of Brazil's newly restored democracy coincided with the country being swamped by cocaine. The industry was seeping into all walks of life, and international trafficking rings were becoming increasingly influential in the trade.

Much of Collor's corrupt money was laundered through Miami – a practice that his own brother revealed in a memoir that provided the final nail in the President's coffin. Miami was the primary source of the ever more powerful weaponry entering Brazil, usually in consignments sent through the neighbouring state of Paraguay. The coordinator of Rio's anti-drug task force, Francisco Carlos Garisto, complained bitterly about the gun trade. 'The United States will sell weapons to anyone, and they don't care if they are going to

Ireland or to Brazil,'[19] he said, adding that 99 per cent of the weapons seized from the Rio gangs originated in Florida.

That didn't quite square with the facts. Two thirds of the pistols and revolvers confiscated from Rio gang members in the 1980s and 90s were in fact Brazilian in origin. The country had been a significant producer of small arms for many years. But the semi-automatic weapons that ensured the drugs trade could at first match then outgun Rio's police were indeed foreign imports.

It was during Collor's first year in office that police in Rio de Janeiro encountered the first semi-automatic weapon, a Ruger 556 manufactured in Connecticut, in the hands of a trafficker from Complexo do Alemão in the city's North Zone. This was the turning point. Weapons such as the Ruger were infinitely superior to those available to the cops. Drug traffickers were now in a position to become an autonomous paramilitary force, which would eventually transform their capacity for violence into political power.

The Rugers, the Colt AR-15s, the Kalashnikovs, and subsequently the Uzis conferred a distinct advantage on the favela gangs in Rio over the local police, who were generally equipped with inferior weapons manufactured in Brazil (in order to support domestic industry and keep costs down). The impoverished police themselves, as well as members of the armed forces, always susceptible to corruption, became important suppliers of weaponry to the gangs.

The AR-15, beloved of the traffickers, cost around $2,000 in the United States. In Rio, the going rate was around $4–5,000, so while Brazilian drug traffickers were making a healthy profit from selling cocaine to the United States and Europe, American firearms dealers were getting a good chunk of the cash back. The logic of the War on Drugs, still firmly embraced in Washington and most of Europe, had created a vicious circle of murder and excess that united the arms manufacturers of America, the traffickers of South America and the coke habits of the middle classes from Berlin to Los Angeles.

The transition to democracy in Brazil and its neighbours during the 1980s and 90s led to the emergence of what one astute observer called the first 'multinational corporation of Latin America and the first example of genuine economic integration: the production, the processing and the distribution of cocaine'.[20]

In 1982, before the illicit cocaine trade had changed the city's economic and social landscape, Rio de Janeiro's murder rate was identical to that of New York City: 23 homicides for every 100,000 inhabitants. Seven years later, in 1989, the New York figure was showing signs of a steady decline. In Rio, it had almost tripled to 63 per 100,000.[21]

These statistics speak volumes about Brazil. Before the cocaine epidemic, people were not being killed in large numbers. The local culture was no more inherently violent than that of North America. Rio's decline, beginning in the late 1980s, was above all the consequence of a policy that had failed over decades: the War on Drugs. First Colombia, then the Caribbean and Brazil, and finally Mexico have paid with the blood of literally hundreds of thousands of men, women and children for a policy of narcotics prohibition which, were it part of a private sector strategy, would have been discarded decades ago as disastrously counterproductive.

In Brazil, these circumstances triggered complex urban conflicts that in the 1990s affected Rio, especially Rocinha and many other favelas, like no other city in Brazil. In terms of overall recorded deaths, this was a low-level conflict. But in the favelas, the homicide rates were comparable to those of countries at war.[22]

At first, the struggle pitted drug traffickers against the police. Then something unique happened in Rio that occurred nowhere else in Brazil: a ruthless war broke out among the traffickers themselves, a war that would transform Rocinha from a poor but peaceful community nestled within the majesty of the Atlantic rainforest into a maelstrom of death and destitution.

The world beyond Brazil's borders was also changing. The United States and Britain had detonated the Big Bang, the deregulation of financial markets that in time would alter the structure of global capitalism and throw a spotlight on wealth inequality. In Eastern Europe, communism collapsed, creating a vast lawless zone, stretching from Yugoslavia in the west to the borders of China in the east, in which a whole variety of mafias would emerge and seek out new commercial possibilities. Huge sums of cash were released into the economy. The world boomed, and cocaine boomed with it.

In 1980, Colombian cartels were exporting around 100 tons of coke to the United States. A decade later, the figure was ten times that amount. The vogue for cocaine reached Europe about half a decade after it had penetrated the brain cells of America's professional classes. Following the revolutions in Eastern Europe and the Soviet Union in 1989 and 1990, the new mafias in that region sought connections with Italy's organised crime groups and through this conduit established relations directly with the Colombian cartels to import ever greater amounts of cocaine to Europe.

As dynamic entrepreneurs, the Colombian cartels responded to this new demand by opening up two primary wholesale routes for refined cocaine through Brazil. The first went north and into the former Dutch colony of Suriname before heading out across the Atlantic. The second went south to Santos.

As a general rule, when a country becomes a major transit route for narcotics, it soon develops a habit of its own, and that certainly applied in the case of Brazil. The length of its borders with Colombia, Peru, Bolivia and Paraguay – all producers of cocaine – is just under 9,500 kilometres. Much of that is thick Amazonian forest, where it is easy to clear small patches of vegetation in order to build the necessary landing strips to import countless tons of fully or semi-processed cocaine and densely packed marijuana from these four western neighbours. By the late 1980s, there were hundreds of such airstrips dotted all over the area.

Controllers of the trade would siphon off a small percentage of what they were pushing across the territory and send the remainder on to Europe. The two largest domestic markets for this recently hip commodity were São Paulo and Rio de Janeiro, the party city.

Because of its location between São Conrado, Gávea and Leblon, Rocinha became the key distributor of cocaine to the youth of the three upper-middle-class districts. Although some young favela residents acquired a taste for coke – or pó, as it is known in Brazil – cocaine was, and is, like elsewhere in the world, a rich kid's drug. Given the country's huge wealth inequality, there were plenty of rich kids willing to pay top dollar for their powder.

The implications of this for Rocinha were monumental. Although the neighbouring favela of Vidigal, on the other side of São Conrado and much closer to Leblon, had taken the lead in supply, Rocinha was simply much bigger, and, crucially, perceived as marginally less dangerous by the young rich kids who wanted both to score their coke and enjoy the cool frisson involved in leaving the safety of the Asphalt for the perceived Bacchanalian excitement of the Hill.

Over the next decade, shootings, torture and excess became common currency, while the overwhelming majority of Rocinha's inhabitants learned to adapt their lives to the new power structure, principally by keeping their heads down, literally and figuratively. Eventually, 60 per cent of Rio's mountainous cocaine consumption would be trafficked through Rocinha. Not only was there money in them thar hills, there were a lot of people who wanted to get their hands on it.

6

UP THE HILL
June 2000

The Don's name is Luciano Barbosa da Silva – known to everyone as Lulu. He is admired throughout Rocinha, but few have ever seen him. Indeed, even some of the people who work for him have never met him. A kid maybe ten years Antônio's junior and with a semi-automatic slung across his chest shows him to Lulu's office.

After twenty minutes or so, Lulu enters the room, smiling, accompanied by three gun-toting 'soldiers', although he himself is unarmed. He is thin and slight, with dark hair and a small moustache on a bony face, but most noticeable of all is the absence of menace. The Don of the Hill is more Wizard of Oz than Corleone. He is also, at the age of twenty-two, almost three years younger than Antônio.

Lulu greets his visitor warmly and asks him why he has sought this audience. Antônio tells him the story of his daughter, Eduarda, and how he can no longer afford the treatment and his everyday expenses. 'My daughter will die if I do nothing,' he explains.

Lulu hears him out without saying a word. At the end of the story, he is brisk.

'How much do you need?'

'In order to pay for the treatment, restore the bathroom and meet our daily requirements – about twenty thousand reals.'

Without hesitation Lulu says, 'I think we can manage that,' and waves at one of his minions, who disappears into the interior of the three-bedroom apartment.

The question of repayment settles on the living room as thick as the fog that sometimes rolls in from the Atlantic. As Lulu seeks to clear the air, Antônio blurts out, 'I will come and work for you. It is the only way I can ever meet this debt.' Lulu appears surprised but says nothing. The minion returns and counts out the cash. Antônio takes the money and shakes Lulu's hand.

'Well,' the Don says slowly, 'if this is really what you want, you can work for security. You can start up here in Rua Um.'

Antônio risks asking a favour, unsure whether it will be received as a reasonable request or an impertinence, given that they have only just met and he has asked for a wad of cash. 'I would prefer to work down in Lower Rocinha, if possible, to be nearer the family.' Lulu doesn't hesitate. 'Sure – go and see the manager in Barcelos and he'll tell you where to start.' The commercial district of Barcelos is one of the liveliest parts of Rocinha, but even so this is a modest beginning. Antônio will be told to stand in an alleyway and simply shout out a prearranged signal if he spots any police.

From Lulu's, he walks back down the Estrada da Gávea to Rua Quatro. He went up the hill as Antônio. He descends as a new man, known henceforth by the nickname o Nem, the Babe. Antônio, the man and his aspirations, is going into cold storage. Vanessa is waiting for him. She does not know how to react. Her daughter has a chance of survival, but she recognises that the family's life is about to change. They have, after all, just said goodbye to the 1990s. And the trickle of cocaine-infused blood that first arrived in the favelas in the late 1980s is by now a fast-flowing river.

Part II
HUBRIS

Two events took place within the space of a year in the early 1990s that suggested Rio de Janeiro was flirting with social and political collapse. The first, in a favela called Vigário Geral, indicated that the state had lost control of its forces of law and order. Rio's police, especially the Military Police, had become as dangerous as any of the drug gangs. The second, the murder of an influential trafficker, triggered internecine warfare across the favelas.

That war edged ever closer towards Rocinha.

1

MASSACRE

1993

The problem of trafficking will only be resolved with blood. It is the only language they understand.

Mário Azevedo, officer of the 21st Precinct,

Rio de Janeiro, 1995[1]

Sometime before 11 p.m. on Saturday 28 August 1993, a phone call came in for Sergeant Ailton Benedito Ferreira Santos. He immediately gathered three fellow police officers and took off in a squad car.[2] The sergeant neglected to alert his superiors that he was heading out, apparently to investigate a claim that there were armed men hanging around the Catolé do Rocha square, less than a kilometre from the police station.

His failure to call into the local command post was no oversight. It meant that he was up to no good. Ailton was well known locally as the ringleader of a pack of extortionists, all officers in the Military Police. Like many PMs, they augmented their pitiful salaries through shakedowns and taking bribes from drug traffickers. Their main hunting grounds were the North Zone favelas of Vigário Geral and its neighbour Parada de Lucas. In local terms, Ailton was powerful, but not without dangerous enemies. During one of his operations a couple of years earlier, he had tried to extort and then killed the brother and pregnant sister-in-law of Flavio Negrão, the man who was now the don of Vigário Geral.

Catolé do Rocha is located some 500 metres from Vigário Geral, which lies on flat ground across from Galeão International Airport. Nobody knows precisely what Sergeant Ailton was doing there that night. Later, Negrão claimed that he was waiting for 67 kilos of coke to pitch up from São Paulo. The sergeant and his colleagues wanted a slice of that rich cake. The police and the media offered a different version. Ailton's mission, they claimed, was nothing so grand. Rather it was a simple excursion to pick up his regular bribe from Negrão's people. In many favelas, part of the profits from the cocaine trade was diverted to local policemen in order to keep them off the traffickers' backs.

Whatever Ailton believed he was going to encounter, he was wrong. The 67 kilos never turned up. It was a trap.

When the squad car pulled into the square, a VW van, a Beetle, and a grey Fiat surrounded it. Ten men emerged, firing relentlessly. Drawing their unreliable Brazilian pistols, the cops were no match for the attackers, who wielded AR-15s and large-calibre pistols. Two of Ailton's colleagues were killed almost immediately, while he and one other managed to find cover behind a parked car. In the passenger seat of that vehicle sat a fifteen-year-old girl, who was there by chance that evening – another innocent bystander in the drugs war. At first the shootout sent her into shock; then, when a bullet went through her leg, into agony.

Ailton and the other policeman were less fortunate. After an exchange of fire lasting fifteen minutes, they were both dead. The assailants threw all four bodies into the back of the police car and drove away, abandoning the vehicle after 500 metres; the petrol tank had been hit during the shooting, and it was already out of fuel. Back in the square, the girl survived, as did the other

50 or so bystanders who were there when the trouble broke out.

Flavio Negrão later claimed that the cop killers were not his men but a team of plain-clothes detectives who wanted the 67 kilos for themselves. He did admit, however, that he had circulated a rumour that the coke would turn up on the square that evening as a diversionary tactic, so that its real route to Vigário Geral would remain secret. The drugs lord denied categorically any involvement in the murders. Even so, police and media reports insist to this day that the four policemen died at the hands of Negrão's gang.

The mood among the Military Police officers around Rio was sombre as their four colleagues were buried with full honours later on the Sunday afternoon. There was growing restlessness among the PM rank and file. Many believed that Governor Brizola, along with his Secretary for Public Security and the chief superintendent of the PM in Rio, was making the officers' lives difficult by depriving them of resources. They were badly paid and were at risk of being killed by the traffickers. The PM officers argued that Brizola, the old leftist, demonstrated much greater concern for the human rights of drug traffickers and other criminals from the favelas. Cop killers, they claimed, were always walking free.

Frustrated by a perceived lack of political backing, and unhappy with their low pay and poor equipment, not to mention the daily dangers they faced, officers of the PM had been gradually taking matters into their own hands since the early 1980s. The rise of the cocaine gangs and the rudderless aspect of the Collor years had added to their sense of isolation and paranoia. Their freelance activities enjoyed the tacit support of their commanders, as well as a large part of the middle class frightened by what they regarded as the menace of the favelas.

These officers formed the core of embryonic vigilante groups, which also recruited prison guards, firemen and former soldiers. The groups, which became known as militias, would succeed in expelling the drugs gangs from a considerable number of favelas, especially those situated far in the north of Rio, away from the cocaine markets of the South Zone. At the same time, they developed into organised protection rackets, with a strong resemblance to the Italian Mafia. Before long, they had seized control of all services into the favelas – water, post, energy, transport and communications – which generated significant profits, guaranteed by their state-issued weapons.

The murder of Sergeant Ailton and his colleagues proved to be a turning point in this whole process.

Almost exactly 24 hours after the events in Catolé do Rocha, a much larger group of 40 to 50 men swung into Corsica Square, just south of where the four police officers had been gunned down. Clad in woollen masks, and black and red shirts with a distinct paramilitary flavour, these men were equipped with much better weapons than Ailton and his team. Setting the tone for the evening, they shot dead without warning an eighteen-year-old lad sipping beer at a drinks stand. From there they walked through the square where their colleagues had been killed, over the bridge crossing the urban train line and into Vigário Geral, where they ripped out the lines into the favela's phone booths.

A few yards from the rail track, a group of workers sat around in a poky bar enjoying Brazil's thumping 6–0 victory over Bolivia in a World Cup qualifying game. Suddenly several of the masked men burst through the door. They announced they were police and demanded to see IDs. Before the customers could pull out their cards, one of the paramilitaries threw a grenade into their midst and several others opened fire. Seven were killed.

At a house opposite, a window slammed shut as someone inside heard the commotion coming from the bar. The assailants ran at the front door and burst into a home where thirteen family members were enjoying an evening together. Amidst much screaming and panic, the killers discussed whether to spare the five children in the house. The oldest, just ten years old, grasped the chance to flee with her four younger siblings, one aged under a year. The rest of the family, devout worshippers at the Church of the Assembly of God, were shot dead, the 56-year-old materfamilias expiring with a bible clutched to her breast.

Five more residents of Vigário Geral were butchered at random that night, making a total of 21. In a decade of bloodshed, Rio had never seen anything like this massacre. The city was still recovering from the horrific events at the Church of Candelária just over a month earlier, when six children and two adolescents who had been sleeping rough around one of Rio's most famous religious landmarks had been murdered in cold blood by another police death squad. The events at Vigário Geral reiterated, were it needed, how far the state had lost control of the police – or possibly how far the state now sanctioned aberrant police activity.

In the early part of the 1990s, Rio's police were rapidly evolving into an autonomous fighting force whose interests may or may not have coincided with those of the state. Whatever the truth, it was no longer performing the job it had been designed for. 'When looking at this period you have to free yourself from the illusion that the police were acting as an agency to enforce the criminal law,' explained a former adviser to the Secretary for Public Security in Rio. 'It was simply one of the warring parties competing for financial control over the favelas and the drugs trade.'

For a brief period, Vigário Geral brought together Rio's disparate communities: businesses, residents' associations, academics, and big media corporations. In a moving display of unity, they organised a Day of Silence, when for five minutes the entire city stopped what it was doing to commemorate those who had died.

Rio's post-war history was a tale of two communities: those who lived in the favelas, and those who lived outside and never entered them. For the latter, the favelas represented a frightening foreign world where great danger lurked. The muggings, the car thefts and the regular chorus of semi-automatic weapons were ominous signs of how the alien culture was gradually seeping out from its confines on the Hill and subverting the Miraculous City.

Attuned to these sentiments, the candidates in the forthcoming gubernatorial elections started to demand more support for the police and more decisive action against the traffickers and the favelas that harboured them. Under pressure, the liberal incumbent, Brizola, eventually announced a new plan, Operação Rio. In conjunction with the federal government, Rio's authorities decided to call in the army.

Nonetheless, Vigário Geral would not be forgotten. The collaborators who inspired the Day of Silence also spawned several of Rio's most remarkable NGOs, who work to this day seeking ways to reduce violence in the city.[3]

Like almost everyone from the favelas, Antônio was shocked by Vigário Geral. He was a law-abiding citizen who was just establishing himself in his first proper job as a magazine distributor for Globus Express. It was hideous confirmation of what most people from the favelas had presumed for two decades – that the police were not police in a conventional sense but a faction at war with other factions in the favelas. The main difference in their approach, so far as he was concerned, was that the police felt no regard or responsibility for the residents themselves. It was a lesson he would remember later: avoid confrontation with the police wherever possible, because it made life much more difficult.

Vigário Geral was controlled by Red Command. Neighbouring Parada de Lucas belonged to Terceiro Comando, the Third Command. Each territory was a no-go area for the other, and if anyone strayed, even ordinary citizens who had nothing to do with the drugs trade, they risked running into serious trouble. Should one of the drugs soldiers cross over, it might precipitate a minor war. The alley separating the two was known as Vietnam.

But after the massacre, the Vigário Geral residents' association appealed to its opposite number in Parada de Lucas. In sympathy with their fellow favela residents, the leadership of Third Command agreed to end their feud with Red Command in Vigário Geral. Such solidarity, however, was very much the exception.

2

ORLANDO JOGADOR

1994

As Demétrio Martins was dragged from the mud-filled ditch where he had fallen and was dumped by the side of the road, he felt as if a frost were slowly descending on his body, followed by excruciating pain, and finally a strong wind that seemed to blow up through his legs and then his guts. It was as though his spirit was rising and he was able to look down at his own corpse below. It was then that he heard God speak to him: 'I have a plan for you.'

His spirit sank back down into his body but he could no longer feel his legs, nor his arms. Try as he might, he could not move his head either. The only body parts that responded to his brain's entreaties were his eyes, furiously darting this way and that. He felt his head being turned by someone's strong hand. Then he saw the face of the preacher who two years earlier had predicted that one day he would spread the word of the Lord from a wheelchair. Now, before falling into unconsciousness, he heard the preacher's voice: 'You are not going to die.'

It would be a mistake to underestimate the attraction and power of faith in Brazil. Not just in the favelas, but across most classes, regions, races and religions. There is little coherence to the belief that spans those geographical and social divisions. Syncretism, the absorption and refashioning of rituals and iconography from one religion into another, has created so many hybrids that individuals and households are practically able to customise their devotional practice.

Brazil still has the largest Catholic population of any country in the world, but Rome is rapidly losing adherents to Protestant churches, particularly to charismatic evangelists, which now account for the faith of almost a quarter of all Brazilians. There are some very big evangelical churches, such as the Universal Church of the Kingdom of God, which has spread its gospel across the world and made a huge amount of money in doing so. But there are also thousands upon thousands of self-styled evangelical pastors, who attract a congregation in their front room or from a soapbox. If you walk down Estrada da Gávea in Rocinha, every third shop front or house appears to be a makeshift church.

Many things have contributed to the success of the evangelical charismatics. In a consumer culture, for example, the fatalism of Catholic teaching, which promises rewards in the hereafter, no longer appeals. Evangelicals hold out the possibility of economic success on earth as well as a spiritual payoff in heaven.

The rapid rise of evangelism in the favelas coincided with the dramatic growth of the cocaine industry. These religious movements often provide a refuge for ordinary people from the regime of violence imposed by both the traffickers and the police. The Church in its various forms is also the one institution that traffickers think twice about trying to co-opt, subvert or destroy (unlike the residents' associations, which are regularly subordinated to the requirements of the cartels). While there is a generous streak of charlatanism among the various self-appointed sects, the work of some individual pastors and churches inside the favelas across Brazil is nothing less than awe-inspiring.[4]

Demétrio Martins' first encounter with the preacher had occurred two years before he was shot. Martins, in his early twenties, had been a prominent trafficker, full of life and swagger. He worked as a senior manager for Red Command in its largest operation, the immense network of over a dozen favelas known as Complexo do Alemão.

It was a tough job that carried considerable responsibility. Demétrio was charged with managing the takings from a large number of smoke shops before the end of the night shift at 8 a.m.

Smoke shops initially sold marijuana – hence their name – and although that drug was still available, by now these pop-up stores were mainly selling cocaine. They varied in size – a young lad with a stash of coke in a backpack was effectively a mobile shop – but in large favelas or groups of favelas like Complexo do Alemão, where the police ventured only occasionally, they were fixed places that did a brisk trade.

Demétrio had to ensure that all the shops were kept well stocked. That meant a lot of cash changing hands in exchange for a lot of coke and dope. But he loved it. He loved the money and he loved showing it off. He loved the respect that money bought him in the community.

His boss, Orlando Jogador,[5] had taught him about the importance of respect. Jogador was the don of Alemão, in control of what was at the time the largest retail cocaine operation in all Rio. To the outsider, the various favelas making up Alemão melt into one another, seeming at times to stretch to the horizon. Between 200,000 and 300,000 people live on and around several giant undulations, immense waves caught in a moment of stasis. To the east, the Catholic Church of the Rock stands solitary on the only hill not covered in barnacle-like shacks.

The respect with which Jogador treated his community added considerable value to his turnover. In the absence of the state, he was the provider of both welfare and justice. And he dispensed these judiciously. People would talk about Jogador, then as now, with a reverence that bordered on the sacred.

Demétrio felt proud to work for such a boss. For all his big-man

posing, though – the jewellery, the guns and the women – he understood that he had to behave responsibly. Orlando Jogador had drilled
it into him: he must think before acting, and the respect due to
him should not come solely from his ability to fire a gun or dispense
large amounts of cash. Which didn't mean, of course, that he and
his 30 gun-toting soldiers were not intended to be a terrifying sight
as they patrolled the favela in the early hours.

Jogador was the first trafficker who instituted what could properly be called a welfare system in a favela. 'He had rules,' explains
Adriano, one of his soldiers, who has long since retired. 'Rules for
us and rules for the community.' With regard to the soldiers, he was
the first to introduce a system whereby anyone who wanted to
leave the organisation could do so without fear of retribution. Some
other dons regarded such a course as intolerable disloyalty, to be
punished by death. Jogador, by contrast, encouraged any man who
found a job outside the business to leave. Not many did, of course,
because the economic benefits in the real world paled against those
offered by the cocaine industry.

For the residents, he paid for medical assistance, basic food
requirements and burials. Given the size of Alemão, this indicates
how lucrative the operation was. 'Huge sums of money were being
generated by the business,' confirms Demétrio.

Then there was justice. Unlike most traffickers at the time,
Jogador instituted an informal court to adjudge, for example,
whether a man had indeed committed rape as the accuser (or often
the mother of the accuser) had claimed. If it was proved to Jogador's
satisfaction that the crime had taken place, then, in the case of
rape, the perpetrator would be executed. The more gruesome forms
of torture and execution that characterised some of the favela
regimes in the decade to come had yet to become regular practice.
A swift bullet to the head was still the preferred method of
dispatching a transgressor.

Thus Jogador dispensed justice – of sorts. But he was still a dictator: he claimed a monopoly on violence and there was no accountability to his rule. Thankfully for the people of Alemão, however, he was an enlightened dictator. Tall and lanky, he is remembered for his bright green eyes and quiet temperament, which has become part of the saintly myth surrounding his memory.

This policy of assisting the residents where the state had simply reneged on its obligations undoubtedly reflected his personal beliefs and morality. But it was also part of his business strategy. He was by far the largest retail trader of cocaine in all Rio, and by looking after the ordinary residents, he ensured a peaceful environment in which to conduct his business. Before long he was responsible for the largest percentage of Red Command's income. This generated respect, but it also engendered jealousy.

One day, Demétrio was with his armed entourage when he was approached by a stranger. The man walked right up to him and, pressing his bible against Demétrio's gun, said, 'This weapon you carry in your hand will only take life if God wills it. And I will tell you something without fear of contradiction. If you do not forsake this life that you lead in the shortest time possible, you will come to Him through pain. You will scream and you will preach the word of God from a wheelchair. Thus spake the Lord.' Demétrio shook his head, stayed his men from assaulting the preacher, walked on and put the incident from his mind.

He remembered it one morning a couple of years later when he had just finished collecting the cash from the smoke shops and was heading home. He told his boys to disperse and had begun walking towards the point where the favela met the forest when he heard a shot. Turning round, he saw the police. Demétrio started running, but the second bullet hit him in the back and he fell. The cops dragged him out to the side of the road, intending possibly to return later to 'disappear' the corpse.

It was then that he felt his spirit leave his body and heard the voice of God. And once it was established that he would never walk again, Demétrio Martins became Pastor Demétrio, and has continued to preach for over twenty years in the same narrow alleyways where he once sold cocaine.

A few weeks after Demétrio was injured, Jogador agreed to see the don of a neighbouring favela. His name was Uê,[6] and he was a highly intelligent, experienced, ambitious and violent man. He controlled three favelas in the neighbourhood, his own base being Adeus, which adjoined Alemão. There had been tension between the two men over the years, and there was a rumour that Jogador had murdered Uê's brother.

Jogador wanted to get relations back on an even keel, so when Uê suggested a meeting, he readily agreed. Uê arrived at the top of the hill with his team of armed backup, ostensibly to discuss the purchase of arms and ammunition. As the most powerful trafficker in Rio, Jogador had access to large amounts of both.

The atmosphere at the meeting was convivial, with both sides drinking and exchanging stories. Suddenly, at just past midnight on 14 June 1994, Uê's soldiers pulled out their guns and mowed down twelve of the Alemão men, including Jogador, who took ten bullets, most of them fired from the notorious AR-15.

Uê's men celebrated wildly, firing their weapons into the air and dragging Jogador's corpse and those of his slain soldiers around the heart of Alemão in a grisly victory parade. They then dumped the bodies in different parts of the city. Half of them, including Jogador's, were left by the nearby metro station of Maria da Graças. This was to ensure that everyone from Alemão got the message that there had been a regime change. But the consequences of this assassination were even more far-reaching. It led to the emergence of a factional struggle between drug cartels in Rio that almost brought the city to its knees and which continues to plague it to this day.

Uê's embrace of gratuitous violence proclaimed how badly Rio had lost its way. The police officer who finally arrested him considered him to be thoroughly evil, albeit extremely intelligent. She believes, for example, that Uê devised the gruesome punishment known as the microwave, where the victim would be 'dressed' in old tyres covered in gasoline and then set alight.[7] The microwave symbolised the degree to which some traffickers had become detached from any trace of humanity.

When people I met in Alemão described the changes after Uê assumed control, it reminded me of a coup by totalitarian forces. Many of Jogador's soldiers fled the complex as Uê's troops, recruited from communities across Rio, moved into the territory. Supporters of Jogador who remained were hunted down by Uê's praetorian guard and either executed or expelled from their favela. Ordinary citizens were forced to swear allegiance to Uê, albeit in a rather haphazard way. People in the favelas are reluctant to talk about the drugs business at the best of times, especially to outsiders. But as Uê consolidated his position, they were even afraid to talk among themselves.

In what may have been an expression of sheer ignorance or a conscious attempt to stir an already bubbling cauldron, the police briefed the media that the leadership of Red Command had ordered Uê to assume control of Complexo do Alemão. They claimed that Marcinho VP, the imprisoned leader of Red Command, believed that Orlando Jogador had grown too big for his boots and that the leadership, or *cupola*, wanted a bigger portion of the dividends from the business.

In fact the opposite was true. Far from delivering Complexo to Red Command, Uê strengthened his friendship with various dons around the city who belonged to Third Command, Red Command's great rival. Third Command agreed to enter into an alliance with Uê, who together with his closest associates formed a third drugs faction in Rio – Amigos dos Amigos, Friends of Friends, or ADA as it is now known.

From the start, ADA opposed Red Command's domination of Rio's drug market, and henceforth many favelas were actual or potential battlegrounds as the city's three factions struggled for supremacy.

As various participants described the war between these different groupings, it put me in mind of the plot of George Orwell's *Nineteen Eighty-Four*, in which the three mighty geopolitical entities Oceania, Eurasia and Eastasia engage in a state of 'perpetual war' through a system of revolving alliances. Some of the bigger agglomerations of favelas, such as the Complexo da Maré, would eventually host all three factions, leading to exceptionally high levels of violence. The Orwell scenario came closer to reality after 2002, when much of Third Command re-formed as Terceiro Comando Puro (TCP), or the Pure Third Command – which broke off the alliance with ADA.

Rio de Janeiro's experience of drug wars was developing in a unique direction. The very geography of the city, with its steep hills, its ravines and its patches of Atlantic rainforest, encouraged the factional divisions once they had begun to develop. Favelas like Rocinha or Vidigal in the South Zone were physically isolated, with natural borders of flora, water or high ground. The sense of individual territories and a highly localised patriotism was much greater in this city than elsewhere in the country.

Furthermore, once the factional fighting became a daily event, the police quickly discovered that this could work to their advantage. The three groupings exerted much of their effort and weaponry on trying to kill each other. This led to the loss of the cartels' most valuable resource: manpower. If a favela was weakened as a consequence of factional fighting, it was more vulnerable to the practice of extortion, which was now widespread among Rio's various police forces. By 1995, the city's murder rate reached a staggering 70.6 per 100,000 inhabitants – not far off Colombia's death rate at the same time, when the Medellin and Cali cartels were at the height of their power.[8] Over 90 per cent of those deaths were in favelas, and 90 per cent of those were males between the ages of 14 and 26.

At the time, it was the most violent city in Brazil. In a country of that size, Rio de Janeiro and São Paulo are virtually next-door neighbours. Yet one is very different from the other. São Paulo is an enormous metropolis, which, along with the eponymous state, reaches deep into Brazil's southern interior. The city is the economic engine of the country, with a population that had already reached 10 million by the early 1990s. The state of São Paulo accounts for about a fifth of the country's population but just under a third of its economic output. Close by São Paulo lies Brazil's biggest port, Santos, the export hub for cocaine heading for west Africa and Europe.

The city's cultural traditions are very different from those of Rio, where the heritage of colonialism is palpable. When João VI, prince regent of Portugal, together with Maria I and a retinue of nearly 15,000 people, fled Napoleon's invading army in 1808, they decamped to Rio de Janeiro, and, to a degree, life in the city still reflects the languid style of the imperial court. Where aristocratic largesse (often debt-fuelled) characterised Rio, it was German, Italian and later Japanese immigration that fashioned the hard-working and acquisitive culture of São Paulo. The *paulistas* identify with the tradition of the bandeirantes,[9] whose courageous and risky penetration of Brazil's interior eventually led to a significant expansion of the colony's territory and the discovery of vast mineral resources (much of which the Portuguese crown managed to squander).

Building on this entrepreneurial tradition, São Paulo has also demonstrated a stubborn separate political identity, and in the last century has sought on at least one occasion to sever its connection with the rest of Brazil through force of arms. This separatism is much less pronounced nowadays, although paulistas often find it hard to suppress their distinct sense of superiority over the rest of the country, and have a spicy cultural rivalry with Rio in particular.

Rio lost its status when Brasília was made the country's capital in 1960. It has never quite recovered. Apart from the prestige, it also lost tens of thousands of government jobs to the brash newcomer. In the eighties and nineties, it also haemorrhaged entire industrial sectors to São Paulo, not least of which was the banking industry. One reason for this was the perceived indolence of the cariocas in contrast to the fierce industry of the paulistas. Another was the almost intolerable levels of violence in Rio's South Zone and centre.

The introduction of cocaine into São Paulo also triggered a dramatic increase in violence there. But wealthy paulistas enjoyed an advantage over their carioca counterparts by dint of the two cities' differing geography. São Paulo is much less hilly than Rio, so that when the great immigration from the north-east accelerated from the 1950s onwards, the new labour force did not populate the empty spaces right in the heart of the city as they did in Rio. Instead, their communities grew up as part of a flat urban sprawl, much further away from the centre and the core residential and business districts.

As in Rio, most of the violence associated with the drugs trade was concentrated in the favelas. But since these were situated on the periphery, the middle and upper classes of São Paulo were less exposed to daily bloodshed and the use of firearms.

Brazil's economic powerhouse was a latecomer to the world of organised criminal groups. The peculiar history of the criminal gangs in Rio who encountered the political prisoners on Ilha Grande during the military dictatorship did not apply in São Paulo.[10] In October

1992, however, Sao Paulo's Military Police and special forces perpetrated a massacre inside a prison that left 111 inmates dead, butchered like cattle. In response, a group of prisoners formed an organisation called the Primeiro Comando da Capital (PCC), or the First Command of the Capital. Its inaugural mission statement, borrowed from the language of the human rights movement, claimed that it had been established to defend prisoners and the people of the favelas. Later on, Red Command gave itself credit for having guided the PCC leadership in its earliest phases, and certainly the rhetoric of the São Paulo organisation mirrored Red Command's early strategy of projecting an image of social liberation for the favelas.

The PCC introduced a strict set of rules and required members to pay a monthly subscription. Failure to make payments resulted in punishment, even execution. In contrast to the more cavalier attitude of the Rio gangs, the PCC, true to its paulista origins, has always kept meticulous records of its income and expenditure. On those occasions when these computerised lists have fallen into the hands of public prosecutors, it makes it much easier to reconstruct both the PCC's financial activity and its membership structure.

In stark contrast to the development of factional violence and competition in Rio, there were no serious challengers to the PCC from within São Paulo's criminal world. Before long, it had started to spread to other states in Brazil, and it also established liaison offices in Paraguay, Bolivia and Colombia. It was on its way to becoming the largest, best-organised and most lucrative criminal syndicate anywhere in the Americas, including Mexico.

One place it made no attempt to infiltrate was Rio de Janeiro. 'My feeling is the PCC took one look at the mess between the factions here in Rio and said to itself, "Thanks but no thanks – I don't think we need to get bogged down in that mess,"' as one Rio police intelligence officer has noted.[11]

It did, however, establish cordial links with Red Command, and as its country-wide operations began to expand, so did its ability to increase its influence over the wholesale market for Brazil in general.

Although Red Command retained its dominant position in the drugs trade in Rio, the newly formed ADA and its allies in the Third Command were providing real competition. Even within Red Command favelas, there were some tensions as the various local bosses tried to fight for more autonomy from Red Command's leadership. One of those favelas was Rocinha.

3

LULU'S LAW
1999–2004

By the beginning of 1999, life was significantly more peaceful in Rocinha. Luciano Barbosa da Silva, known variously as Lulu da Rocinha, or o *Magro*, the Thin Man, had finally assumed control of the entire favela, upper and lower. Since the arrest of Dênis da Rocinha in 1987, a series of dons had controlled the area on behalf of Red Command. The average life expectancy of the Rocinha dons, once they reached the top, was approximately ten months. Their careers were curtailed either by arrest or, in most cases, by murder. During this period, Rocinha was often parcelled out between two or three leaders, all hand-picked by Dênis from his prison cell.

He played a game of divide and rule that created serious friction between the young men controlling Upper Rocinha and those who ran the lower part of the favela. Their authority derived from the stockpiles of weaponry they had accumulated with profits from the cocaine trade. They were generally aged between about 17 and 28. Some were reasonable, while others were near-psychopaths who readily indulged in murder. But once Dênis gave Lulu his blessing in 1998, the atmosphere in Rocinha improved considerably.

Although Lulu was in fact Dênis's cousin, he was quite unlike the majority of traffickers. Born to devout evangelical parents in the north-eastern state of Paraíba, the region that provided more of

Rocinha's inhabitants than any other, one of Lulu's unusual characteristics as a don was his invisibility. Although Rocinhans came to
worship him, they rarely if ever saw him, and few ever spoke to him.

He lived in Laboriaux, at the very top of Rocinha – a district
that is somewhat detached from the rest of the favela. The road to
Laboriaux rises steeply from the peak of Estrada da Gávea. To the
right, Gávea's opulent mansions, with their manicured gardens,
swimming pools, private tennis courts and football pitches, are built
into the lush rainforest. Beyond them sits the lagoon, which is
surrounded in a big circle by the other fashionable districts of the
South Zone: Leblon, Ipanema, Copacabana and Botafogo. If you
turn around, you see Rocinha rolling down the hill towards São
Conrado and the Atlantic Ocean.

Carry on walking up the great hill towards Laboriaux and the
atmosphere becomes bucolic and calming. Although it still looks
like a favela, Laboriaux seems cleaner and tidier. As you reach the
end of the road, the tropical forest begins to envelop you. It is
possibly the most beautiful part of any favela in Rio.

Lulu had built his home just where Laboriaux ended and the
forest began. It was about as far away from the hustle and bustle
of the smoke shops, the guns, the moto taxis, and the thriving
commerce of Rocinha as you could get without actually leaving
the favela. Today the forest is steadily reclaiming and suffocating the
foundations and walls of the house. But in Lulu's day, it was an
attractive, well-appointed middle-class dwelling with stunning
views.

He had a second house close by in Rua Um. This was effectively
the office and headquarters of the drugs operation, and was in turn
not far from the main weapons storage centre.

Few drug traffickers had a clearer vision of their function than
Lulu. Half a decade earlier, sentiment and a deep attachment to
Complexo do Alemão had motivated Orlando Jogador. Just like him,

Lulu understood that as the Don, he had to create a virtuous circle by securing the support of the favela, ploughing part of the profits back into the community and creating a climate of economic growth. It was a conscious commercial strategy. 'I am a businessman,' he would say. 'I don't do war, because war is bad for business.'

During the 1990s, Rocinha had to adapt to the era of the drug lords, but in fact it was for many years a less violent place than others. Located far from the rival nexuses of the narcotics trade – Alemão, the Complexo da Maré and the rest of the North Zone – it was initially spared much of the factional fighting. 'Rocinha was different,' explains Carlos Costa. 'It was rarely characterised by confrontation. The big issue in Rocinha was the commercialisation of the narcotics trade.' Problems did crop up, however, when the dons left home for business or pleasure (which they did frequently). Lulu often disappeared for days, weeks or even months, and when he did, fights broke out between his young lieutenants, police bribes would go unpaid and there would be armed confrontations.

Lulu established a council whose job was to mediate disputes among his own managers and soldiers as well as between his traffickers and the community leaders. He would always insist that they reach a compromise. Parents often brought complaints against his men selling drugs to their children, and Lulu regularly placed restrictions on the sale of drugs to people inside the favela. It was a conscious piece of self-regulation inasmuch as it reduced his turnover but paid dividends within the community. Like Jogador, he encouraged those of his soldiers who wanted to leave to find legitimate jobs, and he would help to set them on their way.

I have spoken to many Rocinhans about Lulu. I never encountered a single one who did not talk of his time in power as a golden age. 'He was incomparable, a person whom I liked and admired and do so to this day,' said William da Rocinha, a former president of the residents' association. 'He helped so many people here in Rocinha, but he also had friends in outside society – celebrities, footballers, businessmen. I've never met another trafficker like him.'

Although Lulu was often invisible, when ordinary Rocinhans approached him, he would always listen and respond. Simone da Silva was returning to Rocinha after a rare trip with her boyfriend into Rio's most upmarket shopping district, Leblon. Simone worked six days a week demonstrating Johnson & Johnson products in a supermarket, for very modest returns. Her boyfriend was wearing the watch she had given him as a birthday gift. She had saved for months in order to afford it. As the bus passed the filthy urban canal that divides Leblon in two, a young man spotted the watch. With a knife bulging through his big orange jacket, he forced Simone's boyfriend to hand it over before leaping off the vehicle. Simone gave chase but failed to catch him. But she did recognise him – he was from Rocinha, just as she was. Under Lulu's law, the local thieves were forbidden to steal from favela residents.

Back home, Simone met a friend she thought could help her. 'I need to talk to the Don,' she said. 'Can you put me in touch with him?'

Following the instructions given, she ventured around 11.30 at night to the bottom of Valão, the Rocinha district named after the open sewer running down it. She couldn't mistake the venue. A large number of young armed men and one or two women were standing in the open air, talking and laughing underneath the dim lights. Individuals came and went, almost certainly bringing in cash from the smoke shops, as midnight marked the end of the shift.

Simone had always avoided contact with anyone she referred to as *vagabundos*, guys in the drugs trade. 'When I got there, I plucked up the courage and asked to speak to Lulu.'

'Who wants to speak to him, and what about?' came the gruff reply from one of the team.

Simone's voice was barely audible: 'I can only discuss it with him.'

She was told to wait, and eventually the crowd parted to reveal a slight man with a moustache sitting on a plastic chair. His face was obscured by shadow, but he was wearing flip-flops, and around his neck was a gold chain with a disc bearing the single letter L in white gold. As was his custom, he was not armed.

'You wish to speak with me?' he said in a matter-of-fact way.

Simone explained that she had been mugged, and described the culprit. Lulu listened carefully and then replied, 'Well, this is a good time, because the thieves are due about now to report to me.' Muggers operating out of Rocinha were obliged to show him the items they had garnered, and explain their provenance. He would then exact a tribute.

Simone stepped back out of Lulu's sight. A couple of minutes later, the thief appeared. She strode up to him and punched him in the chest, demanding the return of her watch, which the thief was wearing. 'Have you told Lulu?' he asked anxiously. 'Yes,' she replied, 'but I didn't know your name.' He returned the watch but told her that if she pursued the matter any further with Lulu, he would come and find her. The threat was clear.

Simone, thrilled to get her precious watch back, thought no more of it. A week later, however, she heard that the thief had been murdered. She never learned whether his death was related to her complaint.

In addition to dispensing justice, Lulu acted as a casual mortgage-broker, lending people money for the deposit on an apartment. This killed two birds with one stone: it was a constructive way of money-laundering, which invested the profits of the drugs trade in the legitimate economy; and it also won the approval of the community.

Critical to his success was the wholesale bribery of the police force, in particular the officers stationed around the favela. Against payment, they would act as his first line of intelligence, warning him if there were any suspicious movements in the vicinity, either by rival drug traffickers or by other police departments.

Paying off the cops brought other advantages. Attempts to extort the residents tailed off, and the atmosphere of calm and prosperity benefited the entire economy. Under Lulu, banks opened their first favela branches; Bob's, Rio's home-grown version of McDonald's, felt the environment safe enough to establish a branch in the middle of Estrada da Gávea; shops selling televisions and other white goods proliferated, and some enterprising businessman even opened the first sex shop in a favela. Above all, it was boom time for three big service industries: Light, the electric company; the moto taxis that buzzed in and out of the alleys like disoriented bees; and the distributors of gas canisters, used everywhere for cooking.

These conditions led to a dramatic drop in the level of violence in Rocinha. By 2002, after three years of Lulu's regime, there were just under 21 unnatural deaths per 100,000 – over a third fewer than the city average. It wasn't yet Vienna or Milan, but it was one of the safest places in urban Brazil.

The upshot was that Rocinha became known under Lulu as 'the middle-class favela' – and so it seemed when wandering around the bustling commercial districts. Yet it was not all a story of burgeoning success. In spite of the banks, the nail bars and the hairdressers, Rocinha still faced enormous social problems, connected with extreme poverty. Along its south-eastern stretch, from Roupa Suja up to the far end of Rua Um, noxious smells, broken masonry and infants suffering from malnutrition are still signs today of social decay and distress as profound as one encounters anywhere in the world. In 2004, a leading think tank revealed that Rocinha scored very low in most of the development indices, especially education, while a fifth of its population lived below the poverty line.[12] Basic sanitation was still thoroughly inadequate, and disease stalked most of the favela like an animal never sated. Nonetheless, where Lulu could help, he did.

While Rocinha was among the safest favelas in Rio, it was, as during Orlando Jogador's time in Alemão, still an enlightened dictatorship with an unaccountable boss whose power ultimately relied on a lot of untrained young men with very powerful guns.

The Don was aware of jealousies, possible betrayals and potential conflicts among his soldiers, but he didn't always handle them as effectively as he might. Beneath the surface, grievances were developing, especially among the twenty-five or so senior managers and security personnel.

Nem had joined the team two years previously, and Lulu was increasingly coming to rely on him – though not as his designated heir. There was no established mechanism for choosing a successor in the event of a don's death or disappearance. Few if any departing bosses left clear instructions as to who should next wear the crown, and this ambiguity often caused problems.

Although Lulu never broadcast it, most people assumed that there were two dons-elect. For Lower Rocinha there was Bem-te-vi, a consummate party animal whom Lulu treated like a younger brother. He was named after the bright yellow bird known in English as the great kiskadee, which perhaps reflected his chirpy personality. Lulu told Nem that Bem-te-vi would be one of the next leaders. 'But I do realise,' he added, laughing aloud, 'that he'll make one unholy mess of the place!' Not many were laughing when Bem-te-vi actually did come to power.

Upper Rocinha would belong to the more level-headed Zarur, who over the years had modified what one observer described as his more brutal tendencies. But there were other pretenders: men such as Lion, a hot-tempered youngster, and Band, who wielded real authority because his father had been a founder member of Red Command. This uncertain future, combined with individual ambition, posed a serious threat to the peace of Rocinha.

Nem was not considered potential don material at this time. He was not a big gunslinger. He was inconspicuous, somebody who carried out his allotted tasks efficiently and without complaint. He was older than many of the others, and, having held down a proper job in the outside world for several years before joining Lulu, he had acquired a greater sense of responsibility.

In the two years since Lulu had advanced him the money to pay for his daughter's treatment, Nem had been assiduously paying off the debt, which was finally cleared in 2004. By then he had moved up the organisation. At 7 p.m. one day in early 2003, Lulu called him up and asked him to attend a meeting right away. 'I thought it odd,' Nem remembers, 'because at the time he was not accustomed to summoning somebody low-level like me in the early evening.' Lulu explained that one of his soldiers had turned up dead in Vila Verde, close by the favela's entrance. 'We don't know who did it,' he admitted, 'so I need you to take over security for Cachopa.' This came in the wake of the unexplained death of a civilian who worked at a local radio station. 'We can't have this mess going on, especially since it's affecting the residents,' Lulu told Nem. 'Your job is to sort it out.'

This was a promotion. Nem had now reached the status equivalent to the 'made man' in New York's mafia. Henceforth he would be in command of three smoke shop managers and about 25 armed men. The agent for Cachopa was responsible for a large part of Rocinha – from Vila Verde up to Dionéia. The area had the second largest turnover of the entire drugs operation after the main commercial region in Barcellos and Valão.

With the elevated responsibility and social status, Nem was

beginning to change. In his personal life, he was slowly assuming the codes and behaviour of the gangster's world that he now inhabited professionally.

By 2002, Simone da Silva, the woman whose watch had been stolen, was the single mother of a three-year-old girl. 'I tried to survive on my own,' she said, 'but money was so tight that I couldn't guarantee to feed my daughter every day.' Although she had been born and raised in Rocinha, Simone's mother had returned to her family home in Paraíba, and it was thought best that she should take the little girl, Thayná, back with her to the north-east.

Simone was slim and attractive, with finely chiselled features, a sharp nose and watchful eyes. One day she was walking near Rua Dois towards work when a young woman she barely recognised came up to her holding a mobile. 'Someone wants to talk to you,' she said, handing her the phone. Simone heard a playful voice say, 'Is that the girl who wears my favourite shirt?' She often sported the distinctive black and red stripes of Rio's Flamengo football team. 'I can see you,' the voice continued. 'I watch you every day going to work. Can we fix a time so we can get to know each other a bit better?' Simone told him politely to get lost. But the mysterious calls kept coming, and a week or so later one of the phone girls told her, 'He's waiting to see you now in Valão.' 'Is he a gangster?' Simone asked, and was told that he wasn't. She had no wish to get mixed up in the drugs crowd.

She walked into the café where Nem was sitting alone. He was extremely polite, and, after a brief exchange, she agreed to have lunch with him the following Sunday. 'That first lunch was fantastic,' she recalls. 'He didn't come on strong, we didn't even kiss, and we stayed until a quarter to midnight, when he said he had to go and finish up his work.'

Simone had no idea that Nem was in the drugs business. In fact, he showed her his old work ID from the magazine distribution company to convince her that he was an upstanding member of the community. 'He also told me he was separated. Of course, I didn't realise then it was all a pack of lies.'

He would always come to her in the early hours of the morning, after his work was over, and stay until mid-morning. He talked warmly about Eduarda, his daughter, but said there was nothing left of his relationship with Vanessa. He claimed that she lived in his mother's apartment, while he stayed on the next floor down.

After a while, Simone started hearing rumours. 'Women would say things like "Don't mess with Simone now because she's in deep with one of the boys." They all knew who he was and what he did but I didn't. I wasn't out on the street much.' One day she told Nem to level with her, and he did. She had promised that as long as he told her the truth, she wouldn't leave him.

A few days later she received a phone call.

'Simone, do you know who I am?'

'No, I don't.'

'I'm Nem's wife.'

'But he told me he's separated.'

'Separated nothing. I sleep with him every night.'

Simone knew that this was not entirely true, because she was doing exactly that herself. Vanessa's tone was aggressive, but only minutes later, she was sitting in Simone's apartment and the two women were eagerly exchanging stories. 'I thought you were just another passing fancy like all the rest of them,' Vanessa said, 'but I decided to get in touch when I realised that he was serious about you.' They agreed that Simone would call Nem and ask him to come over urgently. When he walked in and saw Vanessa there, he freaked out and ran away.

Nem's transition from staid family man to playboy had been swift, though hardly unique. Influential men in a favela are expected to project virility and personal magnetism through their public behaviour. A voracious sexual appetite is regarded as the norm, and no one is surprised if such men sleep with a lot of women. Indeed it would be considered unnatural if they didn't demonstrate their power and control over the opposite sex. When women join forces, as Vanessa and Simone did, the men are sometimes at a loss to know what to do. In Nem's case, he simply disappeared for a couple of weeks, although later the situation would trigger frightening violent episodes. Lulu's behaviour was a slight exception to the rule. He had three relationships in the favela, all of whom got on with each other tolerably well. Just occasionally he also enjoyed affairs with outsiders, some of them prominent celebrities.

But with regard to his team members, none of this mattered to Lulu provided people like Nem were doing their job properly. And Nem was certainly doing that.

The core of Lulu's strategy was clear: keep everything peaceful and business will prosper. As he progressed through the organisation, Nem also began to learn the management of the business in detail, and in particular one of the most critical aspects – accounting.

The issues of security, watching out for police informants and ensuring a regular supply of cocaine into the smoke shops were nothing compared with the problem of keeping track of the money. Lulu was a master at this, and he passed on tips to Nem, who was able to supplement them with his earlier experience as a junior manager at the magazine distribution company. Proper bookkeeping meant keeping clear records of how much you owed and how much was owed to you. As it became more sophisticated, the business would reward customer loyalty by making allowances if cash flow was a problem. In that event, people could always negotiate payment in instalments.

In one respect the new job was something of a let-down. Cachopa was incredibly dull: unlike the commercial districts, there were no bars and few shops, and after about six o'clock the area was dead.

It wasn't long before Nem found this frustrating and ached to join the action down in the centre of Lower Rocinha. 'Lulu prevented me from hanging out with the others like Bem-te-vi,' he says. 'They were an irresponsible bunch, he would tell me, and he didn't want me mixing with them. "I'm very fond of Bem-te-vi," he said, "but I don't want you getting seduced by his party mania."' So Nem had to account for his movements. On one occasion he was invited to Zarur's birthday party. 'You can go there and wish him a happy birthday,' Lulu said, 'but then I want you back at your post.'

From a practical point of view, the biggest problem with Lulu's reign was that the man himself didn't enjoy it. He wanted out from the responsibility and stress of running a favela, even if he was popular. Whenever he could, he disappeared from Rocinha for weeks, if not months, leaving the business in the hands of less competent deputies. Stability was compromised: during his absences, things tended to fall apart.

Alice Avezedo[13] remembers how on one occasion when Lulu was away, her nephew, who was fifteen at the time, started going out with a new girlfriend. Unbeknownst to him, the young woman was already seeing one of the traffickers, who very quickly heard what was going on. The boy was snatched by a group of Lulu's men. 'They took him to Rua Um,' Alice explains, 'and there they began to torture him.'

A week later, Lulu returned. With still no sign of her nephew, Alice, with her aunt and several children, went to Laboriaux to petition him. He received them on his rooftop, listened quietly and then immediately called the men responsible. They turned up with the boy barely conscious, dressed only in his underwear, beaten black and blue and starved for a week. Lulu ordered his immediate release and demanded that the perpetrators apologise to the boy's mother, which they did. Nonetheless, the victim remained terrified and moved away from Rocinha as soon as he could afford to. They had already shaved the girl's head and expelled her from the favela. The incident, one among many such when Lulu was away, demonstrated how precarious the social order was, and how dependent on a single individual to enforce it.

Rocinha from Pedra da Gávea with the Two Brothers Mountain and Ipanema Beach beyond.

Rocinha from the Barra Lagoa highway.

The S-bend, a dramatic hairpin bend on the Estrada da Gávea in Rocinha, and the scene of the 2004 invasion.

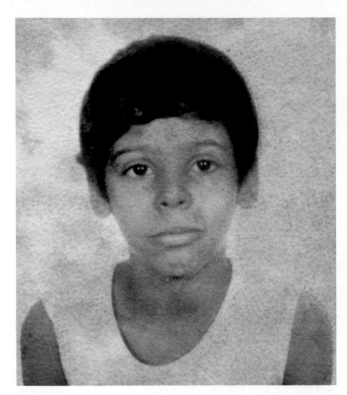

Antônio Francisco Bonfim Lopes was born at his parents' home in Rocinha on 24 May 1976. He has fond memories of his childhood in Rocinha, playing endless games with his friends and running unhindered around the favela. His was the last generation in Rocinha whose earliest memories are free from violence.

Dona Irene, Antônio's mother, with her grandchildren Eduarda and Enzo.

Gerardo Citó Lopes, Antônio's father.

Eduarda and Vanessa, who is pregnant with her and Antônio's second child Enzo.

Antônio on his wedding to Danúbia, April 1st 2006.

Antônio and Fernanda.

Simone and Antônio with their daughters Fernanda and Thayná.

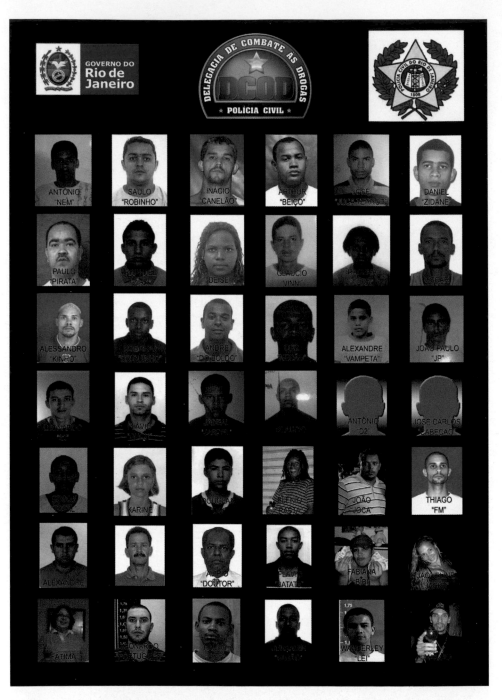

A wanted poster showing key members of ADA (Amigos dos Amigos, or Friends of Friends) in Rocinha, one of the three major drugs factions in Rio, including several of Nem's close associates. Nem himself is shown top left, and Bibi, Saulo and Joca are also featured.

Dênis of Rocinha was the first person in the favela to recognise the business potential of cocaine, and rose to become the favela's first don.

Rocinha bandidos prepare to give a paramilitary style salute for one of their fallen. They took to the rooftops of Rocinha and fired off their semi-automatic machine guns in a direct challenge to the police who had shot their comrade.

The people of Rocinha massed in a huge funeral procession for Lulu, the much-loved don of Rocinha.

The arrest of Joca, who briefly shared the leadership of Rocinha with Nem.

The trial of Dudu, the former don of Rocinha who launched the Easter invasion in 2004.

The funeral of Bem-te-vi, the party don, who was killed by the Civil Police in Operation Trojan Horse.

Members of Nem's band storm the Hotel Intercontinental. Several bandidos pile out of a white van, heavily armed.

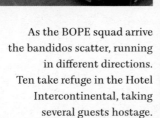

As more bandidos arrive on motorcycles fighting breaks out and the gang hold up a civilian car.

As the BOPE squad arrive the bandidos scatter, running in different directions. Ten take refuge in the Hotel Intercontinental, taking several guests hostage.

After a prolonged siege, the ten hostage takers from the Hotel Intercontinental are captured and disarmed.

Bárbara Lomba, Reinaldo Leal and Alexandre Estelita of the Civil Police who spent four years investigating Nem and ADA in Rocinha.

WANTED: NEM OF ROCINHA
Reward 5 thousand reals.

José Mariano Beltrame, Secretary for Security in Rio State, with members of BOPE, the Military Police Special Forces unit with their symbol in the background.

Nem's journey has taken him from the colourful chaos of Rocinha to the beige walls and militant order of the Maximum Security Federal Penitentiary in Campo Grande. Behind these walls Nem has very little contact with the outside world.

profits in Rocinha and they wanted a greater percentage for them-selves. Dênis refused to allow any such encroachment on his territory and power. His murder, remarked an intelligence officer from the Military Police's special forces, BOPE, was the trigger for all the terrible things that happened subsequently in Rocinha.

Beira-Mar, in particular, was carving out a reputation as the most powerful figure in Brazil's drugs economy. He became the only individual to succeed in lifting himself out of the gangster-like milieu of the favela traffickers and into the wholesale business. He did this by establishing close links with the FARC in Colombia. Until this point, much of the cocaine flowing into Rio was being brought in by matutos, freelance individuals who would physically transport small amounts from Paraguay and Bolivia all the way to Rio on the Atlantic coast.[14]

The matutos ran peculiar risks. First they had to negotiate a viable price from the Bolivian, Paraguayan or Colombian suppliers. Then they had to move the goods across Brazil, avoiding the police, the military and opportunistic thieves. Finally they had to agree a decent price with the traffickers in the favelas. In the early 2000s, a number of matutos were murdered, as though there were a serial killer out there who had a beef with drug mules. These stories never reached the press – they were just names, individuals, some of them Bolivian or Paraguayan, some Brazilian. But those involved in the drugs trade in Rio's favelas suspected that something troubling lay behind the deaths. Lulu concluded that somebody in Red Command owed the matutos large sums of money, and rather than pay their debts, they chose instead to kill them.

This coincided with Beira-Mar's increasing sway over the whole-sale trade delivering into Rio. There is no evidence suggesting any greater connection between Beira-Mar and the deaths of the matutos. But these events certainly strengthened his hand, as they enabled him to extend his control over wholesale deliveries.

At this point Marcinho VP and Beira-Mar began to consider their options if they were to reinforce their influence over Rocinha. Eventually their preference was to return a man known as Dudu to the favela where he had been born and where he would effectively act as their local agent.

The pressure on Rocinha grew after Dênis's death in 2001. Lulu faced demands to hand over a larger percentage of the favela's profits to Red Command's leadership. He refused. By early 2004 the situation was becoming critical. According to police intelligence, Beira-Mar continued to talk covertly with members of Lulu's team, especially those who were perhaps rivals to one of the Don's most likely successors, Bem-te-vi.

The deteriorating situation was deeply unsettling for Lulu. He had already begun to make concrete plans for getting out of Rocinha and the drugs business. In early 2003, he sent an emissary to Luiz Eduardo Soares, who had previously worked as a security adviser to Rio's government and was now doing the same in Brasília at a federal level. He asked Soares if they could come to an arrangement. He explained that he wanted to give himself up, or perhaps more accurately that he wished to escape his current profession and 'retire'. Soares, a gifted anthropologist, writer and political adviser, explained that in his personal capacity he very much hoped that Lulu would be able to retire. Unfortunately, he was at the time also a servant of the state. That meant, regrettably, that should Lulu wish to arrange a meeting, Soares would have no option but to arrest him. He stressed that he wished him well and that Lulu should contact him whenever he needed to.

Ten months later, Soares was attending a Candomblé religious service in Salvador, the capital of Bahia, with, amongst others, the wife of world-famous singer Gilberto Gil. Flora Gil was a close friend of Lulu. As an impresario, she had brought stars like her husband and the hugely popular singer Ivete Sangalo to perform in Rocinha.

Later she helped raise over half a million reals for the construction of a house of culture in the favela. It was a measure of Lulu's charisma that he established friendships with such august personalities.

Soares was engrossed in the mesmeric Candomblé ritual when he felt somebody tap him on the shoulder. It was Lulu. 'Professor,' he said with a gentle smile, 'I managed it! I have got out of the business!' Soares was very pleased. 'And the good news is,' he replied, 'I am no longer in office and so not in a position to arrest you any more. I only need to congratulate you!' As Lulu left the event, Soares's wife warned that the story was probably not yet at an end.

One afternoon a few months later, when Soares was taking a sabbatical in Porto Alegre, the capital of Brazil's southernmost state, Rio Grande do Sul, his phone rang. It was Lulu.

'I have had to come back to Rocinha. They kidnapped me.'

'Who? Red Command?'

'No. The Civil Police.'

While Lulu was visiting his mother in Paraíba, four masked men from Rio's Civil Police had burst into the house and bundled him into their car. The cops had driven 1,500 miles to carry out this mission and they were, of course, completely outside their jurisdiction. That was a mere trifle. Lulu was too important a figure in Rio's complex economy of corruption to be allowed to retire. The police forced him to return to his job as don.

'I thought, of course, that they were going to kill me,' Lulu explained to Professor Soares. 'On the contrary. They said we will kill you if you don't come back to Rocinha. Since you've gone, the place is a complete mess and the violence is spilling out into the neighbouring areas. You have to come back and sort it out.' Try as he might to escape, Lulu was locked into Rocinha and the drugs trade – by the police as much as by his customers, by his soldiers and by the residents of the favela.

So in early 2004, he was back in Rocinha. Soon he found

himself having to deal with a complicated situation that arose around the time of Carnival. This was shaping up to be one of the biggest festivals in years. Tourism was reviving. The *Queen Mary* was one of eight transatlantic cruise liners to dock in Rio for the week of celebration and samba that was due to begin on 22 February. This extraordinary show is rightly considered one of the cultural marvels of the modern world. That year, 80,000 foreign tourists arrived in the city to join 380,000 Brazilian visitors. It was set to be a record attendance. Hotels were booked out, and hundreds of thousands had tickets for the Sambódromo, the avenue down which the samba schools would sashay after a year's ruthless preparation.

Carnival is usually a time when the police and the drugs factions observe an unspoken truce. The cops are needed to maintain order during this immense public happening, of which huge street parties are an integral part. For the traffickers, it is quite simply the high point of the retail year. Major outbreaks of violence are in neither side's interest.

There was excitement in Rocinha that year, as their samba school stood an excellent chance of being promoted from Group A to the Special Group, the premier league of samba. Yet along with the anticipation, new anxieties had arisen.

A month before Carnival kicked off, Dudu, the former don desperate to reclaim his throne, had been allowed out of prison on a weekend release to visit his mother – even though he was designated a high-security risk. He duly failed to return to prison, burying himself instead deep in the Complexo do Alemão where the cops would not find him. As Luiz Eduardo Soares put it, 'Shock horror! Convicted drugs dealer with strong track record in homicide and rape doesn't return to prison after weekend leave.'

The Red Command leaders had given Dudu their blessing to retake Rocinha. They wrote to Lulu instructing him to allow Dudu back into the favela and to accept him as being in joint charge of the trade.

Dudu – real name Eduíno Eustáquio Araújo Filho – was a complex youngster. One of his former teachers described him as 'a big child', who liked to joke with everyone.[15] By all accounts he was a bright and charming teenager, who had, however, fallen in with the thieves' community in Rua Um. In his early twenties, he was arrested and sent down, where he encountered the traffickers of Red Command. On his return, people noticed how he had evolved to become a more dangerous and capricious young man. He began cruising up and down Estrada da Gávea on his motorbike, armed with two large pistols, which he always carried in his belt.

In the early days, Dudu dispensed his violent justice with a breezy cheerfulness. If somebody was standing against his preferred candidate in an election, or they hadn't yet paid for their drugs, or they were going out with a girl he had his eye on, the smiling psychopath would stroll up to them and say simply, 'I'm going to kill you!' He would often be laughing, which might suggest he was kidding. It might also mean he was serious.

But by the time he had become one of the dons of Rocinha in 1994, he was joking a lot less. He became paranoid, and his threats were increasingly earnest. If he believed somebody had betrayed him, his style became more clinical. 'There was the guy on Via Ápia he simply didn't like the look of,' remembers one great chronicler of Rocinha life. 'He just walked up to him smiling and – *boom!* – shot him right in the face.'

Nem's features positively screw up in disgust at the mention of Dudu's name. 'Apart from the killing and everything else, he was a rapist, which just isn't acceptable in a community,' he says.

Rocinhans remember Dudu's brief reign as one of fearful cruelty. Nem's memory serves him well – Dudu was a notorious rapist. Like all other traffickers, his rule was unaccountable, but one law people expected the don to uphold was the unacceptability of rape. Indeed, Red Command itself explicitly proscribed the crime. The caprice of Dudu's terror against men and women alike led many Rocinhans to turn against him very quickly. Unsurprisingly, however, they kept their thoughts to themselves. Reminiscing, they remember this as the darkest period of Rocinhan life since the 1980s.

Dudu lived on Rua Dois, close to the geographical centre of Rocinha. He commissioned a builder to construct a secret cavity in one of his walls, so that if the police came looking for him, he could disappear. The cavity led by way of a secret passage to another house further along the road. This enabled Dudu to slip away when a raid was taking place, leaving the police empty-handed and mystified.

But somebody tipped off the drug squad to the existence of the passageway. So when officers came to arrest Dudu in 1995, they were waiting to snatch him as he ghosted out of his escape house. He received a long prison sentence, and the leadership of Rocinha – determined as always by Dênis from his prison cell – passed to a triumvirate that included Lulu.

Thus, when Red Command instructed Lulu to accept Dudu back into the favela and to appoint him don of Lower Rocinha, Lulu refused point blank. This was an unprecedented mutiny in the ranks of Rio's largest crime syndicate, and everyone assumed it would not go unpunished.

As soon as news emerged of Dudu's flight from prison, the inhabitants of Rocinha started to brace themselves for conflict. Several dozen male residents reported to Lulu's security team for volunteer duty and requested the distribution of guns to loyal citizens in order to protect the favela from attack.

Lulu had begun to rely heavily on Nem for his take on the structure and capacity of the organisation. His lieutenant proved to be a sober counsellor who above all was keen to see guns being used and distributed more carefully. But if his professional life was characterised by caution and shrewdness, his personal affairs were more complicated than ever.

In early 2004, Simone was seven months pregnant with Fernanda, Nem's daughter. Thayná, her first child, had returned to Rocinha from her grandmother in Paraíba after Nem, in a typically generous gesture, offered to pay for her upkeep in the favela. He even adopted Thayná as his own, and the girl already referred to him as 'Dad'.

One afternoon, Simone was visiting her doctor near Via Ápia for a pre-natal check up. As she walked into the waiting room, she immediately spotted Vanessa, who was also heavy with child.

'Simone? Whose is it?' exclaimed Vanessa.

'Erm ... Nem's.'

'Oh no – that can't be right. *This one* is Nem's.'

Right, decided the two women. Enough is enough. Up they marched to Nem's mother's apartment, to find Nem fast asleep after a hard night's work around the smoke shops of Cachopa.

'Guess who I met at the doctor's?' Vanessa bawled at him.

'Goddamit, Vanessa, I got in late. Leave it out. We'll talk later.'

'Simone! And you know what? She's pregnant. And you know who the father is?'

'Whaddya mean, Simone? I didn't know she was pregnant. Whose is it?'

At which point Simone entered the tiny bedroom and with a lashing of irony chipped in, 'You don't know who impregnated me, Nem?'

Nem slammed the door, simultaneously angry and embarrassed. 'Stop all this nonsense or I'll shoot the pair of you!'

'You'd shoot me when I'm pregnant with your child – I don't believe you,' Simone screamed.

This was all taking place to a background of Vanessa forcing open the door and Nem repeatedly slamming it shut in a scene reminiscent of a bedroom farce. 'But I knew this angry side to him,'

Simone said later, 'and at one point I was genuinely frightened that he might actually shoot me.'

Out of sheer fury, it was Simone who eventually became violent, smashing the one window in the flat, after which she was compelled to return to the clinic to get two stitches in her bloody hand.

Once again confronted by angry women, Nem packed his bags and disappeared for a while. 'Yes,' as he remembers the incident, 'for a couple of weeks, I was not only a fugitive from the police but from two women as well!' When the children, Fernanda and Enzo, were born within two months of each other, he remarked how he'd always wanted twins, but if that wasn't going to happen, this was the next best thing. And it was certainly visible proof of his virility, if such were needed.

Although his relationships with women were becoming increasingly complicated, he remained the most steadfast father. Eduarda was by now a lively and extremely intelligent four-year-old, adored by family and friends alike. There was no sign of the Langerhans cell disease returning. Nem was equally assiduous in meeting his responsibilities towards his adopted daughter, Thayná. 'He never let his kids down,' Simone says. 'He would buy them things. He would play with them and read to them. He was and remains a model father.'

Although he still had mixed feelings about his mother with regard to the fate of his father, he admired her commitment to work and family. The two became ever closer. When he had joined Lulu's operation, his mother asked him why he had taken that step. He didn't reply. The most he felt inclined to explain was that he was simply doing an acquaintance a favour, and that he was doing it for his daughter. As time went on and it became clear that this was not a temporary switch, Dona Irene became seized by anxiety, especially at night. Every time she heard the firing of guns, she was terrified that her son might not come back in the morning.

On 22 February, the evening of the big Carnival parade, William da Rocinha was downtown with his wife when his phone rang. Six days earlier, the then 33-year-old had taken office as president of the residents' association. His path into politics had been less than straightforward: from the depths of poverty and drug addiction to the heights of a successful career as a radio presenter and DJ. Once he had kicked the cocaine habit, William had become ever more engaged in community politics, enjoying a constructive relationship with Lulu, who helped finance his funk parties.

As a Rocinhan through and through, he was very aware of the difficulties facing his constituents after Dudu's release from prison, but like everyone else, he assumed that things were unlikely to kick off during Carnival. The phone call on 22 February changed all that. A unit from the Military Police's special forces had just shot dead three adolescents coming out of a funk party in Rocinha.

As the newly elected association president, William rushed to the scene. About 500 people were gathered as police reinforcements were hurriedly mobilised to prevent the fury of the residents from erupting.

The next day, the media all reported the same story: that the three boys were involved in drug trafficking. There was no evidence to support the claim, but the press ran with it all the same. Within a few days William and his colleagues had gathered a dossier of evidence that demonstrated beyond doubt that these were innocent kids out having a good time.[16] Ironically, the police had given the go-ahead for the funk party in advance.

From now on, three hostile forces were prepared for battle – the traffickers of Rocinha; Dudu and his mercenary band; and the Military Police. Everything was primed to explode.

5

THE PASSION OF ROCINHA

April 2004

I t is the eve of Good Friday, and Christ stands in silent defiance. The high priest, Caiaphas, bellows with incredulity: 'Answerest thou nothing?'

His interrogation of Jesus has yet to yield results. From amidst the 80 or so men and women crowding around the high priest and the prophet, a small band of Roman soldiers shuffles forward. Some are wearing flip-flops. They prepare to beat and humiliate the heretic for his insolence. The crowd is growing restless.

The disciple Peter weeps. He has just fulfilled Jesus's prophecy by thrice denying his master. He is standing to one side of the Sanhedrin court that is considering Christ's fate. The proceedings are taking place just by the garage where they park the municipal buses at night.

At the very moment when Caiaphas's condemnation of Jesus at the trial reaches its climax, everyone is seized by sudden terror. The priests, the Roman soldiers, the villagers, the disciples, and indeed Christ himself are forced to duck for cover in response to a sudden crackling of semi-automatic gunfire, followed by an electric burst of flares. Tracer bullets light up the sky in a demonic red. It is, Aurelio Mesquita thinks, as if Satan has dispatched his best legions to disrupt the Passion of Christ.

Everybody knows the rules of the game: find shelter as fast as possible without triggering a panic or stampede. Aurelio reacts quickest. He is the founder and director of the Via Sacra, Rocinha's annual re-creation of Christ's journey to the Cross. A slight but energetic man, Aurelio signals to the actors to follow him to his tiny apartment, just 100 metres away. Thirty people, including several children, cram themselves into a space that in normal circumstances fits about four.

The sound of war proliferates around the theatre troupe. Obviously the dress rehearsal of the Via Sacra has been abandoned. By the entrance to the favela, the battle for Rocinha rages. Some 60 young men have arrived from the neighbouring favela of Vidigal in support of Dudu, armed to the teeth and clad in black, aiming to seize control of Rocinha and its cocaine concession, the most lucrative in all Rio de Janeiro. Twelve people will die this week, and Rocinha will be plunged into a state of chaos that will last for another eighteen months.

Half an hour before the church bells announce Good Friday, Telma Veloso Pinto, a 38-year-old housewife, is driving with her husband and three nephews from the middle-class suburb of Barra to their new flat in Botafogo, an up-and-coming district in Rio's South Zone. Instead of taking the tunnel under the Two Brothers mountain, she decides upon the more scenic route: the coast road that winds between the two warring favelas of Vidigal and Rocinha, and further down to the fashionable beach area of Leblon.

The housewife's nippy Citroën will do nicely for the gangsters from Vidigal, who are requisitioning cars in which they intend to launch their attack on Rocinha. Some five heavily armed men jump out of the forest and signal for Telma to stop. In response, she floors the accelerator, and the gunmen let rip at the vehicle with their semi-automatics. Her husband grabs the wheel and steers the vehicle into the side of the road to stop it. It is then that he sees his wife is dead. He and his three nephews are all injured. Telma is the first to fall in the attempted invasion of Rocinha. Like several still to die, she is an entirely incidental and innocent victim.

As they pack themselves into stolen cars, the invaders assume that they have the element of surprise on their side. In fact, some 100 drug soldiers are positioned strategically around the favela, tooled up and waiting to greet the invasion.

Lulu has become terminally tired of his influential and onerous post. On this occasion, however, he is standing firm. He knows that Dudu, his predecessor and rival, is intent on retaking the favela. He feels a deep responsibility to defend his fiefdom and its inhabitants. The people of Rocinha, too, are desperate for Lulu to win. Nobody has yet forgotten the fear that marked Dudu's reign as don. Nobody wants him back.

Lulu has built up an extensive intelligence network over the years. He has many contacts in the police and throughout the favelas where the cartel to which he belongs, Red Command, is in control. As Good Friday approaches, however, he can expect no mercy from his comrades in Red Command. He has ignored the letter he received from the organisation's cupola demanding that he hand over to Dudu the concession of Lower Rocinha. All he can do is brace himself for the attack.

Perhaps it is in anticipation of just such a development that he has also been cultivating friendships among Red Command's two main rivals, the Pure Third Command (TCP)[17] and ADA.

Most importantly, Lulu has an informant from Vidigal who is part of the attacking force. For two to three weeks he has been leaking information about the invasion plans. By Thursday, Lulu knows that they are going to hit Rocinha later that day – just before midnight.

Nem confirms the news. He too has been tipped off about the impending assault. He commands some 25 soldiers under arms but it is not a well-regimented force. Most are young men in their teens and twenties, usually stick-thin, dressed in regulation football shirts, shorts and trainers or flip-flops. Many are dwarfed by the weapons they carry, and while Nem and the more senior members attempt to instil a degree of discipline in them, when they are out of sight of their bosses, they regularly slide out of control.

The youngsters' path into this career is a familiar one. Their guides are a wayward crew: unemployment, testosterone, acquisitiveness and absence – absence of father figures, of school, of the state and of a future. In the era of globalisation, they are surrounded by images of glamour and material goods. In the favelas, there is only one way to access those things – drug money.

Nem has grown in authority; a far cry these days from the awkward beanpole once spotted by his own brother squatting on the ground clumsily gripping a semi-automatic rifle. During the early days, Carlos would beg Nem to give up his work in the drugs business. He sensed that his younger brother was neither happy with the work nor well suited to it – that he was unsettled by the ever-present dangers. It all ran so counter to his character. But after Gerardo's death, relations between them never properly recovered and so Carlos's advice was disregarded.

Lulu, by contrast, has been impressed with the way Nem has calmed Cachopa and the surrounding areas. When asked to carry out errands, Nem does so swiftly and effectively, accounting, what is more, for every penny taken out of petty cash. Although untrained, he has a businessman's brain by nature.

This evening they have had a difference of opinion. Nem believes that Lulu should station his men at the entrance to Rocinha in order to ambush Dudu's invaders, and he offers to place himself at

the head of the detachment. 'When they try to enter, there won't
be a single one left alive,' he insists. Their intelligence has told
them that the attackers will be entering from the Atlantic side of
Rocinha, not from Gávea to the east. Nem says that his team can
take them out before they actually penetrate the favela. He is
convinced that in this instance attack is the best form of defence
and he pleads with Lulu to allow him to station his gunmen there.
After four years in security, Nem is a much tougher proposition
than when he started. He is certain that Lulu is making a serious
mistake and he tells him so. But Lulu shakes his head. 'Let them
be the ones to fire the first shot,' he says 'and let the world see who
the aggressors are.'

Nem doesn't hold back these days from expressing his opin-
ions and arguing with Lulu if he thinks his boss is wrong. But
when Lulu makes a final decision, he carries out the orders to the
letter.

So at the start of the invasion, Nem finds himself three quarters
of the way up the favela, close to the edge of the forest. Once he
hears the shooting from below, he shouts into his walkie-talkie: 'Let
me head down there, please!' Lulu waits a little longer, until the
fighting has moved to the entrance of Via Ápia, the main shopping
street near the entrance to Rocinha. Only then does he allow Nem
to descend the hill with his men.

At around this time, Fabiana dos Santos Oliveira, a 24-year-old
childminder, is on the back of her husband's scooter, driving down
Estrada da Gávea towards Via Ápia. With the sounds of war fizzing
around them, they are in a greater hurry than usual to pick up
Fabiana's sister from the bottom of the hill after she returns home
from work in the city.

Meanwhile, the invading force should be encountering Rocinha's first line of defence in the district of Vila Verde. Although Lulu wants to ensure that the invaders fire the first shot, he and Nem are banking on them being slowed down by the fighters concealed in this residential area to their left as they enter the favela.

Unexpected and disturbing news suddenly crackles into the walkie-talkie: Dudu and his men have swept past Vila Verde with ease. Something untoward is happening.

The attack force fires its way towards the S-Bend, a dramatic hairpin on an incline a quarter of the way up Estrada da Gávea. Many decades earlier, when Rocinha was not a slum but merely a tiny cottage farm, the S-Bend was the signature moment of Rio's motor-racing course, and the Argentine Juan Manuel Fangio, the greatest Formula 1 driver in history, once swerved around it.

Tonight the S-Bend should be defended by the trafficker called Band, one of Lulu's senior lieutenants, but he has failed to engage the invaders. Nem contacts Lulu again, suggesting that something is amiss. Lulu confirms the alarming information. They have been betrayed. Band is collaborating with the enemy. He was once a valued member of Dudu's operation. Now it emerges that he has maintained contact with his former boss. Lulu tells Nem that if they repel the attackers, he will eliminate Band.

Warned by Lulu to avoid the main road, Nem makes his way around the edge of the favela, through the dark alleys and lanes, towards Cachopa.

Fabiana and her husband turn into the S-Bend, where they are met by a sustained volley of gunfire. The invaders are scuttling the cars they have stolen. Abandoning them on the S-Bend, they start to shoot their way up the hill in the direction of the church. Fabiana is thrown from the scooter when a bullet hits her in the chest. Her husband leaps off to help her but is himself hit in the elbow and has to dive for cover. Fabiana is screaming for help, but the gunfire is so intense that nobody reaches her before she dies.

The exchanges of fire knock out large sections of the rickety electric power supply. Great patches of darkness spread across the favela.

William da Rocinha is talking by phone both to Lulu and to the commander of the Military Police, who has arrived at the entrance to the favela. Lulu asks him to tell the commander that he and his people have no quarrel with the police and will not engage in combat with them. They are only defending themselves from the 'bandits', as he calls Dudu's men. William asks the police to proceed with caution and not to move into areas under Lulu's control. There is, for the moment, broad agreement between Lulu and law enforcement.

At half past midnight, the PM reinforcements arrive. They close the coastal road where Telma Veloso was shot, which connects Rocinha to Vidigal, and the tunnel under Two Brothers mountain. But while this first phase of fighting is in progress, the cops agree not to intervene directly. One armoured vehicle does in fact trundle up Estrada da Gávea, but both groups of bandits leave it alone. They are having enough difficulty fighting each other. Neither wants the police involved as well.

The following day, the police commander explains that the introduction of his men, a third armed faction in the darkness, would in all probability have led to still more civilian casualties. It is a reasonable argument.

Lulu radios Nem again as his lieutenant is arriving at the western edge of Rocinha, where the forest begins. 'Find out what's happening to our boys in Dionéia,' he orders, referring to the district high up the favela, 'and then send them down. We need to cut off and encircle the attackers.' Nem immediately contacts the group and orders them to meet Dudu's army and block their progress up the hill. But when the members of this group catch sight of the invaders, they believe themselves to be outgunned and flee towards their stronghold in Rua Um.

Nem calls them again: 'Where are you now?'

'We're on Rua Um.'

'For fuck's sake, what are you doing way up there? You're a fucking disgrace! Get back down here now!'

But they don't. Instead they head for the forest to hide. Nem makes a mental note of this. He is totting up the failures and tactical mistakes. Above all, he thinks, these kids are too young and inexperienced.

In the commercial heart of Rocinha, Valão, the noise coming from Estrada da Gávea alerts Wellington da Silva to the fighting. Known as Maluquinho, he is 27 years old and one of the country's most famous skateboarders, twice champion of Rio, and Brazilian vice champion. He is a well-known and popular figure in the community and is proud of his friendship with Lulu. Packing a pistol under his T-shirt – which reads *We Want Peace But We Are Ready for War* – he heads towards Cachopa.

When he arrives there at about 2 a.m., he hears the sounds of a party and sees a group of soldiers standing nearby. He signals to them: 'Oi! Guys, guys – it's me, Maluquinho!' This is a mistake. The soldiers are not Lulu's people but Dudu's men, and the leader himself is there. 'You're looking a bit shaky on your pins, Maluquinho,' says Dudu. He shoots him first in one leg and then in his left arm. Maluquinho begs Dudu to spare his life, invoking his two young children. Dudu says that as the skateboarder has been quite clear about his loyalty to Lulu, he is an enemy, and shoots him dead at point-blank range.

Soon afterwards, Dudu and his men withdraw to the forest. It has taken them much longer to reach Cachopa than they anticipated. Few of the invading force are actually local, so the layout of the favela is unfamiliar to them. They decide to lie low for the evening.

Nem comes down to find Maluquinho's body. He radios Lulu to

tell him the bad news. Suddenly everybody's walkie-talkie springs into life to receive a message. It is Dudu, transmitting on all frequencies. 'We will be back tomorrow evening at six,' he crows. 'See you all then!'

6

THE BALLAD OF THE THIN MAN
April 2004

A couple of hours after dawn on Good Friday, anyone who absolutely needs to leave their house creeps out. No shops will open today, and those who have to get to work scurry away as quickly as possible. At 11 a.m., the director, stagehands and actors of the Via Sacra hold a brief meeting. They swiftly agree to scrap that evening's performance – the first time in twelve years that the Passion of Christ has been cancelled. Although deeply disappointed, the artists are united in not wanting to endanger anyone's life for the sake of the performance. They disperse and return home.

The residents' association is spreading the news that an informal curfew will be in place from 5 p.m. Everyone is expecting Dudu's men to carry out a second attack that evening. Lulu and his commanders are less concerned, however, than they were. They judge that although numerically strong, Dudu's force was disorganised and lacking both tactics and strategy. It was almost as if this was first and foremost a demonstration and a warning. Nonetheless, they still make preparations for the invaders' return.

More serious, it seems to them, is the political and media reaction. The newspaper headlines speak of 'the War for Rocinha'. Columnists and leader articles demand decisive action against the 'bandits and traffickers'. The next few days will be more complicated, as the authorities have now ordered a huge police intervention. Some 1,000 extra troops, 350 from the regular Military Police and 650 from BOPE – Batalhão Operações Polícias Especiais, or the Battalion of Special Police Operations – are sent in. The occupation of the favela begins.

BOPE's symbol is a skull with a knife plunged into its crown against a background of two crossed pistols. Its armoured cars are known as Big Skulls. 'Victory over death', promises the force's official hymn, while those BOPE officers who belong to the evangelical churches refer to themselves as 'the Skulls of Christ'.

BOPE has spawned several copies in other Brazilian states, and there are many equivalents around the world. Few, however, can equal the fearsome reputation of the model that has evolved here in Rio. Its origins date back to 1974, during the most repressive period of the military dictatorship. A botched attempt at ending a hostage crisis in one of Rio's prisons, resulting in the death of the prison governor among others, caused a senior police officer to call for the creation of a new unit dedicated to handling emergency security situations.

The first specialist team came into being four years later, and went through various incarnations before it was finally baptized the Battalion of Special Police Operations in 1991.

BOPE is a ruthless paramilitary force that has grown almost symbiotically alongside the drugs trade. It is the government's most powerful weapon for intervening in the business that has so damaged the social equilibrium in Brazil. No expression of state power is as intimidating as BOPE.

As Nem ventures out on the afternoon of Good Friday, the first things he sees are two Big Skulls. He hunkers down in a safe house in Cachopa. By radio, he alerts his teams around the favela. 'If there is an exchange of fire, don't run around wildly because you will be running towards your death – at the hands of either the police or the enemy. Everyone needs to stick together and coordinate.'

Lulu and Nem's people have one great advantage. They know every inch of the terrain inside the favela. Unless you spend many years wandering around this bewildering network of lanes and alleys, it is impossible to understand exactly where in the favela you happen to be. Dudu himself knows the place, of course. But most of his attack force comes from favelas far away, so they have no clear idea of their location at any time. The police have the main roads and districts mapped, but the capillaries, and where they might lead, remain a mystery too dangerous to solve: there is a fair chance that a gun will be waiting at the end.

Rua Um, at the top of the favela, is now crawling with BOPE. This works to the defenders' advantage, as it reduces the points of entry for Dudu's people coming down from their hiding places in the forest. Nem and five others climb up on to the *laje*, the roof of the Cachopa house, to take up their positions.

The lajes are flat concrete terraces common to most favelas that have graduated from the corrugated tin and tent phase to bricks and mortar. They can accommodate huge water butts to collect the rain but also act as a recreational space for the days when the tropical sun renders work impossible. But they are also designed so that when the capital becomes available, the owner can build another floor on top of the building. Favelas like Rocinha can no longer expand outwards, so they grow up and up.

From this position on the laje, Nem and his companions monitor any coming and goings from the forest. Over the radio network, Dudu blasts out a propaganda message: 'Prepare for the Red Command new era.' Nem responds with 'The rapist gang will fail', referring to Dudu's notoriety as a violator of women.

At around 6.30 in the evening, fighting breaks out again, but this time it lasts for only half an hour. BOPE officers kill two soldiers, one from Lulu's gang and one from Dudu's.

During the fighting, a BOPE officer tracks down one suspect

to his house. The gangster isn't at home, but his wife is, along with the trafficker's personal zoo, including a sloth and an alligator. For some reason, the officer releases the wild animals (a bit unfair on the sloth, given that there are shootouts going on). He then turns on the woman and starts beating her up. As he does, the animal-loving trafficker returns home and shoots him dead.

It is a fateful event. The officer was a popular member of his brigade. BOPE now wants revenge.

Lulu's assessment of Dudu's capabilities is turning out to be accurate. The invasion is petering out. Dudu's men retreat to the forest, then back to Vidigal, before returning to their homes. Dudu finds sanctuary in the sprawling network of favelas that is Red Command's mightiest stronghold, Complexo do Alemão.

But the failed invasion has rocked Rio. Easter is dominated by the event. Responding quickly to the media pressure, the vice governor of the city announces that he intends to incarcerate the entire favela by building a huge wall around it. He argues that the three-metre-high barrier would serve a dual purpose: to restrict the movements of gangsters, and to prevent the favela from encroaching any further on the rainforest in which it is cradled.

Most of Rio's large and flamboyant middle class has no direct experience of Rocinha. They never venture into this medium-sized city packed into an area no greater than a large village. They are dependent on Rocinha's inhabitants for much of their service work – cooking, cleaning, driving, gardening, laundry and the like. But at the same time they quietly fear it. Above all they fear that what they perceive to be the dark, corrosive innards of the favela will spill out into their tree-lined districts, bringing with them chaos and violence.

So there is real popular support for the idea of turning the community into even more of a ghetto than it already is. Others, including leading academics and politicians, greet this proposed concrete incarnation of the 'Broken City'[18] with horror and disbelief.

Inside the favela, uncertainty is spreading. Police are crawling through the capillaries and an army of journalists gathers around the entrance, concocting ever more lurid and outrageous stories about Rocinha and its inhabitants.

On Easter Saturday, Nem visits Lulu at the Rua Um headquarters. Here he raises the issue of the organisation of the soldiers. Despite Lulu's even temper, Nem still requires courage to question his strategy. But after the events of the previous two days, he feels he has to speak out. He is concerned about the failure of the security operation in Lower Rocinha – the men who fled and the apparent betrayal by Band. 'Your policy of handing out weapons to the boys just because they have worked for a long time in the smoke shops isn't delivering,' he argues. 'They need to have proper experience.'

Lulu ponders this and then gestures to Nem. 'Okay. I'm going to give you some guns and let you decide how best to distribute them.' Nem's steady accumulation of power means that from now on, there will be a strict policy on weapons – only those who know how to use them responsibly will be permitted to carry them. Those showing them off like a toy around the community – to impress young women and intimidate young men – will have them confiscated.

It is Easter Monday. The invasion is over and cops are now crawling around the favela. Nem is picked up by a police patrol. They are actually looking for another member of the gang with a similar nickname, Neném, who is one of Lulu's principal gunmen. The fact that they do not appear to know who Nem is indicates both that their intelligence is hazy and that Nem is not yet a standout figure in the organisation.

The police demand that Nem betray Neném's whereabouts. To

reinforce their point, they handcuff him and place a plastic bag over his head so that he cannot breathe. In the hope that they will stop torturing him, he claims that he is in fact Neném and that they have successfully trapped their quarry. 'We know your name is Nem!' comes the response. 'And we want Neném,' another officer barks. But Nem believes they are slightly confused and decides that now is the time to negotiate.

Lulu has schooled him in the art of bargaining with the cops – an important tool in the trafficker's kitbag. He has already been called upon two dozen times to secure the release of gang members, including Lulu himself. With his hands cuffed behind his back and the plastic bag still nearby, Nem changes tack. 'Okay, let's talk seriously,' he says. His cuffs are unlocked. The police officer opens negotiations.

'How much can you afford to lose? Fifty thousand reals?'

'I haven't got anything like that.'

'Thirty thousand?'

'Sorry, you're going to have to cuff me again.'

'Whaddya mean?'

'Well, I haven't got thirty K, let alone fifty, so I guess you're just going to have to arrest me.'

'Okay, so how much can you afford?'

'Ten K.'

'Ten? Are you mad?'

'Look, when I give my word, I follow through, and I would rather be arrested than agree to something I can't follow through on.'

'Up to fifteen K and you can go.'

'Okay. I'll have to get a loan for the final five thousand, but it's a deal.'

When Nem is freed on Tuesday, he calls Lulu, who congratulates him on his release and tells him to visit him in the coming days to discuss the 'big decision' he is about to take. Nem suspects his boss is considering a change to Rocinha's allegiance, renouncing the twenty-year link with Red Command in favour of one of its two rivals, TCP or ADA.

Nobody from the organisation has actually seen Lulu in person for several days, and William decides to call him on the radio: 'We have people here on the streets all wanting to know what is going on – whether things are safe or not.' Lulu assures William that everything is under control. He is hiding in Laboriaux, at the very top of the favela, and confirms that things are peaceful there. William continues to receive reports of intense BOPE activity around Rua Um, just below Laboriaux, and so he heads up the hill along Estrada da Gávea to investigate.

Until now, it has been unthinkable that Red Command could lose control of the largest narcotics hub in Rio. Earlier, Lulu discussed the issue with Dênis da Rocinha. From inside his prison cell, Dênis, the founder of Rocinha's drugs operation, said it would taint his honour irrevocably if the favela broke with Red Command, and so he stayed Lulu's hand.

In the aftermath of Dênis's murder in 2001, Lulu and other Rocinha leaders attended a meeting in Complexo do Alemão at which Red Command's cupola denied involvement in Dênis's death and guaranteed Lulu's authority in Rocinha.

For Lulu, the invasion of 2004 means Red Command has torn up that agreement. His loyalty to the organisation is crumbling. The intelligence service of Rio's Civil Police shares Lulu's assessment. The cops believe that the Red Command leadership wants to grab an even larger chunk of the Rocinha spoils than they are currently getting. For his part, Nem believes that Dudu is simply a puppet who would be compelled to hand over the profits to Red Command's leadership were his invasion to succeed.

Red Command's young rival, ADA, is growing at an impressive rate. Unlike Red Command, it has no central hierarchy. Instead, it is an alliance of favelas, each of which has its own leadership. Moreover, its primary focus is on success through commerce, not coercion through violence – although violence remains an indispensable tool.

After speaking to Nem on the radio to arrange a meeting for later that day, Lulu returns unperturbed to the video game he is playing with a childhood friend. The two are unaware that scores of BOPE officers, still smarting from the death of their colleague, are making their way up the hill. The special forces are heading for Laboriaux.

William, too, is making his way up the hill. On arrival in Rua Um, he hears a few shots – not many, though. He spots a Big Skull and takes a photograph of officers carrying out what looks like a body rolled in a carpet. He does not yet know that it is Lulu's body.

The next day, Rio's media report that about a hundred officers engaged in a fifteen-minute firefight with Lulu and another man before the pair were killed. Eyewitnesses from Rocinha will tell you, by contrast, that Lulu and his friend were unarmed and that this was not a gunfight but a carefully planned assassination. The bodies showed evidence not only of bullet wounds but of knife marks as well.

Later that day, a police spokesman tells the media that Lulu's friend was another notorious drug trafficker. In fact he was one of Rocinha's motorcycle taxi drivers, a law-abiding man who had no connection with the drugs business – apart from his lifelong friendship with Lulu, which was his undoing.

People in Rocinha believe that Lulu was murdered in retribution for the BOPE officer killed on Good Friday. William talks bitterly of the murder being ordered directly by the higher echelons of Rio's government.

Under normal circumstances, it is almost impossible for the authorities to move into a favela and arrest or kill a senior trafficker.

The first problem they face is leaks: a competent don always has a reliable network of informers in the police, so he knows about any raid in advance. The minute the police or special forces arrive, dozens of formal and informal *olheiros*, lookouts, will carefully track their movements. Furthermore, in Rocinha there are only two entrances – one at the top, the other at the bottom – and turning from the main drag into one of the unmapped lanes and alleys, whose topography hugely favours defenders, is risky to the point of suicide. Targeted arrests are not an option, and in areas that are so densely populated, any armed confrontation poses a threat to innocent bystanders. Occasionally the police launch opportunistic raids, but only against small fry who are openly selling drugs without due care.

The Easter war enables the police to enter Rocinha en masse. It is only in such abnormal circumstances that the don becomes vulnerable on his own patch. Even then, Lulu has not anticipated his end. 'Remember,' Nem points out, 'there is no death penalty in Brazil. So when there are situations like the one in Rocinha at Easter 2004, the chaos represents an opportunity for those cops who want to avenge themselves to carry out the death penalty anyhow.'

For its part, the government celebrates Lulu's death as a major blow against the drug gangs, suggesting that the people of Rocinha and its neighbouring areas, São Conrado and Gávea, will now be safe again. Whether they are consciously talking nonsense is unknown. Most other people – certainly everyone in the favelas – know that if you kill the king, the courtiers will soon turn on one another in a bloody struggle for the crown. Lulu's undoubted authority has ensured that the latent conflict between Lower and Upper Rocinha has never broken out into the open. Now it will. Many months are to pass before any semblance of security returns to the community.

William is deeply worried. He knows there is no clear line of succession. Lower Rocinha is the terrain of one of Lulu's closest allies, Bem-te-vi, but his authority is contested by another armed group in Upper Rocinha. Band, the *bandido*[19] who failed to defend Vila Verde, is part of this group. The favela is about to enter a period of sustained instability.

7
THE KING IS DEAD
2004

When BOPE kills Lulu, everything changes.

Now murder rates in the favela go through the roof, tripling in the space of three months. They will remain at this level for another fifteen months. Gangsters are killing each other; they are killing police, and the police are killing gangsters; and innocent civilians are also dying or getting injured in the crossfire. The little neighbouring favela, Vidigal, gets drawn into the mayhem. It remains loyal to Red Command and poses a threat to Rocinha's new alliance with ADA. The Easter invasion was launched from here. A repeat performance is always possible.

The news of Lulu's death hits Nem hard. This is the man who came to his aid when his daughter's life was under threat. Over the past four years, Lulu has nurtured and encouraged Nem's career in the business. He has dispensed counsel and justice wisely, listened carefully to criticism, protected the favela and maintained peace. Once more, a father has been killed.

Nem makes a quick decision and calls Bem-te-vi, one of Lulu's vaguely designated successors. 'For Christ's sake,' he says, already exasperated at Bem-te-vi's perceived indifference to the approaching organisational challenges, 'don't you realise what's going to happen? The boys are going to start killing one another – Zarur, Band, Lion –

and then there is Lower Rocinha against Upper Rocinha!' Nem knows very well that Zarur and Lion have never got on well – after all, he has heard Lion refer to Zarur as a tosser and has watched as they almost engage in a shootout. 'It was Band who poisoned Lion against Zarur,' he remembers. 'If it hadn't been for Band, I think Lion and Zarur might have been able to work it out.'

Contemplating the volatility and divisions within the Rua Um crew and the overall tension between Lower and Upper Rocinha, Nem makes a big decision: he wants out. He makes a swift plan to flee the favela and dump his interest in the business. The day after Lulu's death, he collects Eduarda and a heavily pregnant Vanessa, together with a credit card, a chequebook and his driving licence. He is feeling intensely stressed – more so than most people realise. He is leaving Rocinha and the business, but he is also leaving his mistress, Simone, who is about to give birth to his second daughter.

Nem, Vanessa and Eduarda head for the resort of Praia Seca, two hours' drive east of Rio. Nem tells Vanessa that he is finished with the drugs business and that he will begin a new life as a taxi driver. In the previous few months, he has been practising his driving as part of a fall-back plan if things go wrong in Rocinha. Now they have. This is the first of several occasions on which Nem tries – and fails – to escape from Rocinha and the narcotics trade.

News reaches him that the police are threatening his mother because he has not yet paid the 15,000 reals due for his release after the plastic bag incident. He has to return – and to settle his debt, he uses part of the bank loan intended to set himself up as a taxi driver.

At this point, he is virtually penniless – indeed, he is once again in debt. He sees no alternative but to start working for Bem-te-vi. His new boss is a hopelessly indecisive character and has failed to assert his authority with the teams in Upper Rocinha. Worried, and on the back foot, Nem urges Bem-te-vi to take action. 'You must go and tell the boys up there on Rua Um that Lulu named you as his successor.'

Bem-te-vi fails to assert his authority in Rua Um. In Upper Rocinha, Zarur and Lion claim to be cooperating, but their followers regard one another with suspicion. Lion is the front man for Band, probably the most dangerous man in the business.

If you walk up beyond the traffickers' traditional stronghold of Rua Um in the far eastern corner of Rocinha, the cement path eventually turns into soil and grass. Just before the favela ends and the forest begins, there is a clearing, and below that a court on which basketball and football are played. Terreirão – the Big Ground – is bright and pleasant, but it hides secrets, mostly in the form of ashes scattered here after the traffickers have committed murder. The butchering takes place elsewhere. This is where the body parts, already dismembered in another part of the favela, are burned. No body. No crime.

It is here that Zarur and Lion convene a meeting to announce their new joint stewardship of the trafficking business. Bem-te-vi is present but remains silent, thereby implicitly accepting his subordination to Zarur, who appears to be in charge. Bem-te-vi, however, is recognised as top dog in Lower Rocinha while Lion and his bloodthirsty team will manage affairs from Rua Um at the top.

At the same meeting, Zarur confirms Nem's reading of the situation and announces to his supporters that Rocinha has officially broken with Red Command and now swears allegiance to ADA.

Personal rivalries begin to mingle with factional competition to create a particularly toxic mix – although this alchemy is standard elsewhere in Rio. If Red Command's leadership detects strife, it will encourage it, aiming to render Rocinha ungovernable. Of course, BOPE acted as unwitting handmaiden to Red Command when its officers resolved to kill Lulu.

As the lines of authority become thus muddled, there is no guarantee of stability. Rocinha begins to lose its equilibrium as the anticipated and much-feared internal war begins.

Zarur is the first to fall. In late June, he and six of his gang disappear. The police, whose intelligence unit is intermittently tracking the opaque network of disputes among the traffickers, find blood near Zarur's doorstep, but then the trail goes cold. They search the Atlantic forest for evidence, in vain. No body. No crime.

For four months, Rocinha is now truly divided between upper and lower. Nem urges Bem-te-vi to take the fight to Lion. It is quite simply a matter of life and death. 'Either you start to take this seriously,' he warns Bem-te-vi, 'or we are all going to be wiped out.' The new boss is reluctant, partly because he himself is not given to violence unless the odds are stacked unambiguously in his favour.

Nem coordinates the assault on Lion's group. In early October, Lion himself disappears before any fight begins. To this day his fate is unknown, although Rocinhans who express an opinion generally believe that he was not assassinated but rather that he fled (although they may have very good reasons for not telling the truth).

Two days later, Neném, the man for whom the police mistook Nem at Easter, shoots Band at point-blank range, through the eye and in the neck. In the confusion that follows, Neném also takes a bullet to the head, a wound from which he will die a few hours later.

To the outside world, the deaths of Zarur and Band look like business as usual. The police receive intelligence that Red Command has been planning a second invasion from Vidigal in the expectation that Band and Lion would act as fifth columnists. The day after Band's death, Rio's press reports that Rocinha and Vidigal are on a war footing.

Those with a closer acquaintance of the situation expect that Bem-te-vi, as the new Don of Rocinha, will unite the two parts of the favela and that tensions will now relax. Upper and lower do indeed form an uneasy union under Bem-te-vi. But to the disappointment of many, including Nem, the new don is not a good leader. Rocinha becomes even more chaotic.

8

BEM-TE-VI

2004–2005

Fabiana Escobar is awestruck as she approaches Rocinha for the first time. Compared to the modest favelas and lower-middle-class areas where she has grown up, this is a bewildering den of activity. People are shouting, furiously selling all manner of goods; boys are strolling around with semi-automatic weapons. She notices that rubbish is strewn everywhere – along the main streets, up and down the alleys, mixed in with the dog shit and various liquids of unknown provenance. But she is also struck by the self-confidence with which most people comport themselves: there is a brashness she has never encountered before in her home district of Rio Comprido.

Sick with nerves, Fabiana is on a mission she dare not fail. Her husband, Saulo, has been arrested on charges of drug trafficking and has been placed in a jail that is effectively run by Red Command. The police have released tapes to the media, including conversations between Saulo and Bem-te-vi, who now, of course, works with Red Command's rival, ADA, as the new Don of Rocinha.

In the light of Rocinha's factional switch, Red Command has sent out a message to its members declaring all Rocinhans to be *alemãos*,[20] enemies, a designation that carries an implicit death sentence. Saulo's life is in imminent danger.

Saulo acted as a curious hybrid under Lulu, a sort of freelance manager and middle man between Lulu and the matutos. He has been performing the same role under Bem-te-vi. Until his arrest, Fabiana had no idea about his deep involvement with the drugs trade of Rocinha. She is studying at university, with only a year left before graduation. Her life is about to change unexpectedly and profoundly.

Knowing nobody in this buzzing community, she tentatively approaches a sympathetic-looking woman in Valão. 'You want to speak with Bem-te-vi?' the woman responds. 'Well in that case, you'll have to ask that guy over there.' She points to a thin stick of a man wearing an FC Flamengo[21] shirt and flip-flops. 'He is called Nem.'

Barely able to look Nem in the eye, Fabiana repeats her request. 'You want to speak to Bem-te-vi?'

'That's right.'

'Well, we can fix that, but can you let me know what it's about?'

'No. I can't tell you. I have to speak to him alone.'

What comes next is unlike anything Fabiana has ever seen before. A gold pendant the size of a fist swinging from his neck, Bem-te-vi dances towards her at the head of his entourage, his blond quiff standing straight as a rod. Everyone is laughing and smiling, and she later understands why Bem-te-vi and his close friends are called the Band of Gold. With a glass in his hand, metal adorns every limb and digit. By his side swings his pride and joy – an Uzi lacquered in gold.

Bem-te-vi may be the Don of the Hill, but he is not a businessman. The only business he really understands is partying. He doesn't take drugs, but he drinks. A lot.

From Fabiana's point of view, this means at least that he is approachable. She explains that Saulo is her husband and that he desperately needs money to buy his way out of the Red Command cell block and into one where ADA hold sway. Bem-te-vi readily agrees to support her request. Over the next few months, Fabiana is able to arrange everything for Saulo in prison. This includes unscheduled conjugal visits. With Bem-te-vi's cash doing the talking, the prison guards prove most accommodating.

Nobody dislikes Bem-te-vi: he spreads joy, entertainment and money. His reign is like one long conga dance, with many adolescents and young adults joining the fun. The stars of Brazil's national football team occasionally come to the party.

For ordinary working people, it is a less happy experience. Apart from the constant noise, there are also the undesirables Bem-te-vi attracts. For managers like Nem, the new don is nothing short of a disaster. Apart from his lack of interest in the business and his cavalier attitude to money and accounting, he is too ready to engage in shootouts with the police, more for sport than any other reason. Perhaps his greatest weakness is the affection he has for robbers, burglars and thieves. Since the narcotics trade has begun to dominate the favelas of the South Zone, the more judicious and successful dons have kept thieves and muggers on a short leash.

Nem feels a special animus towards these criminals because one of their number fired the shot that led to his father's death. He also believes that a culture of theft and mugging damages business. A high incidence of violent assault scares off potential cocaine and marijuana customers from surrounding middle-class areas. Even more serious is the consequent breakdown in relations with the police. When the incidence of robberies in São Conrado, Gávea and Leblon increases, it makes the police look bad, at which point local commanders come under huge political and media pressure to do something about it.

On 1 February 2005, the two main anchors of the nightly TV news show, *Jornal Nacional*, William Bonner and Fátima Bernardes, do not present the bulletin as usual. Not only are they the most recognised journalists in Brazil, they are also married to each other. The stand-ins for the newscast lead with the story of how a burglar armed with a gun broke into the home of Bonner and Bernardes in Barra, just fifteen minutes' drive from Rocinha. Bonner confronted the thief, who injured the anchor's arm, although he didn't use the gun. The burglar then escaped with a laptop, mobile phones and jewels. Bonner and Bernardes are badly shaken.

The thief lives in Rocinha. There is no reason to suspect that his choice of Bonner and Bernardes' house is anything other than an extraordinary piece of bad luck, given the heat it brings down on the favela. Only an attack on the President of Brazil could have had a greater impact. The damage inflicted on the reputation of Bem-te-vi, of the police, of Rocinha and of Rio is irreparable for several months. This is one humiliation too many for the men and women who run the city's police. Rocinha will be squeezed until it squeals. BOPE is back in town and the level of violence goes up again. More deaths.

The Civil Police (PC), the investigative wing of the Rio force, are instructed to go after Bem-te-vi. Operation Trojan Horse is planned. Over a period of many weeks, the PC observe Bem-te-vi's movements and habits. Much of the new don's time is spent between the downtown commercial areas of Valão and Via Ápia, where Nem is now manager of the smoke shop as well as head of security. By night, Bem-te-vi parties before sleeping long into the afternoon.

It is a measure of how far the Don has allowed his intelligence operation to slip that he has no idea that a police informant has rented a house on the corner of Cowboy Street. The informant is joined by officers from the PC, who are devising a detailed plan. Its execution is set for a Saturday evening, when the streets of Valão are packed full of people.

Walking from his nearby smoke shop in Via Ápia, Nem rounds the corner into Valão to see Bem-te-vi talking to three men. Something about the scene makes him uneasy, and he comes to a halt. He decides instead to order food from a pizzeria. Another customer is in front of him, and as he waits, he hears a gun go off, before a grenade explodes. He rushes out of the pizzeria to see a body on the ground. A number of men have emerged from their hiding place, firing several rounds into the corpse, causing it to jump. The grenade is in fact a smoke bomb, designed to separate Bem-te-vi from his bodyguards, who remain cornered in an alley, unable to see anything through the curtain of fog and hemmed in by armed undercover police officers up on a roof.

The undercover agents are wearing regulation favela dress (football shirts, shorts and sneakers), so Nem assumes they are from Upper Rocinha, come to wreak vengeance on Bem-te-vi for his challenge to Lion.

He then notices the signature gold-plated Uzi on the ground and realises that the corpse must be that of his boss. As Bem-te-vi's entourage attempts to shoot their way out of the alley, one of their bullets almost hits Nem, and he drops to the ground for protection. People are screaming and running in all directions. Nem is on his walkie-talkie trying to organise his subordinates and warning them to expect further attacks. It is only when the squad cars arrive that it dawns on him that this is not Lion's act of vengeance, but the police.

After the body is removed, Nem coordinates Bem-te-vi's soldiers. One police officer later suggests that his quick thinking in this situation is a key reason for his subsequent elevation to the position of don.

The day after the killing, broken telegraph poles, dried pools of blood and smashed windows greet Fabiana Escobar, Saulo's wife, when she returns to Valão. The bar where Bem-te-vi was wont to drink is completely destroyed – shot and bombed to pieces. Fabiana wonders how she is going to continue supporting her husband in jail. If she can no longer afford to bribe the prison guards, he may wind up dead at the hands of Red Command.

Surveying the mess, one local community leader remarks that an atmosphere of trepidation and fear has settled over the favela. 'The war will not end with Bem-te-vi's death, just as it didn't end with the death of Lulu,' he points out. 'This war has only just begun, and we are about to experience worse still.'[22]

The fulfilment of his prophecy comes sooner than even he probably anticipated. The next 24 hours turn out to be a crossroads for Rio, for Rocinha and for Nem.

An announcement is made in Upper Rocinha: Soul Man, Bem-te-vi's brother-in-law, has declared himself the new Dono do Morro. Where Nem has concentrated on the buying and selling of the drugs for Bem-te-vi, Soul Man has been responsible for armaments. His declaration is as much a challenge as a statement of fact.

The truth of what happens next is uncertain.

Fabiana says that before Bem-te-vi's death, she passed a message to him from her husband in jail. Apparently, somebody was selling the tape of a telephone intercept in which Soul Man could be heard slagging off Bem-te-vi. When he received the message, Bem-te-vi wrote a letter, according to Fabiana, in which he declared that Nem and another senior member, Joca, were his anointed successors. If he did write the letter, no copy of it has survived.

Police intelligence make a further claim. They say that Soul Man has been in touch with Red Command's leadership to discuss the possible return of Rocinha into the fold.

O Gringo,[23] a long-time resident of Rocinha, offers much more detail. 'Nem's problem is that he is really smart,' he says. 'In the business, you are penalised for being smart. The killers see you in the spotlight the whole time and they don't like it. Basically, it is jealousy. Some guy like Nem has been in the organisation for just four years and he shoots up the hierarchy. He can look at a pile of drugs on a table and he knows straight away what it's worth. Nem could do it just like that.' Soul Man and his team of bandidos didn't have that capability. 'They would spend two or three days selling on the corner and they had already lost track of the money. But Nem has it all accounted nice and neat within five minutes.'

Soul Man feels deeply threatened by Nem's ability. He orders Joca to come up to Rua Um, saying he needs to sort out some issues about the matutos and their deliveries of coke into the favela. 'Go down to Valão,' Soul Man tells Joca, 'and come back with Nem.'

'He told me to go up alone. That made me suspicious,' Nem says. 'He even specified the route I had to take.' He decides to go a different way and makes it to the meeting with Soul Man. 'He starts to slag off Bem-te-vi. Don't get me wrong, I know he had his faults, but the guy's body was still warm.'

Nem says that he left, irritated with Soul Man for the disrespect he was showing their recently murdered boss, but not overly concerned about anything. 'I meet up with the boys and they say, "Are you crazy? He was going to kill you." I told them to calm down and said there were no big problems between me and Soul Man. Why would he kill me? And they replied, "He doesn't like you and he never has."'

Nem goes off to bed. But others from Lower Rocinha are not sleeping that night. 'So they go up the hill,' Gringo reports, 'with the safety catches off, ready to fire. Everyone is tooled up. That evening Soul Man dies and as many as eighteen altogether go with him.'

That at least is Gringo's version. He says Joca was there but is vague about Nem's presence, and Nem is adamant: 'I wasn't there – pure and simple.'

So who killed Soul Man?

'I can't say who did it because I can't talk about people who are still alive,' Nem explains, not unreasonably. 'Some years later, the guy who did it suddenly started spreading it around that he should be don because he had killed Soul Man.' But although they squared up a little, the dispute ended amicably.

Let us assume Nem is telling the truth – that it wasn't him who built that bridge across the Rubicon. But whether he was responsible or not, by the end of that evening, he was standing on the other side of a river that was running deep red.

If he were to look back across the bridge from where he came, Nem would see himself as the ever-capable consigliere, operating quietly in the background to clear up other people's messes, doing the accounts and ensuring the smooth running of the business. He would also see the impoverished, hard-working family man faced with impossible dilemmas about his baby daughter, and even further back an undernourished boy living in extreme poverty and nurturing his dying father.

Now, looking ahead, he knows that, together with Joca, he is the most powerful man in Rocinha.

Fabiana remembers the moment well. Saulo's wife is acclimatising herself to life in the big buzzing favela. She has left behind her middle-class aspirations and taken up work in her husband's industry, receiving instructions from him during her visits to prison before taking care of business on the outside. She is beginning to love the lifestyle. She has even changed her name. She is now known universally as Bibi Perigosa – Bibi Dangerous. Her transition from polite primary school headteacher's daughter to gangster's moll is almost complete. That evening, after it is confirmed that Soul Man and his allies from Rua Um are dead, she and her friends dance around the bars and clubs of Lower Rocinha, chanting:

HUBRIS

Tá tudo bem, tá tudo bem!
A Rocinha é o Joca e o Nem!
Everything is good, everything is great
Rocinha is with Joca and Rocinha is with
    Nem!

It is Halloween 2005.

Part III
NEMESIS

1

THE GREAT CHANGE
1994–2004

Despite the spasms of police killings, disappearances and murderous factional clashes that culminated in the deaths of Bem-te-vi and Soul Man, the trend across Rio and São Paulo from as early as the year 2000 was towards a reduction in the levels of homicide. The topography of violence was shifting away from these cities towards the impoverished north-east of Brazil. In São Paulo, it was the dominance of a single criminal organisation, the PCC, that contributed to a reduction in violence: the factional fighting that characterised so much of Rio's experience was absent. In Rio itself, the incidence of violence declined through much of the South Zone, including in Rocinha. The period between Easter 2004 and October 2005 was the exception that later proved the rule. Outside the South Zone, towards the northern parts of the city and Rio's urban hinterland, known as Baixada Fluminense, the rate of homicides started to increase dramatically.

The violence in much of Rio was diminishing despite the growth of the militias – the vigilante groups comprising serving and former police and army officers, firemen and other civil servants, which engaged in armed confrontation with the drug gangs. If you had the misfortune to live in one of the favelas in the north or west of Rio, you might encounter drugs factions at war with each other, drugs factions at war with the police, and drugs factions at war with militias.

Notwithstanding this new challenge to public order, the overall death rate continued to decline. Before long, the murder rate in north-eastern cities like Recife, Fortaleza and Maceió[1] would outstrip the historical highs of the southern cities in the 1990s.

The fate of the north-east is another story, but at least, along with the rest of Brazil, it was enjoying the benefits of a most welcome, if unexpected, tonic. After decades of dictatorship and chaotic transition, renewal and optimism were surging out from the federal capital, Brasília, towards the furthest reaches of the country's body politic. Whole regions and classes were reviving after a long period of neglect and deprivation. The sudden arrival of a period of prosperity that saw unemployment fall to record levels and personal spending increase significantly is crucial in explaining why Rio was becoming less violent. Young men in the favelas were turning away from weapons and drugs in favour of education and settled employment.

The surge of domestic contentment radiated out beyond Brazil's borders, enhancing the country's reputation abroad. This was all underwritten by a booming global economy hungry for the agricultural and mineral commodities that Brazil was able to deliver in seemingly boundless quantities.

No longer dependent on the West alone for its exports, Brazilian agriculture presided over a staggering growth in beef and soya bean cultivation. This matched the mouth-watering prospect of an oil bonanza when geologists confirmed huge new finds in the so-called 'sub-salt' fields. President Lula declared the discovery 'a gift from God'. The predicted reserves of around 50 billion barrels dwarfed Brazil's existing accessible reserves by a factor of more than three. The main fields lie off the coast of Rio state, and their discovery led to a sizeable increase in investment there, even if Brazilian politicians were inclined to gloss over the technical challenges involved in extracting the oil. Massive though these reserves are, they sit some seven kilometres beneath a daunting geological Cerberus of ocean, rock and salt. As oil prices fell in the second decade of the century, the optimism that greeted the discovery would appear in retrospect ever wilder.

But in the middle of the first decade, everybody, not least China, wanted to be friends with the commodity giant. Brazil's invigorated sun was beginning to eclipse Argentina's ageing star as the primary source of economic and political energy in the region – even if the two contested the title of most dazzling regional football power as keenly as ever. Under successive governments Brazil expanded slowly westwards through the Amazon and across Bolivia, Ecuador and Peru by planning new transport and trade connections to the Pacific coast. The aim was to establish more rapid access to the markets of East Asia and the west coast of the United States.

Obviously, the ever-growing revenues from commodities was the foundation conferring on Brazil a virtually unassailable advantage over its neighbours in its bid to assert itself as the new pivotal power of South America. But it was the unexpected emergence of two great political figures from the ashes of the Collor administration of the early 1990s that changed the very nature of Brazil's identity and started to erode the chronic lack of self-confidence that had characterised so much of the country's modern history.

The first of these was Fernando Henrique Cardoso, a former sociology professor and one-time Marxist who rarely, however, strayed far from his pragmatic social democratic roots. Urbane, charming and fluent in foreign languages, Cardoso had spent the first decade of the dictatorship in exile, but returned when it was still dangerous to do so in order to devote himself fully to the struggle to re-establish democracy in the country.

As the Minister of Finance in the post-Collor administration, he gave Brazil a gift for which almost the entire country will be eternally grateful: a strategy to combat inflation that actually worked and whose achievements remain in place to this day. As president from 1994 to 2002, Fernando Henrique, or FHC,[2] embarked on the arduous task of reforming the Brazilian state and reducing the chronic levels of inequality that had plagued the country since the early days of Portuguese colonialism.

Despite his huge successes, FHC encountered obstacles on the road to a number of critical reforms. The vested interests of Brazil's powerful, if numerically small, economic elite proved deft in constructing numerous barriers. And the country's constitutional inadequacies, notably the weakness of political parties and the unresolved tensions between the federal centre and the powerful state capitals, also contributed to the difficulties.

These problems notwithstanding, Fernando Henrique's legacy proved a godsend to his successor, Lula, who was finally elected president at his fourth attempt in 2002. Lula competes with Getúlio Vargas, the political inventor of modern Brazil, as the country's greatest politician since the abolition of the monarchy in 1889. Born into poverty in the north-east, and without formal schooling after the age of ten, Lula found odd jobs in Santos and São Paulo after emigrating south on his own aged thirteen. He eventually became a metalworker, emerging during the dictatorship as one of the trade's most effective union leaders. In the latter years of military rule, the unions organised a wave of great strikes whose primary aim was to force the generals' hand into restoring democracy. Lula's role in this movement catapulted him on to the national stage as a resolute but exceptionally charismatic figure whose direct, earthy language contrasted startlingly with the florid Portuguese of the traditional political classes.

In his illuminating autobiography, Fernando Henrique laments the collapse of his political relationship with Lula. The two men had collaborated in the past, but when FHC decided to stand as the social democrat candidate against Lula and his Workers' Party, relations broke down. In truth, the two men's contrasting styles could not have complemented each other better, and their rivalry is perhaps the Achilles heel of Brazil's late-twentieth-century revival. One can only speculate on what they might have achieved as collaborators instead of competitors.

When Lula was finally elected to the highest office in 2002, markets around the world reacted with horror as this firebrand socialist replaced the consummately responsible FHC. Lula confounded their expectations. He kept the economy on an even keel while building upon what FHC had already identified as Brazil's greatest challenge – the eradication of chronic, crushing poverty.

While China was lauded for pulling some 100 million citizens out of poverty from the mid 1980s, fewer noticed Brazil's more monumental achievement flowing from FHC and Lula's policies. In Brazil, 30–40 million people managed to cross the poverty line. Given the much smaller population of Brazil, this was an even greater feat than the Sino equivalent.

The consequences of this golden era for Brazil's political personalities were immense. The primary beneficiaries were the poor, not least those who lived in the favelas of the south. This was especially true of Rocinha. Its isolation from other favelas and its now well-established tradition as a large market, both for the residents and for those coming from outside looking for a bargain, enabled it to ride the wave of economic confidence with a swagger. This growth spurt offered alternative employment to its younger men and women, and so the drugs trade became a somewhat less attractive career path.

The early years of the decade saw record numbers of immigrants arriving in Rocinha from the north-east. The houses crept further up the hill, squeezing into any remaining open spaces, while also becoming ever taller as new floors were built on existing structures.

By its own standards, the favela was growing more affluent. More homeowners started to paint their houses bright colours, giving the area a distinctive and very Brazilian look.

Rocinha had been granted the status of an administrative district within Rio in 1993, separating it from São Conrado and thus also increasing its political significance. The city's declining levels of violence meant that tourists were slowly returning in numbers reminiscent of the 1960s. After FHC had successfully vanquished hyperinflation, Lula tackled the problem of unemployment with equally impressive results. Brazil was a happening place.

The success of its television and film industries played a key part in shifting perceptions of the country in the outside world. Brazilian *telenovelas*, the ubiquitous soap operas that absorb so much of the big networks' airtime, were hugely popular in Spanish-speaking markets, but also developed devoted followings in less likely areas such as France, Italy, the Middle East, Turkey, the Balkans and the Far East. By 1996, TV Globo alone was selling its telenovelas to more than 70 countries for a figure of $31 million.[3] Meanwhile, the film industry was transforming the portrayal of Brazilian social reality, moving away from Hollywood's two clichés of licentiousness and neo-Nazi incubation. Few cultural products have had such a profound impact on domestic and international perceptions of a country than Fernando Meirelles' adaption of the Paulo Lins novel, *City of God*. There was a sense that Brazil was trying to confront its fundamental problems rather than ignoring them as its governments had so often done in the past.

The country was growing up and taking itself seriously. Based on his own energetic travel schedule, Lula developed an independent, highly visible foreign policy, which neither kowtowed to nor alienated the United States and its ever-lurking presence.

All this activity contributed to boosting Rio's economy. This meant that although youngsters in the favelas were less inclined to choose to work with the drugs business, there was, nonetheless, a renewed spike in the demand for marijuana and particularly cocaine. Turnover saw a marked uptick. The drugs trade in Rio and São Paulo benefited from the miracle of the FHC and Lula years as much as any other business – and possibly more so.

Brazil no longer seemed like the old country. Power was shifting. That, at least, was how most Brazilians perceived what was happening. And it felt good.

2
A HELPING HAND
2006–2007

Nem's surroundings do not yet reflect his authority. His office is a desolate room in Valão, near the centre of Lower Rocinha. Unfurnished, with peeling paintwork, it houses a television in one corner and a couple of chairs. His bodyguards hang around here, waiting for something to happen. They handle their guns absent-mindedly. Guns are kept off the street on Nem's instructions. They unsettle people.

But just because he does not yet boast the trappings of power, it doesn't mean that he is not wrestling constantly with the idea and its implications for his new life.

Bibi Dangerous has perforce become better acquainted with Nem, as he has agreed to continue the payments to ensure that her husband remains unmolested in prison. She observes that when facing serious decisions, he is seized by uncertainty. She thinks he is always looking for the advice of a wise head. Perhaps he feels the absence of his mentor, Lulu, who has been dead for eighteen months now. Lulu's leadership was the guarantor of peace and an unhurried yet flourishing business.

Although quiet, Nem is reflecting upon his new situation and the central problem he faces. It is only a matter of weeks since he and his partner, Joca, who controls Rua Um, took power, but already Nem believes Joca is a liability for Rocinha, for the business and, by extension, for Nem himself. 'I will never forget. I was taking my daughter home from school,' he explains, 'so it would have been about five o'clock in the afternoon, when all of sudden they started firing wildly into the air up in Rua Um.' He rolls his eyes. 'I mean,' he adds exasperatedly, 'this was the middle of the day.'

Nem confronts Joca about this, trying to impress on him just how damaging such behaviour will be for their reputation in the community. Joca replies by playing dumb. 'Oh well, I was on one side of the area,' he says, 'and they were far away on the other, so it wasn't anything to do with me.' Either he is lying, thinks Nem, or he is failing to exercise proper control over his teams. Neither is acceptable.

This is tricky for Nem. He has been a friend of Joca's since they were kids. But since he joined Lulu's organisation five and a half years earlier, Nem has been watching power being exercised, learning how a don may best wield it. He recognises that by far his most successful and stable model is Lulu himself. There are three pillars upon which an effective leader builds his dominance: reputation within the community; acceptability to the local police; and authority within his organisation. Joca's behaviour threatens to undermine all three. Observing the situation first from prison and then close up in the favela, Saulo, Bibi's husband, remarks that Joca's behaviour is 'contrary to everything laid down in the annals of crime'. You do not go about frightening ordinary residents in this way: their immediate and reasonable assumption is that a shootout has broken out.

When I ask him about Joca, Nem shakes his head gently. Before Joca took control of Upper Rocinha, he explains, 'there was not a single person who had a bad word to say about him. He was a really nice guy.' He pauses briefly. 'But let me tell you this: if you want to see a person's real character, give them power and give them money. Then they'll show you their true face.'

Apart from the issue of the divided authority between Lower and Upper Rocinha, Nem faces certain specific problems with regard to Joca. 'They had many more weapons up top than we did down the bottom,' he says. Were there a confrontation, there is little doubt which side would be victorious. Nem's primary strategy to deal with this is to try to persuade Joca and his team to moderate their behaviour. But he is also on the lookout for weapons himself. Help with this comes from an unexpected quarter.

During one of Bibi's regular visits to the jail, Saulo tells her of a tip-off he has received regarding a potential sale of weapons in a district in the North Zone. He advises her to approach Nem to suggest that he organise a deal.

Bibi returns to Rocinha and speaks to Nem, using her usual opener: 'Saulo told me to tell you ...' Bibi prefaces everything in this way, because she is understandably reluctant to assume personal responsibility for what may turn out to be one of her husband's hare-brained schemes. Nem likes the idea, but instead of taking the matter in hand himself, he surprises her: 'Bibi, go negotiate this one yourself.' She is taken aback and not a little apprehensive. Still, if the Don has asked her to do it, she has little choice but to go through with it.

Following Saulo's instructions, she contacts the men selling the merchandise. They agree a price – 120,000 reals for four semi-automatic weapons. The sellers tell her to hand over the money, after which they will deliver the goods to Rocinha. This is a preposterous proposal, which the Rocinhans reject out of hand.

Instead, they devise an elaborate plan. Bibi will dispatch an emissary with a down payment of R$45,000. Before this happens, the sellers will send one of their own people to remain in Nem's custody. Once the initial payment is received, the sellers will deliver the four guns to Rocinha and pick up the rest of the money. At this point, their human surety will be released. Everyone seems content, although it is worth noting that the said human surety, a young man, Victor, barely eighteen, is not yet aware of his precise role in all this.

The plan goes disastrously wrong. The sellers take the deposit and make off without handing over the weapons. Bibi is racked with fear as she begins to appreciate the implications. She will be held responsible for the disaster. In her panic, she can only keep thinking, 'Oh my God, I'm going to have to kill that boy.' She sweats as she wonders whether she would be able to bring herself to actually do it. She concludes that if it is a case of her or the boy, Victor will have to go. She curses her husband for having inadvertently trapped her in this unholy moral maze.

Back in Valão, Victor has no idea what is happening. Indeed, he is rather enjoying himself, seduced by the excitement of being hosted by Rocinha's don.

Bibi's return changes all that. When she explains that the money has been stolen, the boy is not slow to grasp the gravity of his situation: unless it is returned, he will die.

He begins to cry uncontrollably. Purely by chance, Nem's security detail is at that moment playing with a genuine samurai sword that Nem has recently received as a gift. Victor collapses in fear, believing that the sword is being prepared to execute him. Bibi notes to herself that if Rocinha were under the control of Red Command, the boy would already be dead.

Nem ambles into the office and is briefed on the situation. The boy goes down on his knees, pleading for his life to be spared. Nem responds without hesitation: 'Okay, let's get one thing straight. Nobody is going to be taking the life of anybody else here. Is that quite clear? I only wish for my money back. Nothing more.'

The boy's relatives, one of whom is an officer in the Military Police, offer to send over what possessions they have in an attempt to make amends. The next day, a clapped-out old car worth about 4,000 reals rocks up in Rocinha with an ailing television and other detritus in the back. Altogether this amounts to about a tenth of the value of the money lost. Nem, however, accepts the offering and releases the boy, who, oddly, becomes a regular fixture in Rocinha for a couple of years, drinking and attending the favela's increasingly popular funk concerts.

The incident is an important lesson for Nem. When it comes to serious issues like the purchase of weaponry, he cannot afford to delegate. He also recognises that by releasing the boy, he has demonstrated weakness within the code of the drugs cartels. He is nonetheless determined to stick by the principle that unnecessary deaths are to be avoided.

Three days before Christmas 2006, Saulo escapes from captivity, having removed an entire air-conditioning unit in his cell and climbed through the hole. At Bibi's request, Nem finds accommodation for her and her husband.

At last Nem can relax a little. Here is a man he can trust – a man with some brains. Saulo is unlike any other trafficker in Rocinha. He was just a few months away from graduating with a degree in mathematics when he was arrested for drug-related activity while working as a postman. But he also nurtures a crucial connection in Rio's world of drugs. His father spent some years in prison, and during this period he came to know Fernandinho Beira-Mar, one of Red Command's most feared leaders.

Although he has a record for violence, Beira-Mar is more focused on his role as Red Command's commercial mastermind. He is the one trafficker from the Rio gangs who straddles both the local domestic market in cocaine and the wholesale market dispatching the drug from its production areas in Colombia, Peru and Bolivia, through its transit zone, Brazil, and on to destinations in Europe and the United States.

Thanks to his father's prison connection, Saulo enjoys a rare intimacy with Beira-Mar. This has one critical implication for Rocinha: even after the break with Red Command and the emergence of ADA as the primary cartel in the favela, back-channel links with Red Command can be re-established. In theory, and certainly so far as their foot soldiers are concerned, the two cartels are at war. In practice, the two leaderships discreetly explore mutually advantageous cooperation.

The uncontrollable virus of hedonism and sensuality is coursing through the capillaries of Rocinha. Quotidian life may be grimy and expensive. People may have to work incredibly hard for minimal salaries. Many sleep on floors or several to a room. The streets may still be smelly with diesel and smeared with animal shit, rotting fruit and commercial detritus. But at night, and especially at the weekends, Rocinha lights up like Broadway. The bars and clubs are packed with young people laughing, gossiping and eyeing up the talent. Inside the clubs, bodies swirl in a medusa bloom driven and directed by the resonating bass of DJs and MCs who, like Brazilians over centuries, have borrowed creative ideas from other cultures and transformed them into something inimitably their own.

The Clube Emoções stands at the pinnacle of the venues. It is a vast hangar with a low ceiling located to the right of Estrada da Gávea, just at the entrance to the favela. This is one of the biggest attractions not just in Rocinha but in all Rio. It is well run and police-free, meaning that thousands are able to enjoy their dance evenings with unhindered access to narcotics. The one thing at which the management draws the line is weapons, and they have always been adamant that they have no relationship with Rocinha's traffickers. This is an unspoken law that the traffickers have almost always respected. To spend a night at a *baile funk*[4] in Emoções is the epitome of cool, especially for the middle-class kids of São Conrado, Gávea, Leblon, Ipanema and Copacabana.

Rocinha's growing reputation as party central has a significant knock-on effect, not just on the drugs trade but on the service industries that flood Lower Rocinha – bars, eateries, souvenir shops and cheap clothes and electronics stalls. All this benefits Rocinha, and it also benefits those running Rocinha. For that reason, Nem and Saulo understand that places like Emoções are to be avoided. They never go there. It is very close to the border between the Hill and the Asphalt, and any difficulties would attract the police. It is vital for the business that the traffickers do not interfere with Emoções.

Nem is concerned that trouble could easily break out. Members of Joca's team often get into fights; as Saulo observes, 'this drives people away from the smoke shops'. It's bad for business. Joca, by now drinking very heavily, is becoming a problem.

There is another issue. Soon after the two men assume control of Rocinha, five visitors arrive separately to see Joca on business. In each case Joca, who dislikes dirtying his hands with trade, sends them down to see Nem. Unlike his partner, he has no notion of accounting, bookkeeping or intelligent supply-chain practice.

The first visitor brings out a notebook. 'Here,' he says, pointing to one column, 'are all the deliveries made to Rocinha.' These represent significant shipments of drugs. 'And here,' he says, moving on to the next, 'is the value of the goods.' Nem has never met the man, although in the past he has heard Bem-te-vi talk about the suppliers. The visitor then explains calmly that payment has yet to be received.

The four other suppliers tell the same story: drugs delivered; payment not made. When all the meetings are concluded, Nem tots up the debts. Most have accrued during Bem-te-vi's administration, but Joca is responsible for some of them. The business owes its major providers approximately R$1,800,000; almost US$1,000,000.

Nem retains his exterior cool while thinking, 'How in God's name am I going to handle this?' He has only ever been in debt twice in his life. The first time was five years earlier, when he borrowed money from Lulu to pay for his daughter's medical treatment – money he successfully paid back on the job. The second was at Easter the previous year, when he took out a small bank loan to pay the rent on the house in Praia Seca where he had hoped to escape the violence of Rocinha.

He checks with Bem-te-vi's managers to ascertain whether the sums demanded by the suppliers are correct. They are.

He really has to settle this somehow. He cannot afford to lose his major business partners at a time when the Rocinha operation is still in the state of chaos inherited from Bem-te-vi and now being perpetuated by Joca. In his first decision as CEO, he arranges to pay the suppliers in instalments over the course of the next year.

Joca is behaving like an idiot. Reports are reaching Nem that his men are intimidating residents, extorting money from them and making other demands. They are kidnapping people and demanding cash for their release. Joca walks the streets with a swarm of armed security. He refuses to talk to residents about their petitions and complaints.

'As soon as Joca started to contest the leadership with Nem,' Saulo recalls, 'they were both hoping that the other would slip up. It's natural, even if they had been friends since childhood and were both brought up here.' It becomes a complex political game. Joca may have the bullish support of the Rua Um crowd and their weapons. But Nem has brains, natural authority and much popular support as well.

Nem invites Joca down to Lower Rocinha for lunch. He cannot understand his friend's transformation. He is immediately worried by Joca's remarks:

'I think somebody may be ready to meet their end up top.[5] And by the way, we've got a cop tied up. He's preparing to meet his maker as well!'

'What cop?'

'Sérgio. Anything wrong with that, old friend?'

'Too right there is!'

After lunch, Nem summons Joca's brother to see him. 'I want you to make damn sure that your brother releases that cop,' he says crisply. 'If they kill him, there will be a showdown. We cannot have a shootout here with the cops.' Nem is already learning that running the business is more complicated and stressful than he imagined. The last thing he wants is a dead cop on his hands. Fortunately, Joca is sufficiently in awe of Nem not to cross him on this issue. The policeman is released 40 minutes later.

'We agreed,' Nem reminds Joca later, 'that together we were going to make a shedload of money. We did not agree to inflict pain on people. Killing cops was certainly *not* part of the deal.'

Nem is not enjoying this. As he did after Lulu's death, he considers selling up and leaving the favela. But before he does, he has one more ploy up his sleeve. He starts choking off the supply of cash to Joca and his people. Lower Rocinha generates considerably more revenue than Upper Rocinha, whose main function is security. It's true that Joca sells a lot of marijuana, but he also wastes a lot of money. In theory, he is obliged to share the profits generated by these sales. But that isn't happening. So in return, Nem decides to hold back on the more significant payments due from the profits of the cocaine trade. His warning to Joca and his followers is implicit yet unambiguous.

The denouement is unexpected. Joca grabs as much cash from the business as he can lay his hands on and flees Rocinha. Some say it is R$800,000, while Saulo later suggests it is a straight million – a large chunk of the money that the business owes the suppliers. Nem is faced with yet another large shortfall. Joca is never seen again in the favela. Before long, he will be arrested in the north-east and sent down on trafficking charges. For traffickers, Rocinha is a safe haven. As soon as you move out of the territory, you run a considerable risk of being arrested.

Although Upper Rocinha's leader is gone, Nem receives a phone call from one of Joca's lieutenants. 'If you want anything to do with Upper Rocinha, you have to deal with me now. Understood?' Nem is tiring of the whole palaver – the Upper Rocinhans spend every evening firing their guns into the air, frightening the locals, goading the police and sleeping with other men's wives and girlfriends. He knows the people he is dealing with are often just kids. But kids with semi-automatics and grenades require delicate supervision.

Nem has been reading a book about Genghis Khan. He is struck by how the Mongolian tyrant based his power by instilling self-belief into the weakest tribes. He pays particular attention to the least confident members of the organisation, those who are little noticed but numerous. He is friendly and open to most people, and this generates loyalty – a loyalty he will need in years to come.

But now the time has come for action. He gathers all his soldiers, and at eight o'clock in the evening, they head up to Rua Um. He also has some supporters in the Rua Um crew whom he has alerted to his plans.

Meetings between two heavily armed factions are always tense affairs. The last time it happened was at the time of Soul Man's assassination, and over a dozen people ended up dead.

Nem notices that the other side has no natural leader now that Joca is gone, and so he starts speaking. 'First and foremost, nobody here is going to die. Understood? What Joca got up to was wrong. But he will not be coming back here any time soon. We have a choice – we can continue arguing with each other and killing each other. Or we can get on with the business of making money. Which do you want?'

Silence.

'I am heading back down to Lower Rocinha now. If I hear that anyone is planning to invite Joca back; if I hear that you have been in touch with him at all; then when I come back, I will not be coming to talk ... Do you get what I mean?'

Silence once more. There are no objections.

Nem has achieved something remarkable. Upper and Lower Rocinha are reunited for the first time in several years. The money is starting to flow as well. Now it is time for his true character to be revealed.

3
TAKING CARE OF BUSINESS
2004–2007

The business still requires a lot of work. The suppliers are not the only ones demanding money.

Rocinha's drugs trade employs 200–300 people, divided quite strictly into a number of different functions. The most low-level employees are the lookouts, the olheiros. Unless you live in the favela, or at the very least are well acquainted with favela culture, you will never spot them. They stand at, or wander around, key points of the slum, watching for any untoward or unusual activity, such as a police incursion or a threatening, suspicious or simply unfamiliar face. Their signals are shouts, whistles, squawks, fireworks, waves and laughs – sounds that send a message from street corners to windows perhaps one, perhaps two floors up. From there the information zips along the stick-narrow alleys, through the lanes and up the hill until it reaches the district organiser.

Traditionally, the olheiros are boys, some as young as eight years old, stepping on to the first rung of the business. In the 1980s and 1990s, school was often an optional activity for the children of the favela, and the kids had plenty of time on their hands. That would change later, although to this day Rocinha has one of the poorest rates of school attendance in Rio.

Nem quickly reaffirms Lulu's law that nobody under the age of sixteen may join the business, although managers sometimes secretly take on underage kids as lookouts nonetheless. The younger they are, the more unobtrusive they appear.

Then comes the processing of the drugs. Young women and men are employed on a freelance basis in small houses and flats known as *endolaçao* centres, 'dollar' houses, so-called because the drugs are divided into little sachets each worth a single real or dollar. With the increase in prices, they have different names: 'Coke for 10' or 'Dope for 5'.

From the dollar houses, the drugs are distributed around the districts of Rocinha by the *vapores*, delivery men who scuttle around the favela making sure that the smoke shops are well stocked. They are paid on a piece-rate basis.

The sub-managers are responsible for the day-to-day running of a small area, usually comprising one smoke shop. Their most crucial role is compiling the accounts for their shop.

Senior managers have entire districts under their control. They have to ensure that the right drugs are sent to the right smoke shops. They also collect the money at the end of the shift and present accounts to the vice dons or the Don himself.

The sale of drugs is a 24-hour operation, although business is fairly slow between about 8 and 11 a.m. Nem notices that because the managers and sub-managers, who do most of the work, are salaried, their earnings are not much higher than those in legitimate employ-ment. The vapores, by contrast, are pulling in much bigger figures.

As Saulo points out, the structure of the Rocinha business is unique in that 'the vapores are not attached to the smoke shop'. They work freelance and not as employees. Within a matter of weeks, Nem issues an order. 'I changed it so that henceforth the vapores were to be put on a salary and that under no circumstances could they expect to earn more money than the managers,' he explains. Greater responsibility deserves greater reward.

The managers' brief also includes liaising with security, the pack of gun-wielding youngsters that became such a frightening icon of favela life in the 1990s and in the first decade after the millennium.

Security is an entirely separate operation from the actual sale and marketing of the drugs. When Nem takes over, he has between 100 and 150 security personnel, or soldiers, under his command. Some, but not all of them, are armed. On reflection, it is quite astonishing how few bandidos are required to police a favela: roughly 100 armed men per 100,000 inhabitants.

They are divided into two principal groups. Many guard the smoke shops, but there is also a separate detail that provides protection for Nem and other senior management figures. Collectively, the security teams are also expected to defend the drugs operation from possible incursions, from rival gangs or the police.

Nem prefers to have older soldiers in his security detail, as they are less prone to the capricious firing of weapons. Soon after he assumes leadership of the business, he pays a former member of BOPE to train up his personal praetorian guard. Initially there are fifteen members of the group, whose sole job is to protect Nem. The numbers grow over the years. This is a disciplined elite squad that is also noteworthy for its habit of wearing uniforms similar to those of BOPE or the Civil Police. 'We did this because of the helicopters,' Nem explains. 'They would sometimes deploy helicopters when raiding the favela, and so if we were wearing police uniforms, they wouldn't be able to distinguish us from the air.'

Finally, senior management in both sales and security all rely on someone known as *o fiel*, the loyalist, or *o braço direito*, the right arm. Over time, Nem employs a few of these, but one man in particular stands out. His name is Wanderlan Barros de Oliveira, known as Feijão, the Bean. Officially not involved in the business, Feijão will play a critical role in Nem's life and financial affairs, and as a political figure within the favela.

Feijão is a childhood friend of Nem's. He has a charming and relaxed manner. He is popular around the favela, always smiling and willing to help. He categorically denies any involvement in trafficking, although many inside Rocinha believe that his close relationship with Nem is not only personal but professional. Early on in Nem's reign as don, Feijão appears to play a role in his transport operation, conveying the drugs boss from place to place by car. For security reasons, Nem is meticulous in not divulging his whereabouts or movements to anyone who does not need to know them.

On top of the substantial debt he inherits from Bem-te-vi, Nem has to pay all his workers. Except for those at the very top, the workers in the drugs trade receive wages comparable to those in the mainstream economy. Most of Nem's employees' families are also indirectly subsidised by the drug industry. If any of his gang is arrested, Nem is expected to pay for his family's upkeep from the business. This involves huge outgoings in his entirely cash economy.

Given all these outgoings, Nem recognises the importance of restoring the business to the flourishing enterprise it became under Lulu. How to do so is a colossal challenge. The police later tell me that he quickly developed an excellent reputation among medium and large wholesalers for being a good payer, and accessible. One of these, a Bolivian, told them, 'Rocinha is like a party – you go with coke and they'll buy it on the spot with cash. You get there, you have women, funk parties and the business is sorted out then and there, cash with no awkwardness.' The dealer then contrasted this with selling in Sao Paulo to the PCC. 'It was terribly tedious,' he remembered. 'You pitched up with stuff to sell and they would then make you wait in a hotel for ten days before they'd see you. At your expense, of course!'

But Nem is also determined to build upon Lulu and Bem-te-vi's tradition of *assistencialismo*, the provision of basic goods, foodstuffs, medicines and loans to the favela residents as a way of ensuring their goodwill.

Assistencialismo is actually forbidden by law, especially as it relates to the buying of votes at election time. But in the absence of a state presence in the favelas, it is a common phenomenon. In many ways, the practice is indistinguishable from Brazil's national practice of *jeitinho*,[6] a quotidian form of corruption that acts as psychological preparation for the monstrous misconduct that goes on at every level of Brazilian business and government.

During his period in power, Nem builds a small football pitch for the community, he pays for residents to make trips back to the north-east to see family, he funds medical treatment and he provides food baskets that are distributed to the most needy.

Unlike in Lulu's time, Nem does not have set office hours when residents can request subsidies, favours or indeed quasi-judicial hearings. While Lulu would only hold court on Tuesday evenings, residents can approach Nem any time and anywhere. Lulu was a mysterious figure – almost mythical for most residents – who liked to keep himself to himself. Nem, by contrast, is both sociable and approachable.

'I expanded certain aspects of the support for the community,' he says. 'For example, Lulu didn't have a system for distributing the food baskets.' Every month, 1,200 residents receive a generous supply of basic groceries. Every week, vegetables are handed out to 600 families. Nem and the business provide the money, and the local community leaders arrange the distribution. 'It was actually Bem-te-vi's idea but he never did anything about it. I was the one who introduced it,' he says.

'The food baskets and the support we gave to extracurricular school activities, such as Thai boxing or capoeira classes, were all accounted for as part of our business expenses,' he explains. 'But burials, prescription costs or if anyone who couldn't afford it needed gas, these were all extra payments.'

Nem financed so many trips for people to visit relatives in the north-east that he thought up another scheme. 'My idea was to buy a van and then just send it up north once a week and people could travel for free,' he says, 'but that was one thing I never actually got round to doing.

'You can go and ask people in Rocinha what they think about me and what I did,' he tells me. So I take up his challenge, and he would be gratified. They consider his generosity and his ability after Joca's departure to reduce the violence in the favela to be his best qualities. Once you have spent some time in Rocinha, people are quite open about this. They do not strike me as speaking under duress, and in any event, Nem's authority is a mere memory, as at this stage he has been in prison for almost four years.

Nem also claims he was so relaxed that residents used to exploit it. 'There was an old woman who asked me to pay for medicine,' he remembers, 'and then I realised she was charging me double what it actually cost! Bloody hell – it's quite a thing when you get old women like that taking the mickey.' But he stopped short of distributing video games. 'Kids would come to see me and ask for this or that game and so I asked them what grades they were getting in school. I would send them back and tell them to pay more attention to their education and not so much to the video games.'

Ordinary Rocinhans are caught between the devil and the deep blue sea. Trust in the police is virtually non-existent. But since Easter 2004, they have experienced the chaos and uncertainty of the gang's violent internal competition. The gangsters have a lot of work to do before they can be sure of regaining the locals' confidence. The business's security patrols are menacing. They comprise teenagers and men in their twenties toting powerful weapons in broad daylight – even if Nem orders this to be kept to a minimum.

Susceptible to the glamour of the gangsta culture – part American import, part home-grown – the soldiers increasingly define themselves by the rewards of money, social status and fame. Social media and the Brazilian culture of frenetic communication are a perfect match. Outside the United States, no country in the world has a higher uptake of Facebook and its once ubiquitous predecessor, Orkut, than Brazil. The young bandits are increasingly driven by a desire to boast of their exploits across these platforms.

The favela is huge. Although from a distance it looks like a compact unit, a few days wandering around its roads, lanes and alleys demonstrates its remarkable complexity. In this environment, policing a community of around 100,000 people is inevitably demanding and fraught with problems.

Nem insists on a number of iron rules. First – as Orlando Jogador once decreed in Complexo do Alemão– nobody under sixteen may join the business. During Nem's five years in power, only one underage boy is taken on (he was fifteen). Secondly, no crack cocaine or *loló*[7] will be manufactured or sold in Rocinha. 'Crack just destroys lives,' Nem says. 'We could see what this was doing in other parts of the city and we simply weren't going to let it happen in Rocinha.' This is strictly enforced and makes a huge difference to social cohesion and stability. As Nem points out, in São Paulo and the North Zone of Rio, where there is no control, crack users establish areas in or near favelas (i.e., largely outside the reach of the police) that become known as *cracolândia*. In these places, desperate young crack addicts congregate, smoke and vegetate. It is a dark plague that infects and destroys thousands of young men and women in the poorest parts of the city, fostering criminality, deprivation and death.

Finally, thieving and petty crime are forbidden, not only in Rocinha itself, but also in the surrounding areas of the South Zone. Apart from anything else, Bem-te-vi's killing by the Civil Police was directly related to his hosting the most notorious muggers and thieves of the South Zone. Saulo and Nem are united on this issue. In late 2007, Saulo has a tense phone call with a senior member of the Rocinha gang's security team. There has been a serious mugging in the fancy area of Leblon and it turns out that the victim has close links to the governor of Rio state, Sérgio Cabral. This is precisely the type of incident that can trigger major armed police intervention: an angry governor, personally insulted, is capable of responding with lethal force. Saulo orders security personnel to go to Vidigal, the neighbouring favela, whither the muggers have fled. He tells them to find the perpetrators, give them a solid beating and return the goods. These are found in a container in Vidigal and promptly returned to the owner. The governor stays his hand. Another close shave for the business.

4

WE'RE NOT ALONE
2007

Bibi Dangerous was furious. She had discovered text messages on Saulo's phone indicating that her husband was seeing another woman. When she confronted him, he denied the accusation vehemently. Every day now, he was leaving home at seven in the morning and not returning until midnight, sometimes later. She was left at home with their two young kids and going stir-crazy. On her Orkut[8] page, she started posting daring photographs of herself holding up large wads of banknotes with comments like 'It's so boring having cash ...' She wanted the world, or at least Rocinha, to know that she was a gangster's moll, proud of it and enjoying the financial fruits Saulo was bringing home.

Anonymous notes were left on her page, taunting her. 'While you're hanging out at home, Bibi,' one mocked, 'your precious Saulo is off screwing other women.'

Angry and increasingly unhappy, Bibi would also show off by taking photographs of herself fooling around with one of the guns Saulo had left in the house. No sooner had she done it than she'd pull the photo from her page, suddenly scared that somebody would see the gun.

Her fears were not misplaced – there were people out there who found Bibi's Orkut page very interesting reading.

In the middle of 2007, she posted a message on Orkut asking her mother to call her. She committed the cardinal sin of including her own phone number. The phenomenon of social media was still relatively new. Brazilians had taken to it like ducks to water, but most had yet to appreciate how public the Internet was. Even if information was posted for just ten minutes, it was archived somewhere, or was being monitored in real time. Nem understood the importance of information control, but his insight was a rarity. Bibi hadn't fully grasped it yet.

Ten minutes later, she removed the number. But it was ten minutes too late. Those somebodies watching had already made a note of the details.

Now it was time for them to listen in. First they heard her chatting to her mum, but before long, she phoned her husband, Saulo. This was what the listeners had been hoping for. They already suspected that Saulo had sought sanctuary in Rocinha after his escape from prison. By eavesdropping on Bibi's phone, and then on his, they were able to start identifying his movements. Unsurprisingly, he never left the favela. Inside the perimeter, no police were likely to violate the sanctuary that Rocinha afforded.

The intercept of Bibi's phone was the opening gambit in Operation Service Provider. Two experienced investigators from the Civil Police, Alexandre Estelita and Reinaldo Leal, were now listening in on every call that Bibi made. Soon after they had Saulo's number, they nailed Juca Terror's. Then Beiço, then Cabeludo, Total, D2, Lico, Vinni.[9] Before long, they were mapping the relationships between dozens of the gangsters running Rocinha.

But they couldn't find a number for Nem. They had been able to identify him as the don, but he was mysterious and distant. Saulo, too, was cautious when it came to using the phone, but Bibi made up for that – not to mention Marcela, Saulo's girlfriend. These two were never off their phones and Orkut pages.

As Nem consolidated his position as sole Don of Rocinha, his natural intelligence and caution quickly asserted themselves. Long before he had reached this position, he had appreciated that telephones and computers were liabilities, to be avoided whenever possible. He could not stop members of his organisation from yakking away on their mobiles – this was Brazil, after all, where effusive verbal communication seems ingrained in the culture. Nonetheless, the infrequency with which the others mentioned him during their conversations suggested that he had warned them to keep gossip to a minimum. If they did refer to him, it was often euphemistically: 'Someone next to God' was a favourite.

Nem assumed, correctly, that the police were monitoring all the gang's communications. More than any other trafficker in Rio, he understood that his future depended on his control of information – and upon the acquisition of new information.

Of course, he needed to use communication devices. He stayed in touch with his team via radio. But he also carried a bag with him wherever he went containing a dozen or more phones, each one linked to a specific contact – politicians, corrupt police and outside informers. For this reason, Estelita and Leal were unable to break through into his closed inner circle of communication.

'He wasn't called the Master for nothing,' the two detectives explain. 'He would see himself as possessing greater wisdom than the others. And he did. Apart from the power invested in him by weapons and fear, he had the power of intellect, which was allied to the power he accrued through his control of information.' A Master, they continue, is a character who has information and knows what he is doing. 'If there were a police operation, he would order his assistants to tell kids not to go to school the following day as there was going to be a raid.' This of course meant that he had been tipped off. 'So the others thought he was like God,' the detectives conclude. 'So far as they were concerned, he just seemed to know everything. And he sort of did.'

The officers may have looked like tough Hollywood cops, with arms like tree trunks, cropped hair, and *Miami Vice*-style stubble around square jaws, but the surface clichés hid characters much more interesting. They were thoughtful and meticulous in their analysis of their targets. Perhaps most striking of all, they did not judge. They tried their utmost to grasp the psychology and methods of the people they were investigating in order to understand how the organisation was structured. They respected intelligence and were contemptuous of stupidity, whether on the part of the police, the bandidos or anyone else involved in this uncertain world of the drug gangs – a world in which a turn into the wrong alley, a misinterpreted glance or a stolen kiss could lead to a casual killing.

They may not have cracked Nem's personal communications, but the cops were far from idle. Within a matter of three months, they had drawn up a detailed organogram of Nem's operation. They also had the names and nicknames of most of the leading players, as well as a rough guide to their background and function within the local branch of ADA.

Estelita and Leal were quick to spot three issues exercising the business. One was the need to purchase arms and ammunition. The second concerned the fears of another possible uprising in Rua Um after Joca's departure, though these dissipated somewhat just over a year after Nem and Joca had assumed power in Rocinha, when ADA supporters in Vidigal drove out the local Red Command team, leading to the re-establishment of fraternal relations between the two favelas. The third was the need to supply and secure their two *esticas*, or 'stretch points', two much smaller favelas, Parque da Cidade and Chácara do Céu. The former was located between Rocinha and Gávea, the latter between Vidigal and Leblon. They were lucrative drug outlets as they serviced the middle-class clientele who wished to avoid the slightly intimidating trip into Rocinha itself. Due to their very isolation from Rocinha, however, the two locations were more vulnerable to police raids. Nem ordered that the two stretch points were to be free of weapons.

Juca Terror, one of Nem's senior managers, had special responsibility for ensuring the smooth running of the business in Chácara do Céu. One day, Estelita and Leal fixed on a conversation he was having with a certain Alexandre Marques. This man arranged with Juca to pick up some money from the smoke shop at the tiny favela. As they were tracking the conversation, it dawned on the detectives that Marques was in fact an officer of the Military Police.

The relationship between Juca Terror and Marques appeared to be long-standing. The detectives later discovered that Marques had explained to his colleagues in the police that Juca was an informer. Indeed, he tailored his phone conversations to make it sound as though that was the case. In actual fact, it was Juca who was paying Marques.

One of their most intense topics of conversation revolved around the status of Cruzada São Sebastião. This was a series of tenement blocks on the north-eastern edge of Leblon. Close to the border with Ipanema, Cruzada is Leblon's only poor area, and was the ideal stretch point for cocaine and marijuana sales to the rich inhabitants living in and around the Asphalt's most desirable postcode. Although very clearly within Rocinha's retail catchment area, Cruzada was not controlled by ADA. This one settlement remained loyal to Red Command, which Juca Terror clearly considered an intolerable state of affairs.

But Cruzada's location posed a certain problem for Rocinha. ADA did have a team of people there, ready to assume control of the retail operation once the sitting leadership was removed. But it was simply not feasible to go steaming into Leblon tooled up and ready for a fight to wrest control of the trade. The police around

Rocinha may have been pliant, but an armed incursion into Leblon (where Governor Cabral also happened to live) would amount to an open declaration of war against the state.

To solve the problem, Juca arranged with Marques that the Military Police would simply arrest the Red Command leader in Cruzada. This they did, and Cruzada fell gently into Rocinha's lap. Juca congratulated the bent cop on his helpful contribution.

For Estelita and Leal, this was a fascinating relationship to track. Marques was not simply a patrolman stationed on the border of Rocinha who had accepted a modest bribe to act as lookout. He was providing hard information about police activity, including when and how raids would take place in Rocinha. The average monthly salary of an ordinary PM officer at the time was just under R$1,800 (about US$750), in a city where the cost of living was comparable to that of many industrial cities in the global north. In certain sectors, like housing, costs were becoming punitively expensive. Many officers were desperate to augment their salary in order to make ends meet. The quickest and easiest ways were criminal: either you took money from the drug traffickers, or you joined one of the militias controlling the favelas in the North Zone. Alexandre Marques had chosen the former.

'We concluded,' Estelita says, 'that after the taking of Cruzada, Rocinha wanted to control all the favelas of Zona Sul all the way to Chapéu Mangueira, which is just beyond Copacabana.'

Nem concedes there is some truth to this. 'Look, we did want to push Red Command from there, but nobody would make a move on a community if the people there were happy with what they had. Cruzada was very unhappy with Red Command, just as Vidigal had been.'

Slowly but surely, Estelita and Leal were building up an immense storehouse of information about the extent and sophistication of Nem's operation in Rocinha. They don't mind admitting that they were impressed by its scale.

5
BOOM TIME
2007

Officers Estelita and Leal were tucking into lunch in the eatery around the corner from the station in Lapa, a down-at-heel but funky district twenty-five minutes drive from Rocinha. As was his wont, Leal was satisfying his large frame by ravaging a basket of prawn *pasteis*, the irresistible Brazilian pasties made all the more tasty with a liberal sprinking of hot chilli sauce. 'Boy, can that man put it away,' laughs Estelita about his colleague. 'I had to drag him off when the phone rang.' But the call was sufficiently important to persuade even Leal to forget his midday meal.

It was August 2007, and the wiretap on Saulo's phone had lit up. It was his right-hand man. 'Saulo – bad news I'm afraid,' the caller told his boss. 'The factory has blown up and a fire has broken out. It was an accident and two of the guys have been badly burned. We've sent them to the hospital.' Saulo wanted to assess the damage. 'What exactly is on fire? Has the equipment been damaged?' he asked. 'Uh uh, nope,' came the reply. 'It's just the wooden stairs leading up there that are burning.'

Leal looked at Estelita, who raised an eyebrow. 'Whaddya think?' he asked. 'I think the hospital,' Estelita replied.

The officers jumped into their car and headed towards Miguel Couto, the nearest hospital to Rocinha. They arrived to find the two workers who had been admitted with burns. Estelita introduced himself. 'So what happened, lads?'

'Oh nothing,' one replied casually. 'We were having a barbecue and the lighter fluid caught fire.'

Estelita and Leal spoke to the hospital staff, who obligingly handed them the results of the forensics gathered from the two patients. These showed that under their nails was a mixture of cocaine and precursor chemicals, required to transform coca paste into its more familiar powdered form. Less than two months into their investigation, Estelita and Leal had stumbled across a cocaine refinery in Rocinha. Bingo!

Saulo was even more enterprising than they had first imagined. Along with his family connections to Beira-Mar, the Red Command leader, it appeared he had brought another valuable resource to Nem's business. He may not have finished his maths degree, but in the University of Crime that is Rio's prison system, a friendly narcotics expert had taught him how to transform cocaine paste into powder.

Paste has the consistency of cake icing and is the interim stage of processing between the coca leaf and cocaine powder. Following his escape from prison, Saulo had suggested to Nem that he establish a coke kitchen, or refinery, in the favela, to which the Don clearly assented. This important business decision would have a huge and positive impact on the turnover of Rocinha's drug trade. Before long, not only would it be able to boast that it supplied some 60 per cent of Rio's entire cocaine consumption. It would also be the only favela capable of providing other areas and factions with the processed drug.

Back in Rocinha, Saulo was counting the cost of the accident. The equipment appeared to be safe, so they could get the kitchen up and running again without too much difficulty. But they had lost quite a lot of paste, possibly as much as several hundred thousand reals' worth. That at least was what he indicated to his wife, Bibi.

Estelita and Leal knew roughly where the refinery was located, but they wanted to take a closer look. 'The thing is,' Estelita explains, 'you can only go in with about three hundred men.' Serious police work in the favela was not easy. The cops couldn't simply walk up to somebody like Nem and arrest him. First, the bulk of the Military Police patrolling the perimeters were in Nem's pay, and their job was to warn him of any imminent raid. Second, if a small number of cops entered the favela without authorisation from the traffickers, they would be dead before they got within a mile of him. The authority of the state only extended into the favelas when its representatives appeared in numbers and heavily armed.

So for Estelita and Leal to investigate the details of the refinery, it needed to be part of a much larger cover operation, and it was arranged that a couple of hundred Civil Police would enter the favela in an apparent swoop for drug stocks.

When the police went into a favela on an investigation, all activity came to a halt. Kids would stop playing. Shops appeared to close early for the day. The residents would simply disappear. It was a creepy experience as the two officers headed ever deeper into the favela. Apart from their own, breathing and movement fizzled out.

From the wiretap, Estelita knew to start looking near Rua Dois. 'As we were crouching by a wall, I see a dense clump of wires at the entrance to a house. Follow the crumbs and you'll find the loaf. So I say to Leal, "Hey, brother, look at all those power cables – it's not like the other houses."' Refineries require a lot of electric lighting and ventilation, and the cables reflected that. Apart from the power supply, all you need is some buckets and the right kind of chemicals.

'We go up some narrow stairs and place a camera just under the door. The first thing we see is a glass jar of acetone and one of hydrochloric acid.' Bingo.

They were being watched, of course. Every time the police entered the favela, Nem mapped their routes. He would note very carefully which alleys and lanes they habitually used, which ones they didn't know about and which ones they appeared to avoid. In time, he assessed that the police were aware of some 70 per cent of the ins and outs of Rocinha. This was invaluable information and a marker of how seriously he took his own counter-intelligence operation.

Once revealed, the existence of Saulo's coke grotto led to the nature of the investigation changing. Operation Service Provider morphed into Operation 200, which concentrated on identifying exactly what each member of Rocinha ADA actually did in the gang – a requirement in Brazilian law when it comes to prosecution.

It takes a lot of precursors to produce significant quantities of purified cocaine. As in many countries, Brazil restricts the amount of precursors (they have many other, non-criminal uses) individual citizens can buy. Generally this is a quixotic policy that is difficult to monitor. In Rocinha, Saulo's refinery staff obviated these restrictions by paying dozens and dozens of individuals to purchase their monthly allowance in different parts of the city. It was simple and foolproof.

Rocinha did not have to buy in the paste in bulk. Matutos nipped back and forth between Paraguay, Bolivia and Rio, carrying a kilo or two of paste in their backpacks. Saulo even admitted that they were turning down requests from wholesalers offering to supply paste because their freelancers were more than covering their needs.

Estelita and Leal's most important findings were that one kilogram of paste, which cost some US$3,500, rendered the same weight in pure cocaine, which sold for $8,000. They were also able to ascertain that the single smoke shop in Parque da Cidade, a small satellite favela of Rocinha, turned over $1,250 per day, amounting to more than half a million dollars a year. In addition, Saulo confirmed that they were selling to other favelas, including some Red Command areas.

Meanwhile, Nem's policy of keeping guns off the street and avoiding violence where possible was also paying dividends. Under his leadership, the homicide rate dipped even lower than during the halcyon days of Lulu. It was comparable with rates registered in the neighbouring middle-class districts, and bore almost no relation to the other great centres of drugs and weapons, the Complexo do Alemão and the Complexo da Maré.

Of course, the turnover from the smoke shops did not represent pure profit. Along with employment costs and casual expenses, there was the need to keep the Military Police quiet. According to the Gringo, Nem's philosophy was simple: the business could only work if everyone was happy. The Gringo reckons there were probably some eight police vehicles stationed around the favela. Two or three were parked between Gávea and Upper Rocinha and five or six in or around the entrance down below. The first job of these police was to inform Nem's people if there was any sign of outsiders heading in numbers towards the favela. 'You know, a message like "We've just seen this number of vehicles heading your way from Gávea. The team appears to be armed." I mean teams from the other factions,' the Gringo explains.

On average, the Gringo paid each cop 50 reals per shift. Those working near the commercial district of Barcelos would expect more. Some, like Alexandre Marques, had a much deeper, and hence more expensive, relationship with ADA. Furthermore, when there was a command change in the 23rd Battalion of the PM (the precinct with responsibility for Rocinha), the figure would go up, as it did a couple of years into Nem's tenure as don.

Then there was the welfare programme – food, medicines, rents and loans for residents in distress. 'Nem and the team paid for a whole lot of things in order to persuade the locals to keep their mouths

firmly shut,' explains the Gringo. 'But you mustn't be in any doubt
– it was far better than the way it was done in some of the other
favelas, where silence was guaranteed by guns and intimidation.'

Nem had learned his trade from Lulu, and he never forgot his
master's business strategy. This is a company, Lulu would say, and
you have to pay your suppliers, your employees, the family of anybody
who dies, the family of anyone arrested, parties and celebrations
– Children's Day, Mothers' Day, New Year – and, of course, money
for the police.

The business was stressful and complex, but it was working
exceedingly well. There was relatively little pressure on Rocinha
from the police. The residents were happy with the stability that
Nem had brought to their lives and the whole favela was becoming
more prosperous by the day. Rocinha's experience was not that
dissimilar to what was happening in Brazil in general.

6

NEM'S BRIDE
2004-2006

While Bem-te-vi was in power, Simone and Nem split up. Not for the first time, nor for the last. One morning, when they had been apart for about three months, he pitched up at her house at four o'clock. He was looking angry. 'Simone,' he said, 'who is Marcos?' Simone said she didn't know. In fact, for the last few months she had been cultivating a friendship with a young man she had met at a party. He asked to see her phone and showed her some of Marcos's messages. But then something much more disturbing happened: he took out a CD and told her to put it in her player. It was a recording of Simone's phone conversations with Marcos. Apparently he had been conducting an investigation into the alleged infidelities of the partners of gang members and had managed to bribe somebody in the police to wiretap the wives and girlfriends in order to gather evidence. When I ask him about this, he says he was bluffing – he didn't actually have the recording. Simone seemed to believe him without needing to hear the evidence.

By now he was already very angry, and little could sway his conviction that she had been seeing someone. 'So you've decided to make me look an idiot?'

'I never did.'

'You were cheating on me!'

'I never touched the guy. Never kissed, never hugged – no intimacy whatsoever.'

Nem went berserk. Simone had just replaced all her furniture – new sofas, new fridge and a new cooker. He trashed the lot. He then radioed his security team and told them that they were to stay outside her flat to prevent her from fleeing while he went to fetch a pistol to kill her.

About a dozen armed men patrolled outside the apartment, while four or five were stationed on the stairs leading up to it. Simone, now in genuine fear for her life, scooped up her two daughters and pleaded with a neighbour who had just arrived in Rocinha from the north-east, explaining that her husband had threatened to murder her and begging him to allow her to escape through his window. 'He's not a gangster, is he?' the neighbour asked. 'No, not at all,' Simone lied.

Simone went to hide in the apartment of a friend who happened to be heavily pregnant. On the way, little Thayná, her daughter, said, 'You go alone, Mum, Dad wouldn't dare do anything to me.' Simone dismissed the idea of leaving the girl because it meant she'd have to come back for her. And right now, she needed to keep well away from Nem and Rocinha.

On the street, Nem had let it be known that he would pay a reward of R$100,000, a staggering amount of money, for anyone who located Simone, who, he said, was fleeing Rocinha with his children. He had kept her phone and was going through all the numbers, trying to work out where she might be concealed.

Infuriatingly for Simone, she had her period at the time and so asked her pregnant friend to pick up some tampons. By pure chance, Nem happened to be outside the supermarket when this woman two months from giving birth walked out carrying the tampons. He recognised her immediately, even though he had seen her with Simone only once. The woman had no choice but to lead him to his quarry.

By now, however, Nem's anger was abating. When unleashed, his fury reached an alarming pitch, but it subsided quickly and was usually followed by remorse – as it was now. Instead of exacting retribution, he replaced every last bit of the furniture he had destroyed. The subject was never mentioned again, and he and Simone resumed the relationship they had abandoned several months earlier.

There was, in its own perverse way, a principle behind this. If there was even a hint that the girlfriend of a bandido had been involved with another man, it would be regarded as an intolerable stain on his honour, regardless as to how many women he had on the go at the same time. Furthermore, as most of Nem's ex-girlfriends discovered, this unwritten law applied after the relationship had ended as well. Circumspection was a matter of life and death.

Simone herself was given to the occasional flight of violent anger. Soon after the furniture-smashing incident, she was taunted by Nem's latest squeeze, Raquel (with whom he fathered another child), at a party on Rua Um. While Nem's back was turned, Raquel gestured to Simone that Nem was her man and hers alone. Loser, she seemed to be saying.

Simone was working at a bakery at this time, and she noticed that Raquel walked past it every day on her way to and from work. One day, she leapt out from behind the counter and attacked her. 'I saw her and I just went for her big-time,' she confesses. Her mother witnessed the event and shouted at Simone to stop, as Raquel was considerably younger than she was. 'If she's old enough to sleep with somebody else's man,' Simone barked back, 'she's old enough to take a beating!'

In the long run, it was probably Vanessa who had the worst deal of all. She was looking after the children and she had no prospect of finding another partner. Now that the man she had married had become the Don of the Hill, all other men regarded her as a no-go zone. Nobody would dare look at her, let alone ask her out.

Although committed to keeping gang violence to an absolute minimum in Rocinha, Nem rarely deviated from the macho traditions that characterised many parts of Brazilian society, including the favelas. This was not only a cultural inheritance. It was also a matter of political power. He believed that he had no choice but to behave high-handedly, even violently, towards his several women in order to sustain his authority. Women, he believed, could bitch and moan as much as they liked behind closed doors. But in public their behaviour must take account of his position as boss.

In 1997, a thirteen-year-old girl fell pregnant in the Complexo da Maré, one of the most sprawling and dangerous communities in all Rio. During her childhood, her home favela was the scene of regular shootouts both among rival drug gangs and between the gangs and the police. It was an informal rule that nobody went out after about 9 p.m. because the possibility of being caught in the crossfire was so great.

Perhaps these early lessons in survival had contributed to her strong will and self-confidence. Her mother found her daughter's pregnancy extremely distressing, pointing out that she was only a child herself. But the girl defied her mother, adamant that she could provide for the baby. She found a job in a bingo hall. Schooling appears to have played a largely incidental role in her life. The father-to-be was an eighteen-year-old gambler and thief who was too deeply involved in the local gangs for the liking of the girl's parents. He was unlikely to be much help once the child was born, which was one of the reasons why the girl continued working until just before she gave birth.

Her parents had named the teenage mother Danúbia, an unusual, possibly unique name in Brazil and beyond. They had the idea from a neighbour who had travelled the world. He had often spoken to them about a long, beautiful river that ran through many great cities that he had either visited or lived in, and they decided to name their child after that mysterious stretch of water. After she had given birth, life was a struggle for Danúbia, although, as a winningly attractive bottle blonde with high cheekbones, a generous mouth and a perfectly proportioned little nose, she had many suitors. One or two of them were well-known characters from Maré's underworld.

Things changed in early 2006 when a girlfriend from Rocinha invited her home after the two women had been to a pop concert. By now 21 years old, Danúbia had never seen anything as exciting as Rocinha. It was like Maré but without the permanent tension caused by the warring drug factions. And the downtown area was much livelier than the equivalent areas of her home favela, with plenty of bars, retail opportunities and nail salons.

It was during that visit that she first ran into Nem. At the time, although separated and in the process of getting divorced, he was still officially married to Vanessa. 'Actually, he told me he wasn't married,' Danúbia says matter-of-factly, 'and that he lived on his own. Later he took me back to his place.' The trappings of power and success added to his charisma, even if he liked to kid himself that it was his natural magnetism alone that made him so attractive. 'There was one time when these two girls just started chatting me up because they thought I was so interesting,' Nem claimed. 'They had no idea who I was.' When he told me this, I thought he protested too much. He may have believed it, but he was deceiving himself if he did.

Danúbia was a feisty party girl. She knew almost instinctively how to make the most of her beauty, although when I met her as a prison widow in Campo Grande, she retained a youthful naivety that lent her a genuine charm. The first time she met Nem, they just talked. A week later, she received a message from her friend saying that Nem wished to invite her back to Rocinha. Her friend would organise a barbecue. Danúbia accepted the invitation, and that evening she and Nem became lovers. Within a couple of months they were planning to marry.

Nem was crazy about her, compulsively buying her chocolate, flowers, clothes and anything else she desired. Almost from the minute he met her, Danúbia remembers, 'he appeared jealous. He didn't like the idea that I was working at the bingo hall, where there were all sorts of guys hanging out. So he quickly tried to persuade me to give it up and move to Rocinha, which I did.'

Vanessa was already fed up with Nem and knew that their marriage was over. But it wasn't until Simone witnessed the intensity of his relationship with Danúbia and the pride with which he displayed her in public that she understood that she too had joined the ranks of his discards. 'I thought at first she was just a passing fancy,' Simone said. But then she ran into the couple one time at the party venue known as the Bubble. 'When I saw her being introduced to everyone like a queen, I knew that was it.'

Danúbia's mother continued to advise caution. She had seen the consequences of her daughter's previous relationships. She felt that Danúbia had been damaged enough by wastrels with dubious professions. And she knew very well who Nem was. Not for the first time, however, Danúbia dug her heels in, and on 1 April 2006, she and Nem were married. She still has a letter he wrote her in which he told her that he would always commemorate the date 'not as April Fools' Day but as the day he found true love'. She adored the status of being his wife. Her beauty and presence combined with his authority and money turned them alchemically into Rocinha's golden couple.

7

NEMESIS

1997–2009

I n late 2006, the recently elected governor of Rio state, Sergio Cabral, appointed a new man to eliminate the rot in Rio's security apparatus. José Mariano Beltrame was visiting his family down south when Cabral issued him with an unexpected summons to return to Rio. When he arrived, the governor and his advisers quizzed him about the security situation. Although he knew that he might be in for a big job, Beltrame was not inclined to ingratiate himself with anyone. Because of his work in drugs enforcement, he knew Rio well – and he knew that its policing was a mess.

In his disarmingly honest fashion, he said as much to Cabral and the others. There was no cooperation whatsoever between the Military and Civil Police, he declared, which made the coordination of operations almost impossible; many favelas were at daggers drawn with each other and exceptionally volatile; there were serious problems with corruption; and there were politicians involved with the militias. Public security, he concluded, had essentially been discarded. Police operations were reactive in purpose and form and not designed to solve any of the underlying problems facing the city. Furthermore, the next two years would see FIFA and the IOC decide on the venues for the 2014 World Cup and the 2016 Olympic games respectively. Brazil stood a fair chance of being awarded the former, and Rio was in the early stages of preparing a full-blooded bid for the latter.

Beltrame returned home assuming he would hear no more about it. A couple of days later, Cabral called him and invited him to join his cabinet as Secretary for Public Security. Beltrame accepted.

For a decade from the late 90s, Beltrame had been an integral part of a small but highly effective team of intelligence officers within the Federal Police engaged in mapping the routes through Brazil being developed by the wholesale drug traffickers. He would criss-cross this enormous country, tracking huge consignments of cocaine that were either en route to São Paulo or Rio, or in transit to Istanbul (one of the early distribution points for coke destined for the European market) or later Amsterdam. He was involved in around 450 operations, which led to the confiscation of 20 tonnes of cocaine, 50 aeroplanes, and some 1,100 vehicles, as well as the arrest of about 1,200 people involved in international trafficking.[10]

One of his targets was the notorious Rio criminal Fernandinho Beira-Mar. In 1997, he spent long periods staring into Paraguay from his lookout post in Brazil. The border was a hot, dusty road. Watching him from the other side was Beira-Mar himself. It was not just Brazil Beira-Mar was wanted in; as probably the most notorious drug trafficker in South America since the brothers who ran Colombia's Cali cartel had been arrested, he had the Colombians, the Europeans and, of course, the Drug Enforcement Administration of the United States on his tail. In Paraguay, however, he was safe – he had the local authorities in his pocket.

Beira-Mar would chuckle and acknowledge the presence of the Federal Police with a wave, knowing full well that Beltrame and his colleagues had no authority to cross the road and arrest him. And why would he return to his home country? He lived a life of luxury in Paraguay. For the moment, he was safe and able to organise the wholesale cocaine trade across Brazil and into Suriname, from where the goods would travel on to various destinations.

Beira-Mar's wife, Jacqueline, would move back and forth between the two countries and Beltrame would always make sure she was trailed once inside Brazilian territory. But there wasn't much the Federal Police could do about Beira-Mar himself. It would be another four years before the Colombian police, working with Beltrame's colleagues, along with the DEA and the CIA, succeeded in seizing him deep in the Amazon in a place called Dog's Head. Well-connected to the FARC, the Colombian revolutionaries and coke producers, Beira-Mar had assumed he would be safe in Colombia. But from here he was deported to Brazil, where he has been in jail ever since.

Beltrame was from Rio Grande do Sul, hence a *gaúcho*, one of the most distinctive cultural communities in Brazil. Until the nineteenth century, descendants of Indians, Portuguese, and African slaves ruled the pampas, the fertile lowlands that straddle north-east Argentina, Uruguay and Brazil's southernmost state. They were joined by hundreds of thousands of immigrants from Europe, chiefly from Germany and Italy. Beltrame's family was from Italian peasant stock. They were respected in the small town he grew up in, but they were not wealthy. He and his siblings excelled in school and exploited their educational opportunities to the full. After passing the rigorous exams to join the Federal Police, Beltrame also trained as a lawyer. Although he never knew where his work would take him next, he would return home regularly to spend time with his family.

On one such trip home in May 2002, he received a phone call from the maid who worked for his younger sister. The maid was distraught but managed to blurt out that his sister's ex-husband, who was subject to a restraining order banning him from approaching her, had tricked his way into her home. A few moments later, the maid heard two shots being fired.

When Beltrame arrived at his sister's apartment, he was greeted by a terrible sight. 'It was a macabre scene: Ana Eunice had fallen with her feet against the side of the jacuzzi, soaked in blood, and Joao Alberto was by her side. There was nothing to be done. They were both dead. He had shot my sister in the neck and immediately killed himself with a bullet to his jaw, which hit the bone and then went through his brain.'[11]

Even before he could grieve, Beltrame was faced with a difficult decision: what to do about his two nephews, aged seven and eleven. If he were to take responsibility for them himself, it would effectively mean his career being marooned – all the experience he had gained, his detailed knowledge of the Brazilian drugs trade, would return with him to his small town in Rio Grande do Sul. Yet the children had been in the apartment at the time of their parents' death, and he understood the immense trauma they had suffered.

To his great relief, his elder sister, a respected Brazilian diplomat stationed in Uruguay, agreed 'to sacrifice her career in favour of mine'.[12]

A year later, Beltrame was transferred to Rio to become part of a small intelligence team that was given the task of monitoring and mapping the criminal groups operating in the city. It was called Mission Support. Its members were told to keep a low profile, chiefly because they did not want to alert the many corrupt officers of the Federal Police – and, of course, the PM and the PC – to their activities.

It was an exacting period for Beltrame, dealing intensively with the worst aspects of Rio life, living in barracks and missing the support of his family. But during the next three years, he learned a lot about crime and corruption in Rio. Of course, he immersed himself in the ins and outs of the factional struggles among the trafficking gangs. But he also concluded that the enduring hostility between the Military and Civil Police was rendering null any attempt to bring the situation under control. Furthermore, he came to the realisation that until the state engaged with the favelas and their inhabitants in a positive way, addressing their economic and social concerns, the battle against violence would never be won. Favela inhabitants, he observed, felt nothing but fear and contempt for the police, and until that changed, Rio would be damned.

8

THE BATTLE FOR RIO
2006–2008

Four days before José Mariano Beltrame was due to assume office as Secretary for Public Security, the city caught fire. In a series of gruesome assaults in the lazy days between Christmas 2006 and New Year 2007, bandidos belonging mainly to Red Command gunned and firebombed their way around the city. The primary targets were vehicles and stations of the Military Police.

The havoc began without warning as dozens of young gunmen coordinated attacks in more than twenty parts of the city. The death toll would eventually reach nineteen. The most horrific incident occurred just north of Complexo do Alemão in the early morning of 28 December. A group of fifteen masked men stopped a long-distance bus carrying 28 people from Rio state's northern neighbour, Espirito Santo, to São Paulo to the west. The driver was forced to halt as he drove along Avenida Brasil, the huge arterial road that transects Rio east to west. Using petrol and Molotov cocktails, they set light to the vehicle and watched as the desperate passengers tried to break windows to escape. 'I don't know how, but I gathered my strength, got myself into the aisle of the bus and jumped through the window,' one female victim of the attack reported. 'I felt like I was being toasted.'[13] Seven people were burned alive and another one died two days later in hospital. Those who escaped had to drag themselves across Avenida Brasil under fire as the gangsters took potshots at them.

Elsewhere, women and children were hit by machine-gun bullets as the gangsters shot at anything resembling a police car or foot patrol in busy thoroughfares.

According to the prison intelligence service, Marcinho VP, the most senior Red Command boss, had given the orders for the mayhem to take place. In an embarrassing revelation for the outgoing governor, Rosinha Garotinho, it emerged that intelligence had received information about the possibility of impending attacks some time earlier but had not acted upon it.

It seemed that the attacks were a response to the encroachment of the militias upon some of Red Command's bastions, in particular Adeus, the favela that borders its greatest stronghold, Complexo do Alemão. Red Command regarded the militias effectively as an offshoot of the regular police forces, which was why they resolved to target them in this way. They may have drawn their inspiration from a similar series of assaults mounted by the PCC in São Paulo earlier that year. For two or three days, Brazil's economic capital was more or less locked down as the PCC and the Military Police battled it out around the periphery of the city. Over 120 people died. The Rio attacks resulted in fewer casualties but were less discriminating geographically, with many of them taking place in the city's business and administrative district.

Rocinha during this time was peaceful. Red Command's battle against the local government was not its concern. Furthermore, business was in fine shape and nobody wanted to interfere with it. The value of Nem as a figure who brought stability and calm to a community nestled among Rio's wealthiest areas was perfectly clear to Beltrame. 'Rocinha under Nem was never an especially violent place,' he concedes. 'They were always much more interested in making money.' At the turn of 2006, it must have been a huge relief that the largest favela in Rio was not touched by violence: the city's security forces were already stretched to breaking point.

Nem believes firmly that the government has every reason to thank him for his composure. 'Had I agreed to join in,' he thundered, 'they could not have stopped us. Just imagine: ADA, Third Command and Red Command raiding and torching the city of Rio de Janeiro? Not even if they'd called in the army.' The government's good fortune, he is convinced, lay in the assessment he made on day one. 'I knew that it was wrong from the very start.'

If Beltrame hadn't yet grasped the complexity and size of the task he was about to take on from 1 January 2007, he certainly understood it now. The pressure on him, and on the incoming governor, Sérgio Cabral, was enormous. The *New York Times* reported that the attacks were a warning to Cabral and his new team not to confront the traffickers, while the BBC quoted residents saying that it was as if Rio was now at war.

Aside from the natural anxiety of ordinary cariocas, the city was scheduled to host the Pan-American Games in the summer of 2007, and Brazil could not afford any disaster to strike at that time. In October of the same year, FIFA would be deciding on the venue for the 2014 World Cup, and if Rio continued to be described in the international media as 'one of the most violent cities in the world',[14] it could wreck Brazil's chances of being chosen. Having won the trophy more times than any other country, and being generally considered the greatest footballing nation on earth, Brazil was desperate to win the tournament on their home territory.

President Lula immediately offered to divert federal resources to the Rio government. A large number of the Military Police's rickety old vehicles were replaced, and CCTV cameras started going up across the city. Lula had just secured re-election as president and was at the height of his popularity and influence. Brazil's reputation was rocketing across the globe. Securing the right to hold the World Cup was confirmation that the country had turned a corner. There was, everyone believed, no return.

In the wake of the attacks, Beltrame and Cabral resolved to give Red Command a bloody nose. Beltrame had identified the Complexo do Alemão 'as a veritable regulatory agency of crime' in the city. He dispatched a large force into the area to root out drugs, guns and senior gang members. The force didn't stay, so Red Command was able to reconstitute itself quickly, but the action was well received elsewhere in Rio as a sign of resolute intent. Media interest focused on one character in particular: Inspector Leonardo Torres of the Civil Police. Known as the Thunder, he was photographed Rambo-like smoking the stub of a thick cigar as he prowled around Alemão. Governor Cabral liked this image so much that he persuaded a manufacturer friend of his to produce a series of Action Man dolls in the Thunder's likeness. More attuned to the sensitivities of favela residents, Beltrame persuaded Cabral that this was unlikely to win hearts and minds. The idea was quietly dropped.

But the operation to cleanse Alemão was seen as a temporary measure. A new long-term policy was needed to secure Rio's future, one that involved the state making amends for its disgraceful neglect of the favelas and Rio's poor over the previous several decades. In late 2008, Governor Cabral unveiled the new strategy: pacification, known in Portuguese as *pacificação*, or more commonly as UPP, the acronym designating the police units involved (Unidade de Polícia Pacificadora, or Police Pacification Unit).

Pacification was ambitious. There had been attempts in the past to mount similar programmes, but none had ever garnered the requisite political support. This was different: the elections of 2006 had produced a federal government that was an ally of the coalition now in control of Rio state and, within less than two years, in control of Rio municipality as well. For the first time in years, there was an opportunity to introduce a bold security policy without petty party squabbles hindering its development.

In his election manifesto, Sérgio Cabral had promised to do

something about the lamentable security situation in Rio. He had no specific policies in mind, but after his victory at the polls Cabral commissioned a diverse group of private and public sector consultants and advisors to develop ideas about overcoming the chronic shortcomings in Rio's public security.

Over eighteen months, two imperatives emerged. The first was to do something about the appalling state of the police. One poll conducted in 2007 registered that a staggering 92% of cariocas had limited confidence in the Military Police. The Civil Police fared little better – 87% had little or no trust in them.[15]

The other was the need to re-establish state control over the favelas by deploying and maintaining a strong police presence in territories controlled either by drug traffickers or by militias. While this, the advisers argued, was an expensive proposition, the stability it created would generate more than adequate revenues to cover the costs.

The primary goal of pacification was not to rid the city of the drugs trade, centred in Rio's favelas, but to halt the violence and reduce the number of weapons in circulation. Beltrame was quite explicit in separating the two ideas. He recognised that the huge demand for narcotics across Rio's various communities; the proximity of the city to the areas where the drugs were produced and refined; and the incalculable profits to be made from this commodity made suppression of the trade a quite unrealistic goal.

But although unable to eradicate the drugs, he was convinced that he could lower the rates of violence, even though this implied confronting the drug cartels and attempting to remove, or at the very least reduce, their influence.

The strategy involved the special forces, including BOPE and the Brazilian military, whose deployment, if deemed necessary, would amount to a demonstration of shock and awe in the favelas. The principal aim was to decapitate the drugs gang running each individual territory by arresting, killing or expelling its key figures. Following this initial invasion, new police units would be established throughout the favela.

In theory, once these new units had gained the confidence of the community, their work would be followed up by something called Social UPP, a programme that envisaged the establishment of health centres, crèches, schools and other social services, to demonstrate that the state harboured benign intentions as a complement to its iron fist.

Beltrame himself always denied that there was any relationship between Rio hosting two sporting mega-events and the introduction of pacification. Certainly his rhetoric, which was consistent and impassioned, suggested that he considered the neglect of the favelas to have been nothing short of immoral and criminal. He embraced the new policy idea with verve. 'For fifty years, the state chose to abandon the favelas. The whole world knows that Rio has been a divided city with these islands of criminality. Everyone knows that we have to occupy those islands. And this occupation has simply given an opening for the formal city to enter into the informal city. Taxi drivers know this; politicians know it; sociologists know it; journalists know it; everyone knows it. But until we chose pacification, it hadn't been done – because of politics and because of corruption.' By the standards of Brazilian politicians, these were candid and emphatic words. It remained to be seen whether they could be turned into reality.

There was a striking footnote to the violent events that swept Rio in late December 2006. The intelligence reports not only suggested that Red Command wished to intimidate the police and the militias. They also claimed that the group may have wanted to exploit the chaos to reassert its control over Rocinha.

Nem and ADA played no part in the December violence. Why would they? Thanks to their policy of reducing violence and generating economic activity, Rocinha was enjoying an extraordinary renaissance. Unlike Alemão and the other Red Command strongholds, it was rapidly becoming one of the coolest places in the city.

9

ROCINHA'S GOLDEN AGE
2007–2009

One day, a young woman was walking around Lower Rocinha with a capuchin monkey dressed in a tailored waistcoat and dinky cowboy hat. An officer from the Civil Police spotted the woman and her simian escort. 'Quite a catch,' he thought. Like others who worked the Rocinha beat, he was aware that Nem owned a pet capuchin monkey. Chico-Bala was a well-known figure around town and was happy to take a stroll with most Rocinhan residents.

Nem adored the monkey and the monkey adored Nem. Chico-Bala would sleep with his arm or tail curled around Nem's neck, and once a week Nem gave the monkey a thorough clean using Johnson & Johnson's baby shampoo. Danúbia liked pets too, and although Nem was unable to provide her with her first choice, an ocelot, he did present her with a snake.

Chico-Bala was a trusting sort who was friendly with all comers, which was why he was strolling around Lower Rocinha with the girl. Equally, he didn't put up a fight when the police officer ordered the girl to hand the monkey over.

Nem was furious when he learned that his pet had been kidnapped. After a short period, he received a note demanding about $75,000 for its release. He dispatched Urso, appropriately a large bear of a man, to track down the missing monkey. Urso was an environmental officer who worked with animals in Rocinha and elsewhere. Oblique messages delivered from the Civil Police hinted at Chico-Bala's whereabouts, so Urso followed the trails. He went to the North Zone. He went to a fire station. He went to the head-quarters of the Federal Environmental Protection Wild Animal triage unit. But Chico-Bala was nowhere to be found.

When he realised that the monkey had gone for good, Nem received a series of replacements. None of them quite filled the hole in his heart, but each had its own endearing peculiarities. One was especially fond of riding around on moto taxis – the most popular form of private transport in Rocinha. A moto taxi would pull up at Nem's house in Cachopa and the monkey would leap on the back for a ride.

Unbeknownst to either Urso or Nem, Chico-Bala himself had in fact died soon after he had been kidnapped. He fell out of a cop car several miles away on Avenida Brasil. It remains a mystery whether he jumped or was pushed.

Chico-Bala had been a popular character around the favela. When Nem arrived at a baile funk, the monkey was often an integral part of the grand procession. Sometimes Nem would be wearing his Flamengo shirt and shorts. Sometimes he would sport a large gold chain and disc with the word MESTRE[16] standing out in white gold. In front of him was his praetorian guard, armed and marching in formation; then came Nem himself, sometimes riding, somewhat incongruously, on a small motorcycle. Chico-Bala would be perched on his shoulder, dolled up in the waistcoat and hat. Behind these two was the second half of his security detachment. As he approached his *camarote*, the VIP marquee from where he would watch a concert, DJs would start rapping songs in his honour:

É a Rocinha e o Vidigal, está tudo monitorado
  deixa eles vir, está tudo palmeado
É calibre avançado, está sempre pegando fogo
É o mano MESTRE e seu elenco fabuloso
A cada dia o nosso poder aumenta e a nossa
  fama
Se expandiu por todo mundo, a mídia não se
  cansa em divulger
Que bandido na Rocinha, tem a vida de luxo
Nós anda de Hornet por toda comunidade e as
  novinha jogam na cara com vontade
Cheio de ouro e o bolso cheiro de grana portando
  OKLEY, LOCOSTE, DOLCE GABBANA
E quando a chapa esquenta nós estamos sempre
  preparados
Nosso poder de fogo é de calibre avançado
E o MESTRE montou um elenco Fabuloso pra
  defender a nossa mina de ouro.

In Rocinha, in Vidigal, we're totally covered
Let them come, we're in control
The big guns are always on standby
For the man MESTRE and his fabulous team
Every day our power grows and our fame
Spreads across the globe, the media doesn't tire
  of reporting
That Rocinha's bandit lives a life of luxury
We move around on Hornets and the babes
Throw themselves at us, covered in gold, pockets
  full
Of cash, wearing OKLEY, LACOSTE, DOLCE
  GABBANA

And when the heat is on, we're always standing
    ready
With our firepower and big guns
And the MESTRE has built a great team to
    defend our gold mine.

These rituals, in which the young people of Rocinha revelled, conjured up visions of a Roman consul attending an entertainment in some far-flung corner of the Empire.

By early evening one Saturday in August 2008, a sea of young people had swept into Rocinha. Nem and Danúbia were already in their camarote awaiting the arrival of Ja Rule. A few weeks earlier, an old friend of Nem's living in the United States had contacted him, explaining that the New York rap artist would soon be performing in Brazil and that he was interested in taking his show to Rocinha. 'Apart from anything else,' Nem says, 'I wanted to demonstrate to the outside world that this community was essentially a safe place, not some lawless outpost where every second person was carrying a gun.' Of course, it also benefited him at home, because no other favela could boast that it was able to attract a big international star.

Not even Rocinha had ever really seen anything like Ja Rule in concert. Next to Nem's camarote was that of the former Brazilian World Cup footballing star Romário, and next to his was that of the radio station O Dia FM, which would be broadcasting the event live. The atmosphere became yet more fevered when the controversial evangelical pastor Marcos Pereira turned up with his entourage – men and women all dressed in beige suits.

Pastor Marcos insisted on visiting Ja Rule in his artist's caravan, which may have slightly unsettled him, given that the singer had been drifting around Rocinha in a dense cloud of marijuana smoke. Nem was also introduced to Ja Rule, although the meeting was more a matter of protocol than anything else, as the language problem proved more or less insuperable. But once the party started, after a three-hour delay, it was a rip-roaring success. The reviews across the Brazilian media were uniformly ecstatic.

The impact of Rocinha's rise as a venue for cool events and a destination for cool people was tremendous. Whether consciously or not, Nem was creating Brand Rocinha. Before long, he had agreed to host a Gay Pride event, something that would have probably been unthinkable in most other favelas, not only for security reasons but also because in many ways people from the favelas are socially conservative. The Gay Pride march indicated how the permissive atmosphere of Rio's South Zone had to a degree permeated Rocinha's consciousness and lifestyle.

This was now the favela that everyone wanted to visit. It had a deserved reputation for being safe. It had a vibrant economy and nightlife, and everyone wanted a piece of the action. A trickle of tourists soon grew to a steady river as tours became more organised and local entrepreneurs seized the commercial opportunities.

Nem and Danúbia moved into a house in Cachopa, which was certainly grand by Rocinha's standards. The new dwelling comprised three storeys, one of which was the party area on the roof. The decor was a strange mixture of contemporary minimalism and 70s furniture reminiscent of the lounge in Mike Leigh's play Abigail's Party, including a well-stocked bar and a large widescreen TV. But it is preposterous to compare it to the luxurious modernist apartments of the upper middle classes in Leblon, Ipanema and Copacabana, with their infinity pools and huge terraces. By those standards, Nem's place was a poky suburban house with a paddling pool.

There was no question, however, that the couple were the most exalted in the favela. Nem had by now acquired several nicknames, of which the most telling was simply Presidente.

When he talks about those days now, he is keen to impress on me that this golden age and the power he had accrued never went to his head. He describes how he continued to pick up his kids from school, and says that nothing would prevent him from his weekly kickaround with his childhood friends on a Friday afternoon.

But Nem's depiction of himself as an ordinary guy who just happened to run an extensive drugs business doesn't fit with the huge gold chains, the entourage of gun-wielding youths, the trophy wife, the praise-singers and the VIP seats at every live concert or rave. The fact is that he exercised immense authority over a community of 100,000 people, and he understood that these trappings of power were critical to his success. Many Rocinhans liked having a flamboyant leader who offered stability, some prosperity and a strong sense of local patriotism. One thing of course that neither he nor anyone else can get around is the fact that his power depended ultimately on guns and a monopoly of violence. 'It wasn't a democracy,' he agrees, 'but at the same time it wasn't a dictatorship, because I would always explain my reasoning to ordinary residents.' And as leaders go, he was very accessible. People could and did take grievances to him whenever they wanted.

Nonetheless, he was boss of the favela's only effective police force, one that boasted significant economic interests and involved him in taking tough decisions. The issue of the X-9s, or informants, was probably the most serious.

One late afternoon, Urso was at home in Parque da Cidade, a tiny favela outpost of Rocinha just by Gávea, when he received a call from Carlão, one of Nem's senior security people, telling him that a moto taxi was coming to pick him up to take him to Cachopa. Urso harboured a grudge against Carlão. He had procured a beautiful iguana for him at the gangster's request and Carlão had then allowed the reptile to die from neglect.

When Urso arrived in Cachopa, Nem was playing foot volleyball on the basketball court close to his house. Urso sat in the stand while Carlão stood below brandishing an AK-47. When Nem had finished his game, he said casually, 'Okay, let's get this business sorted out.'

Another of Nem's team, Little Fatty, took out a laptop and pulled up a set of photos of Urso posing with a group of policemen. Urso was a master of Krav Maga, the Israeli military's hybrid martial art, and in the course of his work he trained both policemen and gangsters. 'I always made it clear to everyone that this is who I am and this is what I do,' he tells me. 'I did not discriminate.'

Looking at the photos, Nem said to Little Fatty, 'Okay, tell us again exactly what you told me.'

'I said I think he's an X-9,' replied Little Fatty, showing everybody the photographic evidence.

'Carry on,' said Nem, at which point Carlão walked up to Little Fatty and slapped him hard around the head.

At this point it dawned on Urso that he was witnessing a kangaroo court, and that he was in the dock. He came down from the stand, convinced that he was about to die. He was weighing up whether to use his lethal Krav Maga skills to defend himself when Carlão turned to Nem and asked, 'And what about this one, Mr President?'

Fiddling with a revolver, Nem said, 'I am going to say the following out loud so that everyone hears it. I know very well who my friends are inside Rocinha and outside. Cabeça is my friend,' he announced, pointing to his fellow foot-volleyball player. 'Kobra Khan is my friend.' This was his personal nickname for Urso, in honour of both the character from *Masters of the Universe* and Urso's facility with wild animals.

'My heart was going tick-tick-tick-tick-tick at high speed,' remembers Urso.

Nem continued, 'I know everything about everyone. You think I don't know who the X-9s are? Here in Rocinha?' A cold silence descended on the court. 'If I want to, I will send for them, understood?'

'I could see that Carlão had been just waiting to have a go at me,' Urso recalls. But once Nem had spoken, Carlão fell silent. Nem's commitment to gathering information about Rocinha, the business, his employees and the residents had come to Urso's rescue. As Urso made to leave, Nem said, 'Don't forget to pick up the vaccine for my monkey!'

'I still thought I might be in trouble as I left Cachopa,' Urso recalls. A group of armed young men watched him as he walked away. 'All cool?' he said, trying to disguise his fear. 'All cool,' they confirmed. 'But as soon as my back was facing them, I was more frightened than I've ever been in my life. I thought, I'm going to die with a bullet in my back.'

Nem punished Little Fatty because he had levelled the accusation in the hope of earning himself some reputational capital in the organisation. Such behaviour was common, but as the incident demonstrated, it carried risks. Little Fatty was taken off somewhere and beaten up; Urso saw him alive after the episode, so he knows he wasn't killed.

In 2009, Nem reached the zenith of his influence. He was at the top of the Hill. He had already been in sole control of Rocinha for about four years – which for a drugs lord is a long reign. But the greater his reputation, the more attention he attracted from the Asphalt below. It wasn't just the police who were beginning to track his every move. The wider Brazilian public was becoming aware of Nem and his mythical status within Rocinha.

In particular, one tenacious journalist, Leslie Leitão, developed a fascination for the favela. Not only did he cultivate many cops and lawyers around the city, he also nurtured his contacts inside

Rocinha, including some close to the leadership of ADA. On more than one occasion he confounded the efforts of detectives Estelita and Leal. The two police officers had learned through their wiretaps that Saulo and Bibi were holding a birthday party for their young son, outside Rocinha in Tijuca. It was rare for Saulo especially to leave the favela, because he was a fugitive. The party would be an excellent opportunity for the police. Before it took place, they staked out the venue and managed to insert a series of listening devices and cameras. They regarded it as one of their most daring and potentially fruitful intelligence operations.

But on the morning of the bash, Leitão published a story about how one of Rocinha's drug bosses would be holding a party that afternoon. As a result, Saulo and Bibi ducked their own son's birthday celebration. Estelita and Leal were both furious and baffled. How could Leitão have possibly known about it?

Another time, a set of cops mounted a raid against Nem's house in Cachopa. Nem's contacts in the police had, of course, given him advance warning, so they didn't find him at home. However, during the operation they removed a book of photographs belonging to Danúbia, including what became a famous pose of Nem's wife standing by a helicopter offering airborne tours of Rio. It would appear that somebody from the police had leaked the photos to Leitão, who published them in the Rio newspaper *O Dia*.

Nem's anger at Leitão's reporting matched his appreciation of the media's power. In response to the publication of the photographs, he ordered members of his team to drive around the South Zone and buy up the entire print run of *O Dia*. I ask him whether this is true. 'Oh yeah,' he laughs as he remembers. 'Put a match to the whole lot!'

And was it as everybody says, I continue, because you didn't want Danúbia to be upset by the photos appearing in print? 'No, that wasn't the reason,' he replies. 'It was because there was a photo of *me* among them.' And that was a security issue. He didn't want to be recognised on the Asphalt. Burning the papers was a quixotic response – the photo was, of course, already on the web.

10
POLITICS
2008–2010

President Lula's most famous policy innovation was the *bolsa família*, the family purse or family grant, which guaranteed a cash payout to families under a certain income level, provided they could prove that their children were attending school full time. A second impressive strategy to boost the condition of Brazil's poorest communities was the Programme of Accelerated Growth (PAC), which focused on infrastructural developments, mainly in the favelas and areas of rural poverty.

In addition to making life easier for residents, with new roads, schools, sports facilities, health centres and crèches, the PAC would of course have a Keynesian impact by providing jobs for local workers. It was an extremely good use of federal resources and Rocinha stood to gain a great deal from it.

A sudden injection of cash into a community, however, arouses the interest of various parties who hitherto may not have had much time for somewhere like Rocinha. These parties include companies who wish to tender for infrastructural work. They also include political parties, for whom Rocinha, given its size and growing influence, was a rich potential source of votes.

Nem too had an interest in representation. He had consolidated his position as the head of ADA in Rocinha; his social programme was running smoothly; he was able to show off his beautiful wife; he was an excellent and generous father; and he was the patron of much of the entertainment that was making Rocinha famous, even beyond Rio. He now believed that as a key member of the community, he should have a voice in the politics of the favela.

In 2008, an election to the municipal assembly was scheduled to take place, and two candidates emerged from the field. The first was William da Rocinha, the former head of the residents' association.[17] The other was a man known as Claudinho da Academia, who ran the local samba school, a position of some influence. Like William, he had been born and raised in Rocinha.

Nem was keen to see a local person represent Rocinha in the assembly, and he offered money to support both candidates. William refused to accept the cash because of Nem's position as don. But Claudinho had no such qualms. With Nem's money at his disposal, he was able to have hundreds of T-shirts printed. His own name was on the back, but equally importantly, the names of President Lula and the recently elected governor of Rio, Sergio Cabral, were on the front.

His association with the two political leaders and with Nem meant that Claudinho would have a hard time losing the vote. Nem, indeed, is convinced that his decision to put his weight behind Claudinho's campaign was decisive in securing victory. 'He wasn't very well known in the community at the time,' he explains, 'but his ratings started to improve once people twigged that he was my friend. And to my mind, that's why he won ... At one point, he came to see me saying he was going to move and live somewhere else, so I told him straight, "You are assembly member for Rocinha and you are going to live in Rocinha. If you mess up with the people here, you're messing up with me as well."'

Inside the community, Claudinho was not shy in advertising his connection with Nem. Outside, he was feted by Cabral and Cabral's deputy, Fernando Pezão.[18] It is conceivable that Pezão and Cabral had no notion of Claudinho's connection to Nem, but if they really were ignorant of it, their political intelligence apparatus was woefully inadequate. Cabral and Pezão didn't get where they were by not doing their homework, and it is hard to believe that they would have paid no attention to information uncovered in a raid by the Civil Police on Nem's house in the middle of 2008. The PC claim to have found a letter from Nem in which he wrote that he would not tolerate the defeat of his candidate (Claudinho) in the elections to the municipal assembly.[19]

With his new involvement in politics, albeit indirect, Nem was silently crossing a line. It was certainly a tradition that the dons in the favelas would closely monitor the activities of the local residents' associations and of those who administered them. But backing a representative to the municipal assembly and later to the state assembly was novel in the politics of Rio's drugs cartels.

A few months earlier, Nem had lost the expertise and acumen of Saulo. His colleague was seeking to leave the business, rather in the way that Lulu had tried to do more than once before his death in 2004. Saulo was tired of the stresses and strains and of his complicated personal life in Rocinha, with Bibi, his wife, and his girlfriend Marcela, not to mention his two kids. So he extracted the family from Rio and moved to a resort in the north-eastern state of Alagoas, where, ironically, he was arrested shortly afterwards.

Effectively alone and heading in a new direction, Nem was vulnerable and in danger of overreaching himself. He was not a man who enjoyed taking decisions on his own, although he is adamant that ever since the death of his father, he had been extremely decisive. In any event, he liked to consult people whom he believed to be his intellectual equals before embarking on a course of action. Now, in the absence of Saulo, others saw this as an opportunity to exercise their influence over him.

William of Rocinha suspected that Nem had come under the sway of a group of revolutionary leftists, represented by members of the Movimento Sem Terra, the Landless Movement, which defended the rights of both dispossessed peasants and those migrants into the urban areas who were itinerant and homeless. More importantly, one of William's political supporters suggested that Nem was being persuaded by his new advisers to expand his ambition in Rocinha beyond the drugs trade and to involve himself in the other economic mainstays of the favela, such as the gas and transport businesses.

While investigating Nem, Detective Estelita came to the conclusion that the politicians 'saw the opportunity to use the power of the trafficking organisation to place themselves in a position of influence in all aspects of favela life. They could leverage money from retail businesses, from the taxi vans, from the moto taxis, from the gas trade ... It became a sort of militia structure.' Since cocaine had altered the social economy of the favelas in the 1980s, Red Command, Third Command and ADA had essentially made their money from drugs. The new model that some believe Nem was adopting was that of the militias, the right-wing vigilante groups in the North Zone whose revenue came from the wholesale extortion of the communities they controlled.

Nem has always refuted the accusation and reacted to it with considerable anger. One person, however, who he does not deny having an ever-deeper relationship with at this time is Feijão, the Bean, his right-hand man. The two men had been friends since childhood, and Feijão was godfather to one of Nem's children. Elected in 2010 to the leadership of the residents' association, Feijão was not formally a member of the business, but Nem trusted him with the money from his drugs operation. Indeed, Feijão was charged with but found not guilty of running a money-laundering scheme on Nem's behalf.

Matters became further complicated when Claudinho, Nem's man in the municipal assembly, died of a heart attack in 2010. He was only 39 at the time and had just begun his campaign to stand for the assembly of Rio state. Had he been successful, this would have represented a considerable step up – one that might have resulted in Nem's influence extending still further.

Instead, Claudinho's supporters put their weight behind another rising politician, who also enjoyed the backing of Cabral and Pezão. Standing against the new candidate was William da Rocinha. Before the election, William explained, Nem called him to his office and offered him ten times his potential salary as an assembly member if he agreed not to stand for election. William declined but lost nonetheless.

Nem has always insisted that his backing for Claudinho was motivated solely by his desire to see an authentic Rocinhan voice speaking out for the community in the municipal assembly. That may be the case, although Claudinho was a poor choice. He rarely made an appearance in the assembly and spoke even less frequently. When he did, his performances were lacklustre.

Was Nem's decision to involve himself in politics the moment at which he overreached himself? After Claudinho's death, the Workers' Party and its ally, Sérgio Cabral, parachuted in another politician, who had no previous connection to Rocinha. From this point on, Rocinha's representatives tacitly exploited the indirect relationship with Nem in order to underpin their otherwise weak credentials in the favela. Nem himself appeared to gain very little from this. He now says that having had time to think it through, he can see that 'the government was able to use me in many ways'. A number of people benefited from his political and financial backing but they were never likely to risk their own careers or necks should Nem need them in return.

I have been given detailed descriptions of how Rio's political establishment engaged both obliquely and directly with Nem in order to secure influence over the favela, its electorate and its economy. But while these are convincing descriptions, I cannot support them with documentary proof or sworn testimony, as witnesses are too scared to talk. They are quite clear in explaining that it is not Nem they are scared of, but people in government. Nem insists that 'I know secrets which if I told them would bring down several grand political careers.' But hard as I try to persuade him to divulge those secrets, he won't. I think that Nem too is scared, but I don't doubt him for a minute.

In August 2010, something happened that meant he would need friends in high places. But when the chips were down, the friends were nowhere to be seen.

11
THE HOTEL INTERCONTINENTAL
August 2010

In the early hours of a Saturday morning in August 2010, Nem explains, he is returning from a big party in the neighbouring favela of Vidigal. He is tired and has decided to slip away before the rest of his team. He takes one of the ubiquitous vans that until recently criss-crossed Rio day and night, ferrying people from the favelas to and from their place of work.

As he gets out of the van between Rocinha and São Conrado's shopping mall at around 6 a.m., an officer of the Military Police comes around from behind the back of a parked bus. The policeman has a semi-automatic slung at an angle across his chest. Nem has a pistol. The two men lock eyes and freeze momentarily. Even if the PM officer doesn't recognise Nem specifically, he must know that he is a bandido from Rocinha.

'Steady,' Nem says gently. The officer starts reaching for his rifle. 'Don't do it,' Nem says. 'Don't do it, because all hell will break loose if you do.'

The officer stops. 'Okay, steady,' he agrees.

'Okay,' replies Nem. 'You go your way and I'll go mine. We've both got families waiting for us.' The officer nods his assent and the two men walk off quickly in opposite directions.

This is the closest Nem has ever come to being directly engaged in a shootout with the police. He is tense and frightened, but demonstrates, not for the first time, that in an extreme situation he is able to think quickly and avoid the worst. The PM officer is taking the rational route out: Nem might kill or injure him, or he might kill and injure Nem, but in either event the noise of the exchange would attract more bandidos from Rocinha, and it is hard to see how he would escape with his life. He knows that Nem is right when he talks about all hell being let loose.

Nem is much relieved by the outcome, but still disconcerted. The experience has left him uneasy. It has been a bad start to the day.

This bizarre encounter has required all the sangfroid at his command, but as Nem continues to calm down, the situation on the streets begins to deteriorate. At around 7.45, he hears the sound of uncontrolled shooting coming from the direction of neighbouring São Conrado, and he knows straight away that his boys must be involved. The phone rings, and already he is busy trying to ascertain exactly what is happening.

In fact, phones are ringing urgently in quite a few places. Detective Inspector Bárbara Lomba is looking forward to a quiet weekend at home in Barra. The call for her comes at about 8.15 a.m. It's an old colleague who happens to live in São Conrado. 'Bárbara,' he says, 'do you know what on earth is happening here? There is one hell of a firefight going on.'

While making the coffee, Bárbara is able to talk it through with her husband. He too is a police officer, and knows the score. They have a six-year-old son, but she will obviously have to scrap her plans for the weekend. On a positive note, as a detective inspector in the Civil Police, she is not expected to take up a position on the front line of an active operation like this.

Now 35 years old, Bárbara has risen steadily up the hierarchy in the past decade and is regarded as one of the most judicious and effective female detectives in the Civil Police. The daughter of two doctors, she graduated in law before casting around for something to do. 'My parents had always stressed the importance of public service,' she explains. 'They were extremely committed to public sector health, and this issue of service was ingrained in me.' Her training led her to the police. One of her first courses involved training on the police computer system. Her instructor was a certain Alexandre Estelita.

Eight years later, she is heading a team of eight, which includes Estelita. He and Leal are already in the third year of their investigation into Nem and the ADA organisation in Rocinha. The camaraderie and efficiency of the three police officers is unusual. Although younger than Estelita and Leal, Lomba is regarded by the two men as an ideal boss, and they are not slow to acknowledge their admiration for her.

Although the team will not be expected to place themselves in the middle of the shooting, their presence is essential in order to analyse the volatile situation as it unfolds. They will be in charge of taking witness statements when the incident is finally over.

Under Lomba's direction, Estelita and Leal have gathered huge amounts of evidence on Nem and his followers. In that time, she has observed the lengths to which Nem will go to avoid confrontation. An unrestricted shootout in a middle-class area is simply not his style. If, as is likely, he and his men are involved in the event, something must have gone very wrong. And to try and work out why, she will need Estelita and Leal – if she can find them.

A few minutes later, the phone rings in Cabo Frio, two hours' drive from Rio: 'Estelita, we're going to have to get down there now,' says Bárbara. Estelita is tired. His first reaction is to dismiss it. Shots in São Conrado, he thinks, probably just some fun and games in Rocinha. And then there is the prospect of the commute on a Sunday.

Leal is at home in Copacabana with his wife. A tinge of ginger in his hair, this gentle giant is even jollier than Estelita. His darker side comes out at night, when his alter ego takes the stage as the lead singer of a heavy metal band that goes by the English name Unmasked Brains. But like Estelita, he is a sharp observer both of his environment and of human psychology. He and Estelita have developed such an understanding that they often finish each other's thoughts. When Leal gets called in, he does what he always does to get to work – jumps on his bicycle and pedals to the station alongside Rio's most famous beaches.

The Secretary of State, José Mariano Beltrame, has just come off the phone in Ipanema, a short drive from where the fighting has broken out. He knows that BOPE is on its way to São Conrado. Early reports of a policeman being hit are coming in. This is not the first time he has woken to an emergency, but with casualties already reported, he needs to act fast.

Officer José Melo of the Military Police is lying on the ground with a bullet lodged just above his knee. He and his colleague have crawled round to the back of the squad car. Their vehicle provides cover against a barrage of bullets coming from the direction of the Atlantic Ocean. But they need another car to protect them from the shooting coming from behind them. Normally when bandidos move between Vidigal and Rocinha, the Military Police are paid off in advance to ensure that they will not interfere with the caravan of gangsters. But Officer Melo and his colleague are, by chance, out of the loop. They have not been told to allow the team through. This turns out to be an extraordinary piece of ill luck for Nem. It is almost as though the gods have decided to start playing with him.

Out walking their dogs, jogging, or buying the milk and papers, the ordinary folk of São Conrado have scattered in a tremendous panic. The officers are hunkered on Avenida Aquarela do Brasil, a broad leafy avenue with its two lanes separated by a small concrete central reservation. Luxury residential apartment blocks flank both pavements. Behind rises Rocinha. In front, 300 metres to the south, is a gorgeous sandy beach and the Atlantic.

It is from this direction that the main threat to the officers is coming. Forty or so members of Nem's cartel are at the bottom of the Avenida, by the ocean. Some of them are under the influence of drugs, some are drunk, and all of them are starved of sleep after having spent the entire night partying in Vidigal, barely a mile away. Several bandidos have piled out of a white van, while 30 or so have arrived on motorcycles, two to a bike, with the barrels of their semi-automatics pointing defiantly in the air.

Within minutes, another PM squad car veers off the major highway that separates Avenida Aquarela from Rocinha. Before the car can double back and under the highway, it too comes under fire, the officers inside sustaining light injuries. The bandidos then run past the Sendas supermarket to reach the entrance to their redoubt, Rocinha.

The first BOPE squad arrives in a Big Skull, and scoops up Officer Melo from the ground. They also spot a woman face down on the pavement close to where the gang was. They radio in to report that somebody is down.

With BOPE and reinforcements pouring in, the gang splits up, running in different directions. Most of them succeed in escaping, but a group of ten seek refuge in the nearest building: the five-star Hotel Intercontinental, which backs on to São Conrado beach.

Geert Poels, a Belgian tourist who arrived in Rio for the first time the day before, emerges from the elevator in the Intercontinental. He is with his brother, Bart, and they are looking forward to breakfast. As the lift doors part, the two of them are startled to see 'several Chinese people running into the lift opposite the one we were coming out of'. They then see 'some nine young men in shorts and T-shirts coming in the main hotel entrance and wielding large-calibre weapons. About four of them had backpacks, one of them had a ninja scarf wrapped around his head so you could only see his eyes, and they all brandished either pistols, semi-automatics or grenades.' A member of the gang comes over to Geert and puts a gun against his neck, forcing him and his brother into the kitchen, where they surprise several members of staff. The gun remains at Geert's throat.

Rogério 157, a senior member of Nem's security detail, starts dialling. He first sends the message up to Rocinha that ten of the gang are in the Intercontinental and are holding a number of hostages. Then he dials again. He spends most of the next two hours talking on the phone.

Several miles away, in Tijuca, journalist Claudia Mônica is fast asleep, enjoying the lie-in she has been waiting for all week. She is dragged out of her slumber by her mobile ringing. Angry at being disturbed, she looks at the number, doesn't recognise it. She throws the mobile down and tries to go back to sleep. It rings again. She thinks it is a friend who has threatened to play a joke on her. 'Go away, I'm trying to sleep,' she moans down the phone.

'Claudia, Claudia – it's Rogério ... you know ... from Rocinha ... Get down here, Claudia, we need your help. We're in the Intercontinental – we have some people here.'

In recent months, Mônica has been producing a series of television documentaries in Rocinha. Nem knows about them, although she is clear that he has had no editorial control over the pieces. She has got to know several senior figures in ADA, including Rogério. Ten minutes later, with her phone running out of juice, she is heading in a cab to São Conrado, keeping Rogério on the line.

Back in Rocinha, Nem is beside himself with anger and frustration about the unfolding crisis. It took him only moments to understand how deleterious the impact of an event like this would be on his carefully managed strategy for the favela, and his response to Rogério is unambiguous. 'Tell them to hand them-selves in now and release the hostages unharmed!' He then calls Feijão to fix a meeting with him in Valão. They also agree that Feijão, who is after all boss of the residents' association, should head down to São Conrado to help negotiate the hostage release and the surrender.

Now it is Nem's turn to get dialling. He picks out a phone from his bag of mobiles and calls his most trusted lawyer, who is just arriving into Santos Dumont, Rio's inner-city airport, on a flight from Brasília. 'I need you to get over here as fast as possible,' he says.

Firemen have by now reached the female body lying on the ground. News is already breaking across the media: first in Rio, then nationally, and then around the world. They are all reporting that the dead woman is a local São Conrado resident returning to the Avenida in a cab. This is wrong. The deceased is in fact Adriana Santos, the 42-year-old deputy manager of one of Rocinha's smoke shops. She was with the gang members getting out of the van. It is not known whether she was killed by a police bullet or by one of her own.

Claudia Mônica is given permission by the BOPE negotiators to enter the hotel. She has to walk in with her hands tied behind her back (at BOPE's request). The police hope that her presence will calm the gangsters and reduce the possibility of further fatalities. For the police, this situation is extremely tense. Mounting a raid to free hostages in a hotel carries with it far too many dangers, and so they need to keep all possible conduits open. For Claudia, mildly hung-over, it is the weirdest and most perilous assignment she has ever undertaken.

Inside the hotel kitchen, another hostage, Italian Beatrice Albertini, notices that the atmosphere has calmed. 'I think each of the eight men holding everybody in the kitchen possessed at least two or three weapons,' she later remembers. 'One semi-automatic and two handguns per person, and three of them had grenades strapped around their belt.' The bandidos attempt to reassure the guests: if they stay calm, nothing untoward will happen to them.

Beatrice notices that several of the hostage-takers are pulling wads of paper out of their rucksacks and burning them. 'They also took out the SIM cards from their mobile phones and started destroying them,' she adds. Elsewhere, out of sight of the hostages, two of the gangsters are systematically wrecking the hard drive of a laptop computer they have with them. Nem insists that there were standing instructions to destroy it, because it was on this machine that he conducted his affairs with other women, and the last thing he wanted was for Danúbia to find out. When forensics finally get their hands on it, they are unable to retrieve a single file. Later on, Nem tells the detectives that the only information concerning the business on the computer was some details of a .30 calibre weapon that they were purchasing.

Back in the Civil Police station Bárbara, Estelita and Leal have been following the drama. 'It wasn't until the events at the Intercontinental,' Estelita explains, 'that it dawned on us the import-ance of Feijão to the organisation.' Feijão delivers a clear message on Nem's behalf to his subordinates: 'Give yourselves up immediately and do not harm anybody.'

In the hotel, Claudia Mônica notices how Rogério and his colleagues do not blink at the prospect of having to take one for the boss. 'I was struck by their absolute loyalty to Nem and their immediate recognition that arrest and imprisonment is part and parcel of their work. I sincerely think they would die for him,' she opines.

After two hours, Rogério gives the orders to start releasing the hostages two by two. Finally the gunmen give themselves up into the welcoming arms of BOPE, who take them down to the station.

Detectives Lomba, Estelita and Leal now have to start the arduous task of working out what on earth has just happened.

The headlines the following week are understandably merciless. For Rio de Janeiro, which has been confirmed as the host city for the 2016 Olympics, it is a huge embarrassment, especially since there were foreign holidaymakers among the hostages. The BBC, CNN and the news agencies spread the drama across the world. The letters pages in the main Brazilian dailies demand resolute retribution, including a call to invade Rocinha and bring Nem and his soldiers to justice.

Unbeknownst to most people, the authorities are in fact stepping up their engagement with pacification. Plans to enter Complexo do Alemão, the great stronghold of Red Command in the North Zone, are already well advanced. So concerned are Beltrame and Governor Cabral about the threat posed by Red Command in Alemão that they have requested and received the consent of President Lula to deploy troops and equipment from the Brazilian army and navy to secure the perimeter of the sprawling network of favelas.

Some people, including Detectives Lomba, Estelita and Leal, believe that Nem was with the group of 40 as they came home from Vidigal that Saturday morning; that the incident with the Military Police officer with whom he came face to face actually happened as he was trying to escape the initial outbreak of shooting. But as with so many rumours that fly around about Nem, nobody is able to present any evidence to back up such theories.

Nem understands the gravity of the situation. 'How do you think I felt about it?' he says. 'I knew I had to close this thing down, and close it as quickly as possible.' Even with his quick thinking and the decision to send Feijão down to negotiate a surrender, he knew at the time that it was probably too late. 'This incident was the one failure of my leadership,' he admits, 'and I couldn't afford any fail-ures. This was when the gods decided the time had come to play with me.'

He does not have the public relations capacity required to spin his way out of the events at the Intercontinental. Beltrame may be planning to launch the operation to bring Complexo do Alemão under the control of the state. But after August 2010, the smart money is on Rocinha moving right up the agenda for pacification. With dramatic headlines stretching from Rio to New York to London and even Beijing, Nem becomes the most wanted criminal in Rio overnight.

His spirits are faltering. A cold film of despair seems to creep across his body. His lawyer turns up. The one person he feels he can trust 100 per cent. When he arrives, Nem gets down on his knees, beseeching. He is in tears. 'This is getting too much to bear,' he says. 'I need you to get me out of this life.'

The time has come for a rethink.

PART IV
CATHARSIS

1
FIRST CONTACT
September 2010

t's just a five-minute walk beside the Lagoa to Barra highway to reach São Conrado's Fashion Mall from Rocinha. Beyond the burly, silent men in black suits who watch the entrances to the mall lies an air-conditioned environment of almost perfect sterility. Some shops are high-end purveyors of fashion in which heavily made-up women, nervously thin, wait for their occasional wealthy customer. Other outlets are more typically Brazilian: slightly chaotic affairs with an idiosyncratic selection of bric-a-brac, books, Havaianas, toys and stationery – all usually themed in blue, green and yellow. Punctuating everything nowadays are the minimalist centres of mobile phone providers with their soothing shades of blue and purple, which seek to render their impenetrable offers and deals more seductive.

The food court dominates much of the first floor. In one of its coffee shops, Rio state's Deputy Secretary for Intelligence, Rivaldo Barbosa, sits and waits for a lawyer to arrive. Strolling around the mall unobtrusively are twenty plain clothes officers from his intelligence corps. Barbosa is preparing for a sensitive encounter and one where he might reasonably expect some unwelcome surprises.

This is the second day in a row he has waited at the Fashion Mall, but although a tense business, it is unlikely to throw Barbosa, one of the most methodical policemen ever to work in Rio. During his training as a meteorologist in the Brazilian air force, he learned to rely on statistics, mathematical probability and carefully drawn-up plans. Now he has brought the skills with which he forecast the weather to his work as a detective. In the nine years since he joined the police, his talents have seen him rise up the hierarchy at light-ning speed. He will tell you loudly and robotically that 20 per cent of murders take place between 6 and 9 a.m. and that, perhaps surprisingly, Thursday is the number one day for them. He pores over stats in an attempt to understand the human drivers of desire, jealousy and aggression. Some time ago, José Mariano Beltrame noticed his methods and seconded him to work in his intelligence directorate.

Using his probability yardstick, albeit provisionally, Barbosa has concluded that, on balance, today's unusual meeting is worth a shot.

After the lawyer failed to turn up the day before, Barbosa made an interesting telephone call. He spoke to Nem, newly designated Public Enemy No. 1, who confirmed that he was considering whether to hand himself in to Barbosa and that he wanted to discuss the matter. More than two years later, I speak to Senhor Barbosa to get his version of the phone call. But he refuses to confirm or deny that it ever took place, although he does concede that the meeting with the lawyer happened. Both Nem and his lawyer are adamant that Nem and Barbosa did indeed talk both by email and by phone.

The idea under discussion is as astonishing as it is unprece-dented: a senior leader of a drugs operation in Brazil wishes to negotiate his own surrender. Some lower-level gang members working as police informants have done so in the past, but never somebody of Nem's seniority who is not working as a nark.

Ironically, Nem has encountered some difficulty in trying to find a contact inside the police. He has already tried through his lawyer to negotiate with a senior officer in the Federal Police, but to no avail. The officer did say that if Nem were to send him precise details of all the policemen he had ever bribed – names, dates, amounts – then he might consider talking. But neither Nem nor his lawyer considers this a serious response.

Nem is finding the job of don increasingly hard to bear: managing all the competing egos in his organisation, as well as coping with the trigger-happy tendencies of some of his team and the demands made by other businesses in the favela. He is quite simply suffering from the usual stresses associated with a high-pressure management job – except, of course, the issues of life and death come up much more frequently in his profession than they do elsewhere.

Two years previously he identified a successor and groomed him to take over the top spot. 'Dani was really smart,' Nem explains. 'He would occasionally stress me out because he would humiliate the others, so I would have to give him a dressing-down now and then. But he had real leadership qualities.' However, Dani was murdered in late 2008 at a party in another ADA-controlled favela, Morro dos Macacos. After that, Nem says, he never came across anyone else with the requisite abilities to take charge of Rocinha in his place.

But now if he is to surrender, he must have a clear successor in place. If he doesn't, he insists, Rocinha will collapse into civil war again. He is determined not to repeat the mistakes made by Lulu and Bem-te-vi. He has settled upon a young but competent member of the business called Tadpole. But he will need a bit of time to ensure that all parties buy into his decision.

He has never told me, but I am confident that Nem was also squirrelling away sufficient funds to ensure a peaceful retirement. That must amount to a significant sum of money as he is responsible for the welfare of seven children, an extravagant wife, and his mother; some of his ex-partners may well receive handouts also. So if he can get away with a decade or so in jail, it surely wouldn't be such a bad payoff?

There are of course good reasons why no don has taken the leap of faith involved in offering his surrender until now. The move would engender suspicion among his colleagues, in both ADA and the other factions, including possibly his contacts in the PCC, the São Paulo organised crime leviathan. To insiders and outsiders alike, it might appear as though he has already been working with the police for some time, which would make his life in jail precarious.

Nem explains that his motivation for handing himself in was to ensure his family's security. With him on the outside and wanted by the police, and pacification approaching, he felt his wife, his children and other relatives were not safe. Several of those close to him suggest that he was worried about his own security too – that he himself might be killed by either a rival or the police.

Nem confides to those close to him that if he were to give himself up, he would never return to the world of drug trafficking.

That he should seek out Beltrame's office is all the more remarkable given that he is now probably the longest-serving and most successful Dono do Morro in the short but complex history of drug criminality in Rio's favelas. He enjoys broad support in Rocinha itself. He has reduced the level of violence to a new low. His rule has contributed to a vigorous economic boom in his community. And his regulations have led to a significant reduction in petty crime, thieving and rape throughout much of the South Zone, notably São Conrado, Leblon and Ipanema. By even talking to the Deputy Secretary for Intelligence, he is taking a big chance. If anyone finds out, it could raise the suspicion that Nem is actually working as an informant.

He is not alone in engaging in risky behaviour. Rivaldo Barbosa believes that he too would be subject to unwelcome scrutiny if he were to accept Nem's surrender, even though his boss, Beltrame, has agreed to the talks. Obviously, on one level it will be hailed as a success if Nem is arrested. But as Barbosa himself admits, Nem and ADA eschew confrontation in preference to corruption. Indeed, Barbosa considers ADA's commitment to bribery over violence to be nothing less than an ideology, which starkly differentiates the organisation from Red Command.

If he should bring Nem in, tongues might start wagging. How long has Barbosa enjoyed a relationship with Nem? What has been the nature of that relationship? During fevered times in Brazil, it is hard to stop the rumour mill. The egregious corruption of government officials since colonial times has ingrained a deep cynicism among the public. Almost every civil servant is a target of surmise, conjecture and jealousy, whether deserved or not.

But Barbosa has an incentive too. If he were the man to bring in Nem of Rocinha, it would be a big feather in his cap. Who knows, it might just clear his path to the top job as boss of Rio's Civil Police.

In any event, Barbosa needs to drive a hard bargain. He needs more than just the man himself. So he insists that Nem give up some of the semi-automatic guns that are stored in Rocinha. Something in the region of 30 should do the trick. Nem indicates that he is prepared to organise a handover of some ten weapons that he has for his own personal security. But that is all. They seem ready to agree on this.

Barbosa claims he wanted Nem to give every single detail about the policemen he had corrupted – names, dates, amounts. Otherwise, no deal. Nem insists that never happened; as he said before, 'I'm no snitch.' He would not compile a list.

Nem, too, has his conditions. He wants his family to be safe and protected – possibly even with a name change. And he wants guarantees for his own security once incarcerated.

They do in fact agree on most of the details, but then, according to Nem, towards the end of the phone call Barbosa says, 'As soon as you hand yourself in, we will start planning for the pacification of Rocinha. We will be there in two weeks.'

'The minute he said that, it was over so far as I was concerned,' explains Nem. 'I told Barbosa that I would need some time to sort things out inside the organisation. But instead, he wanted me to be arrested or for me to hand myself in, and then two weeks later, they move in.' There would then, Nem continues, be further arrests, confiscation of weapons and drugs. 'And everyone would think that I had given up the information. Forget it.'

No deal.

2

THE TAKING OF ALEMÃO
November 2010

n mid November 2010, the battle for Rio flared again. At dawn and throughout the day, at dusk and throughout the night, bandits emerged from the shadowy lanes and alleys of the favelas and on to the main thoroughfares of Rio. They stopped traffic, they opened fire, they mugged drivers and their passengers and set buses ablaze. Casualties began to mount and the pressure on Beltrame to do something about this anarchic violence grew with it.

In one attack, a group of young men, arbitrarily firing their semi-automatics, shouted out the battle cry: 'We are the team from Borel.' Five months earlier, Borel, which sits next to the middle-class district of Tijuca, became the eighth favela to be pacified under Beltrame. Although relatively small, with around 20,000 inhabitants, it was a critical hub for Red Command and a symbolic marker, home to some of the most belligerent members of the organisation. When the police were ordered to launch the pacification programme in such places, they hoped to arrest as many traffickers as they could find. In most instances, however, the gang members fled in advance of the invasion. Why would they wait to confront the immense and unforgiving power of BOPE and other special forces deployed in the first days and months? They could simply find temporary refuge in one of the dozens of other favelas controlled by Red Command.

The pacification of each favela absorbed hundreds and some-times thousands of police officers, all of whom had to be taken out of service elsewhere. After several months, the initial occupation would give way to the installation of a pacification unit, comprising a dedicated team of police officers intended to reassure residents that the state was now a permanent presence in their area and the traffickers would not be back.

Of course, most residents were as suspicious of the police as they were of the traffickers, if not more so. Opinion polls regularly show that between 60 and 70 per cent of Brazilians have no confi-dence in their police forces. That percentage is much higher in the favelas. For three decades, the police had offered the favelas a diet of corruption, chicanery and arbitrary violence. It left an aftertaste not dissimilar to the fare served up by the drug cartels. But in most cases the residents had known the traffickers since they were chil-dren, and on the whole they were confident that they would not suddenly strike them down. The exception might be the dreaded stray bullet.

Because the police had such a bad reputation in the favelas, Beltrame decided to staff the pacification units with largely inex-perienced recruits. He reasoned that they had yet to be ensnared by the corrupt and violent networks that had grown like malign tumours in so many of the forces at his disposal. These recruits, it is true, were relatively callow, but most of the actual commanders of the units were former BOPE officers, a fact that would prove to have serious consequences, not least in Rocinha.

Most of the favelas first subjected to pacification were in the South Zone or close by. These boasted some of the highest cocaine turnovers because of their proximity to middle-class customers. This strategy had a disproportionate impact on the fortunes of Red Command, in that more of their favelas had been targeted for early pacification than those belonging to ADA or the Pure Third Command.

When the Red Command bandits expelled from favelas like Borel escaped in advance of the invasion, they sought refuge in the very heart of the drugs and guns trade in Rio – the complexes of Alemão and Penha. These two agglomerations bordered each other to form a staggering ocean of poverty comprising over twenty individual favelas. Apart from their combined size, they were also close to Rio's major land, sea and air transport hubs, which conferred a significant advantage on the controlling drug cartel.

The ranks of drugs soldiers in Alemão and Penha were swelling with the refugees from Borel and elsewhere. They enthusiastically joined the frightening attacks that spread across Rio in November 2010. The media were quick to claim that this was an outburst of angry frustration on the part of the traffickers, a result of pacification's success in disrupting Red Command's drug trade.

Police intelligence reported something different. Apparently, Red Command bosses gave the signal for the attacks in the middle-class residential and business areas to express their displeasure at the decision to transfer a group of senior Red Command leaders, including Fernandinho Beira-Mar, from their prisons in Rio to jails in other states. In Rio's most notorious facility, Bangu, it was relatively easy to manage the day-to-day business of the drug trade by paying guards to allow in mobile phones. It would be harder to communicate from the penitentiary in the state of Paraná, far away from the action on the ground, especially since security in federal facilities was much tighter than it was in municipal jails like Bangu.

The migration of bandits to Alemão also pointed to an uncomfortable reality, which would dog the pacification programme at every turn: suppress the cartel in one favela and it would simply pop up elsewhere within days. There were, after all, just under 1,000 favelas in Rio. If you had been run out of your home favela, there were plenty of others to choose from, especially if you had a gun or two. It was not long after pacification started that the authorities in the neighbouring cities of Niterói, across Guanabara Bay, and São João de Meriti, in Baixada Fluminense, were complaining bitterly that they were having to deal with an upsurge in drugs-related violence as a consequence of pacification in Rio's South Zone, as the bandits found refuge with them.

Originally Beltrame had intended to launch the pacification of Complexo do Alemão in late 2011, but in the two years since the inauguration of the programme, he had become convinced that his constituents would regard pacification as mere window-dressing until he steeled himself to enter Alemão – the big one. Some 300,000 people lived in the twelve favelas that comprised the complex. If the most significant nexus of violence in the city could be pacified, then places like Rocinha would surely follow.

On Tuesday 23 November 2010, the Rio-based O *Globo*, the most influential newspaper in the country, published an editorial which concluded that the Pacification Programme 'cannot solve the problem simply by expelling the traffickers from one area, only for other areas to discover that they have become hostages to migrating violence ... Rio's police need to recognise the absolute necessity to engage with what could be the mother of all operations against crime in Rio – the occupation of Complexo do Alemão, headquarters of trafficking and the known refuge of those gangsters who have been forced to leave their own favelas which have been rescued by the Pacification Units.'

Perhaps the leader writer was being prescient. More likely, Beltrame's office had tipped off the paper.

The government of Rio de Janeiro was about to launch probably the world's most challenging campaign in what the Pentagon has dubbed MOUT: military operations on urbanised terrain. Some believe the development of this novel doctrine is an essential foundation of new security strategies to deal with the rapid and chaotic growth of cities across the world (especially in the global south).

Others argue that it is simply a way of keeping the poor penned in – and poor. Either way, it is becoming a dominant form of warfare, along with the use of drones and other robotics. Already over 54 per cent of the world's population lives in cities – and that is set to grow to about 75 per cent by the year 2030. The migration into urban areas places the growing levels of inequality in starker contrast than ever before, often resulting in instability – especially when the wealth gap is augmented by cultural characteristics such as race or religion.

Using armed force in cities is exceptionally dangerous: the possible consequences for members of the public are obvious. Furthermore, in slums around the world, those who are being attacked enjoy the advantage of knowing the terrain intimately. And the more densely populated an area, the less valuable heavy weaponry becomes.

So when it became clear that Rio's government was intent on entering some of the largest slums in the world, it wasn't only Brazilians who were interested in monitoring the outcome. It was of fascination to military and security experts everywhere.

Before attempting to go into Alemão itself, Beltrame and his advisers agreed that they would have to enter neighbouring Vila Cruzeiro, considered one of the most dangerous favelas in the city, and affected by some of the highest levels of deprivation. Lying just north of Alemão in Complexo da Penha, Cruzeiro backed on to a protected wedge of the Atlantic tropical rainforest called Mount Misericórderia. By controlling this area, Beltrame's forces would possess a key vantage point, enabling them to enter and occupy Alemão.

But nobody presumed that they could just stroll into Vila Cruzeiro and the other favelas in Complexo da Penha. Beltrame and his advisers understood early in their planning that not even BOPE had the resources to secure this territory.

So he and Governor Cabral made a fateful decision: they requested the support of the Brazilian armed forces, and President Lula agreed.

This was the first time that the government had approved the domestic deployment of the Brazilian military for security purposes since the end of the dictatorship. Needless to say, it was a highly sensitive issue.

In Vila Cruzeiro, only the marines took part, quite specifically because the navy agreed to lend the police several M-113 armoured personnel carriers and their drivers. BOPE's famous Big Skull had one vulnerability – rubber tyres. In enclosed urban environments, it was relatively easy to disable the vehicles by destroying their tyres. The M-113s, by contrast, had caterpillar tracks, and when Beltrame ordered the assault on Cruzeiro on the morning of Friday 26th, these virtually irresistible monsters crushed and tossed aside the burning cars and motorbikes the traffickers had fashioned as barricades as if they were made of paper.

Helicopters filming the invasion of Cruzeiro soon spotted dozens upon dozens of young men scrambling over Mount Misericórderia in order to reach the safety of Alemão. Some were carrying cash, some drugs; most were armed. One man was shot in the leg and dragged across a dirt track by his comrades only to be left by the side of the road. Protected by the might of the amphibious M-113s, a vanguard of BOPE officers fanned out around Cruzeiro, establishing control within a mere two hours.

While this was in progress, Red Command members were continuing to commandeer vehicles and police stations around the city. More than 30 buses were set alight that day, and shooting was recorded across Rio. Fear, and a sense that cariocas might be returning to the violence of the 1990s, was heightened by the excited military rhetoric used by both the police and the media. *O Globo*'s banner headline on 26 November read: 'D-DAY'. The atmosphere thickened with an apocalyptic haze.

The day after special forces went into Cruzeiro, the Brazilian army entered the fray, with hundreds of soldiers taking up position around Alemão to block all 44 points of entry and exit. Throughout the 21 favelas of Penha and Alemão, hundreds of small shops put up their shutters, all public services came to a halt and terrified residents hunkered down in their inadequate shelters.

A massive squad of officers drawn from all three police forces moved slowly into Alemão as armoured helicopters whirred menacingly in the skies, spotting potential traffickers and giving cover to the ground troops. The entire operation was broadcast live on television from helicopters, and from cars and cameramen on the ground. It was an extraordinary twenty-first-century spectacle: the armed might of the state attempting to assert itself in a territory for the first time in decades of neglect against a group of tough desperadoes and tens of thousands of ordinary people who lived around or below the poverty line. José Junior, the mediator from the NGO Afroreggae, had tried but failed to secure a negotiated surrender, and the fear was that the firefights would intensify.

The force ranged against the traffickers was, quite simply, so immense that resistance would have been futile. Instead, they tried to escape. Despite the army having encircled the entire area, dozens managed to flee down water pipes and through tiny alleys leading into favelas outside the complex. At least one trafficker was reported to have walked out through the front door, as it were, dressed convincingly as a pest control officer.

There is no question that the taking of Alemão was a dramatic turning point in Rio's history. José Mariano Beltrame's status (and with it his power) was growing all the time. Of course, the military action was only the first step in making the city more secure. Beltrame himself had always stressed that he was not aiming to shut down the drugs trade (he simply didn't possess the resources), but to reduce the number of weapons in the favelas. Similarly, he had no illusions about the residents' commitment to the state as it made its presence felt in their home territories for the first time. If the government failed to provide further infrastructural improvement, better pay and decent jobs, it would find it difficult to instil any loyalty among the inhabitants in the long term.

To the credit of the security forces, not a single death was registered during the taking of Alemão, although there were several injuries on both sides, and over 30 traffickers were arrested. Perhaps most astonishing of all, if the police were to be believed, along with 50 semi-automatics confiscated, they found 40 metric tonnes of cocaine and marijuana.

There was much work to be done. But for the moment Beltrame was content, in his genuinely modest fashion, to accept the plaudits for the smooth success of Alemão. Yet as he remarks, within days of the operation he was being asked the same question by almost everyone he met: 'So what about Rocinha?'

3

CONFESSIONS
January–April 2011

At 4.30 p.m. on 13 January 2011, two intelligence agents await their host in an apartment deep inside Rocinha. They are dressed casually in grey T-shirts and jeans, but the informality cannot disguise their slight nerves. There is a knock at the door. Nem walks in and the two shake his hand. If anything, he appears more nervous than the spooks, which is odd given that he is on his home turf. He places two pistols on the table in front of them. It's a disturbing opening – Otávio and Renata[1] are unprotected, unarmed, and aware that if anything goes wrong here, their bosses will deny any knowledge of their mission

'Well,' Otávio smiles in the hope of breaking the ice, 'here we are unarmed, and you're tooled up!' Nem is fearfully apologetic. 'How rude of me,' he says, flustered, and slides the two guns over on to the agents' side of the table. In a reciprocal gesture, Otávio pushes the weapons aside so they are in front of nobody – a surreal moment for the agents.

A few days earlier, down at the 15th Precinct, Detective Estelita had been chatting to a man from Rocinha. In passing, he said, as he always did to anyone who might be linked to Nem, 'You can tell your boss that the only way he is going to get out of this mess is if he gives himself up. Someone really needs to tell him that.' Instead of scuttling off, the man looked Estelita in the eye and replied, 'You know, he has talked about turning himself in several times but he has no one to discuss it with.' The man then asked if Estelita could talk to somebody 'high up' who might be able to explain to Nem in person that he is just a criminal businessman and not an evil killer. If Estelita could find somebody with sufficient authority, 'he'll probably give himself up.'

Estelita paused, slightly shocked. He certainly couldn't imagine walking into a favela to chat to a don. But he did agree to pass the message up the chain.

Estelita's boss, Bárbara Lomba, was sceptical but she agreed to give it a go, thinking that this would be the last of it.

But a little later she received a request for all the information she and her team had on Nem. It was a sign, perhaps, that something was moving. Somebody in the highest political circles had given the go ahead, although that was the last Bárbara heard of it.

Now the two intelligence operatives are staring across the table at the man himself. For the last two months, they have been studying his business, his organisation, and his life in minute detail thanks to the remarkable dossier compiled by Estelita and Leal. And yet there is still so much to learn. They grasp immediately why the Civil Police detectives have found it so difficult to penetrate Nem's communications network. One minion is charged with carrying his phone bag with the dozen or so mobiles in it, each dedicated to another trafficker or a corrupt policeman, or anyone else with whom Nem needs to speak securely.

The first meeting takes place in a small two-room apartment in Cachopa. Along with the table, there is a sofa and a television in the rectangular living room where they talk. Nem sips Johnny Walker Black Label throughout.

Otávio and Renata will want at some point to broach the idea of Nem giving himself up, and how that should work. But they have no intention of pushing it – this is a unique opportunity for two people who normally live deep in the shadows and they are happy to chat about the business, its employees and its mechanism. Nem obliquely reveals his preferences for particular individuals in the organisation.

Nem begins to relax. He realises that his interlocutors are not looking for a bribe. They actually want to converse, and he has never had the opportunity to chat with two highly intelligent government officials who don't appear to be judging him and who actually know what they are talking about. Before long, he is happy to discuss the possibility of handing himself in.

But first he tells them his life story. He talks of Eduarda, her illness and the necessity of borrowing money from Lulu. He talks about the disputes within the favela, the shootouts, the cocaine, the corruption, his family, the money, the support given to the community, pacification – he does not hold back. He talks often about God and the guidance he receives from above. Slowly but surely, he unburdens himself. He only has one rule – he refuses to implicate anyone else in criminal activity.

Outside the favela, in an anonymous building in Rio Centre, anxiety is growing among Otávio and Renata's colleagues. They surely can't have been in there for so long without running into trouble. But in Cachopa, the two barely notice as five hours pass seemingly in an instant. The three agree to meet again. The two spooks finally drive back to the office at 10 p.m. It is easy to read in their faces their feelings of suppressed elation. They think that their work is on the verge of bearing the most unexpectedly sweet fruit.

The next meeting, two weeks later, also takes place in Cachopa. Nem is at pains to make the agents feel at home, offering all manner of refreshments and suggesting that he organise a barbecue at some point. As Otávio and Renata tell me about this, I can't avoid conjuring up the peculiar image of Rio's most powerful and charismatic drugs boss passing round the grilled beef with hot pepper sauce to a pair of iron-faced intel operatives who are explaining to him how they intend to arrange his arrest. Perhaps with the same vision in mind, Otávio and Renata politely decline the offer of a *churrasco*.

To this day, Nem retains his affection and admiration for the two agents. 'They are the only two decent government people I've ever met,' he says. 'They were serious, intelligent and they always kept their word.' Nem often gives the impression that he was starved of decent conversation, that he craved some intellectual stimulation and that he relished the opportunity to discuss matters in depth in a way that didn't often happen inside the organisation.

He seems perfectly ready to discuss the conditions for his surrender. In contrast to the earlier discussions, these two are not demanding a list of the names of corrupted policemen. They do want to see some of Rocinha's guns handed in, but Nem does not baulk at this, explaining once again that he will deliver up *his* guns but that he has no authority over other people's. His main concern, he reiterates, is his safety and that of his family.

The agents suspect that Nem is tired. They reckon the job is imposing a tremendous strain on him: the responsibilities, the tensions, the security issues and, yes, the violence. It is all becoming too much. He is adamant that in the event of his surrender or arrest, he will not resume his career in the drugs business after his release from prison. And the two make it perfectly clear that there exists more than enough evidence to ensure a long stretch inside. Nem has had enough, they believe. But he is worried and frightened by the possible consequences of surrender. He has to take immense care as he weighs up his options.

During the second meeting, Nem really opens up. There are some remarkable exchanges. He tells the story of how he ordered his soldiers to deliver a rapist to the Military Police. His men returned and said that the PM officers were demanding 10,000 reals. 'No,' said Nem, infuriated. 'We don't want them to release the guy. Go back and explain that we want them to arrest him!' But the guys explained that the officers wanted 10,000 reals to *arrest* the rapist. 'What sort of a world are we living in,' Nem asks Otávio and Renata despairingly, 'when you have to pay the cops to arrest criminals?'

The agents leave that meeting with a strong sense that Nem is shedding his outer skin to reveal the inner man – Antônio, the hard-working and unassuming guy he put into storage eleven years earlier when he took the long walk up Estrada da Gávea. Their confidence is growing that he is about to hand himself in. He is talking more and more about his fate being in the hands of God. The details of their conversations are relayed back to their immediate boss, and these then go up the chain of command. A breakthrough is on the cards. 'I can assure you,' Otávio tells me, 'he was a hair's breadth away from giving himself in.'

At which point, the gods allow Chance on to the stage once more. Just after a third meeting between Nem and the two agents, the chief of Rio's Civil Police resigns for having leaked details of a federal investigation into corruption involving some of his own units. A successor is appointed. These events trigger the curse that perennially debilitates police forces around the world: miscommunication, born of confusion, of incompetence, of skulduggery, of jealousy, or of a wicked brew of them all.

Amidst the chaos of internal change, nobody informs the intelligence team that Polinter, a specialist Civil Police unit that cooperates with police agencies beyond Rio's borders, is about to swoop on Rocinha.

In April, Polinter issues arrest warrants for several people, including Nem, his mother, his wife, Feijão and others, on charges of money-laundering, centred on two shops in the favela. Nem and

Danúbia escape the big police raid that precedes the announcement of the charges (in all probability somebody leaked details of the operation), and eventually the case is dropped for lack of evidence.

But it is a drawn-out affair whose reverberations crash against the delicate negotiations taking place between Otávio, Renata and Nem. This changes Nem's calculations. With an arrest warrant issued against his wife, there is the danger that their daughter 'would be left without a father and a mother'. The talks continue, but they are less relaxed. The venue for the fourth meeting changes from Cachopa to Rua Dois. This time the three are no longer on their own. Nem asks if Feijão can join the discussion. Otávio and Renata are no longer feeling quite as secure as they were previously. In public, Feijão has always presented himself as a civilian whose relationship with Nem is based solely on the fact that they were childhood friends. He projects the image of an upstanding citizen, democratically elected as president of the residents' association but with no substantial links to the traffickers. His comportment during these meetings, however, makes it perfectly clear that he wields considerable power in Nem's operation, if not as a soldier then as a senior consigliere. This, the agents believe, is a man actively seeking power.

From Nem's point of view, he needs all the support he can get, and Feijão is one of the few people close to him who is both intelligent and trustworthy. Nonetheless, in retrospect Otávio and Renata assess that his introduction marks the point when the tide turns against them. Feijão doesn't say much. Instead he briefly shakes his head or winces when he hears something he doesn't like. The agents think this is enough to sow doubt in Nem's mind. The security of Nem's family would be at risk, Feijão suggests, if he were to hand himself in. 'It was only at this point that we began to realise just how significant Feijão had become,' Otávio remarks. They do not consider his influence benign. Feijão needs Nem, and he is not going to permit the state to staunch the source of his power.

In addition to all this, the pacification of other favelas in the South Zone has unsettled Rocinha. São Carlos, an important ADA-controlled favela, has been under police occupation for two months by now. Many of its traffickers have sought Nem's protection and moved to Rocinha.

On 29 April, the day after the penultimate meeting with the agents, a man pulls up on his motorcycle by the steep hill leading from Rua Um to Laboriaux. It is 5.30 a.m. and all is quiet. Suddenly a car screeches to a halt beside him and four men bundle the motorcyclist into their car before driving off at speed. The victim is Foca, a prominent trafficker from São Carlos. Hours later, the kidnappers demand a ransom of R$1.4 million for his release. It falls to Nem to organise a whip-round of money and jewels to meet the demand. ADA hand over some of Foca's own flamboyant gold jewellery, including four rings spelling his nickname in white gold and a huge chain upon which hangs a gold sculpture of Jesus.

'This was a real challenge,' remembers Nem, 'and actually a huge risk for whoever did it.'

But for Nem it is also a warning. If outsiders can just drive into his territory and abduct a well-known bandido, it is a sign that his control is slipping.

Nem and the spooks will meet one final time, but before they do, another unexpected event will unsettle everyone still further.

4

LUANA AND ANDRESSA

9 May 2011

am tramping up the narrow path leading away from Dionéia, near the top of the favela, and into the rainforest when my guide suddenly starts singing in a soft, melancholy falsetto:

O Obaluaê! Protect me with your hat.
The plague is running across the land as
    the star runs across the sky.
If an old man comes along the way, give him
    your blessing.
God bless me, Obaluaê!
God bless me, Obaluaê!
I have come without food and I beg the
    sacred spirits to come to my aid.
It was the spirits who helped me.
It was the divine sacred spirit.
Blessed be the Lord, our master.

The guide falls silent and then gestures towards a clearing, about twenty metres in diameter. 'This is where it would happen,' he tells me quietly. 'Many years ago, there was a local temple here, and the people would leave offerings for the spirits of the forest in the house of Caboclo.'

Around the open space cluster the deep green trees and bushes of the Atlantic forest. Parakeets squawk and the yellow-breasted bem-te-vi trills his onomatopoeic song. Capuchin monkeys cackle, while tiny creatures rustle gently in the undergrowth. In between the sounds, the silence is crystalline. Some of the plants contain poison. I grab on to an apparently harmless stem to steady myself and a nasty thin spike penetrates my skin and sinks into my flesh. When nature remains undisturbed, however, the place exudes an almost divine tranquillity.

Before we enter the clearing, the guide becomes still more circumspect. First he prays to Exú, messenger of God. On another occasion, he might then raise a glass of sacred *vinho da Jurema*. Centuries ago, practitioners of Umbanda assimilated the indigenous hallucinogenic drink into their own rituals. My guide bows to Oxóssi, spirit of the hunt, of the forest and of the life force. Finally, he appeals to be granted the protection of Obaluaê, whose straw head-gear hanging down over his face will protect us from disease, pestilence and death. 'It is necessary,' my guide explains, 'because in recent times, very bad things happened in the temple.'

At the back of the clearing there is a tree, and a patch of ground where the vegetation is faded. This was where they butchered bodies on a slab of stone. 'Most were already dead when they arrived here,' the guide continues, 'but some arrived still alive and were placed against the tree before being shot.' Bullet holes in the trunk are still visible.

As the body was being dismembered, the blood would flow into a small brook that would continue down into Dionéia, Cachopa and other parts of Rocinha. The limbs and torso would be put into a wheelbarrow and the head placed on top before being pushed off to a different part of the favela for incineration. Other victims were put through the 'microwave', alive or half dead, trapped in petrol-soaked tyres, which were then set alight.

As they say in Rocinha, those who are brought to this place don't come back.

'Nem was not here when I witnessed this,' my guide insists. Since starting my discussions with him, I have tried hard to establish if there is concrete evidence linking Nem to murders in Rocinha during his rule. Some people have been adamant that he was directly responsible for a number of deaths. They will not, however, put their name to the claim – for entirely understandable reasons.

And throughout most of his time as Don of the Hill, no charges relating to murder or assault were ever brought against him.

Then Rio's public prosecutor alleged that on 9 May 2011, two young women came to the clearing above Dionéia, never to return.

According to the charge sheet, four members of ADA, two from Rocinha and two from pacified favela São Carlos, brought Andressa de Oliveira, 25, and Luana Rodrigues de Sousa, 21, to this place and murdered them. Their bodies, the prosecutor claimed, were burned and reduced to ashes.

In addition to the charges brought against the four, Nem was accused of having directly ordered the death of the two women. 'As soon as these ridiculous charges were brought against me,' he says, 'I put my plans to hand myself in on hold.'

According to the police investigation, Luana had been staying with Andressa in an apartment on Rocinha's Rua Quatro. A couple of weeks earlier, she had split up from her boyfriend, Ronaldinho, because he had been beating her up.

Luana was from a small lower-middle-class area of São Conrado. She had worked as a model in the past. Articles published after the two girls disappeared never failed to include a photograph of her. She was, without question, an attractive young woman. In those reports, she was also always described as having a bubbly and warm personality. By contrast, no photos of Andressa were ever published.

Indeed, she was frequently not even mentioned by name in the media. Andressa was black, and not a model.

The state's case was based on witness testimony that suggested Andressa was an entirely incidental victim of whatever actually happened. One witness, one of Andressa's sisters, observed that Luana had gone out with traffickers, football players, policemen – 'in short, anyone who ... she may be able to make use of'.

In their turn, people appeared to make use of her. According to almost all the testimony in the case, Luana worked as a mule for ADA. She would take drugs from Rocinha to other favelas around Rio. The cartels understood the advantage of employing pretty young women to transport their wares, as they were less likely to be stopped by police.

A few days before the two girls disappeared, Luana, it seems, deposited 25,000 reals' worth of marijuana at Andressa's flat. She was due to take the drugs to a favela in Tijuca, north of Rocinha. According to witnesses, Andressa's boyfriend, Thiago, allegedly a crack addict, discovered the marijuana when he was dismantling the cupboard in which it was stored. Andressa warned him not to touch the drugs and this time hid them under her bed. The following day, when Luana came to pick them up, the bag was empty. She called the traffickers to explain what had happened, clearly implicating Thiago as the thief. The traffickers tracked him down and demanded to know what he had done with the drugs.

On Sunday 8 May, Andressa's thirteen-year-old sister, Juliana, who was staying with her at the time, testified that Andressa had explained to her how the following day she 'would have to account for the loss of the drugs to Nem' and three other traffickers. It seems that the organisation had demanded Andressa's apartment 'as compensation for half of the value of the drugs'.

At 5 p.m. in the afternoon of the 9th, the prosecutor argued, Juliana bade farewell to Thiago and her sister and headed off to babysit for Andressa's friend Fernanda. This was the last time that anyone prepared to testify saw Andressa. According to Juliana, Fernanda later 'spotted a group of some six traffickers heading up the hill at Dionéia carrying a shovel, an axe and a gasoline canister, along with a piece of wood with nails sticking out of it, used by traffickers to beat and torture their victims'.

Apparently Thiago escaped the ultimate sanction of the traffickers' kangaroo court; he later turned up at Rocinha's health clinic requesting treatment for the consequences of the severe beating that he received at the hands of the bandidos. Why they would release Thiago is one of several puzzling aspects of the case. He was the person who, according to all the testimony, was most obviously guilty of having ripped off the traffickers. And yet he got away with it? Peculiar to the point of being incomprehensible.

The public prosecutor further alleged that although the traffickers released Thiago, they then shot the two women, Luana and Andressa, before taking the corpses up to the clearing and burning them according to the principle of 'no body, no crime'.

The officer of the Civil Police who led the investigation into the case visited the clearing with a forensics expert, reporting a find of two animal bones, one human bone, one flip-flop, one tennis shoe and a bracelet. Witnesses later identified these items as belonging to Luana and Andressa. The forensic examination broke several of the fundamental rules of scientific examination, and the investigator in question has since been fired from the police for having manufactured evidence in another murder case.

During Nem's five years in power, there had been rumours aplenty of murders, summary executions and casual assassinations. Influential characters such as the man who once controlled half of the lucrative gas concession in Rocinha, Lucas do Gas, had gone missing before turning up dead. Some people ascribed such deaths to Nem. The media frequently represented him as an indiscriminate killer, but all these claims were based on hearsay. Nobody has ever provided evidence for them.

When I confront Nem with the accusation, he becomes incandescent. 'Why on earth would I kill those two girls?' he asks rhetorically. 'And what evidence is there that I was anywhere near this place – apart from hearsay communicated by a thirteen-year-old girl?'

Although the evidence was paper thin, the magistrates referred the case for a trial by jury, and at the time of writing, Nem is waiting to hear when it will take place.

As José Mariano Beltrame understood, one of the consequences of the state having ignored the favelas, allowing them to rot in the rancid juices of poverty, disease and violence for so long, was that Brazil's criminal justice system had no purchase inside the favelas at all. And the inverse was also true – people in favelas didn't care what the outside world thought about them. 'For fifty years,' one Rocinha resident told me soon after I started living in the favela, 'they didn't give a fuck about us. So why with all this sudden interest on their part should we suddenly give a fuck about them?'

Nonetheless, the police did, over the years, make some attempts to understand what was happening inside the communities. Estelita and Leal's patient and meticulous investigation into Nem's organisation is probably the most sophisticated, if an extremely rare, example.

Another important innovation was introduced in 1995: a hotline known as the *disque denúncia*, with anonymity guaranteed as callers leave details of crimes committed, or perhaps of unusual movements of the cartel in a particular favela. The disque denúncia has on the whole proved a very effective tool in helping to map the contours of criminal activity in Rio, but, more controversially, it is used as evidence in criminal trials even though there is no way of substantiating the claims that are phoned in or the motives of the callers.

The police also habitually cultivated X-9s, informants inside the drug organisations. The cartels considered the X-9s the greatest threat to their security, and if informants were exposed, they would be killed, usually in a brutal fashion. On one occasion, Vanessa, Nem's first wife, falsely accused Simone, his lover, of revealing to police where he had concealed himself on a certain day. Although lacking any reasonable proof, Nem was so sensitive to the accusation that he beat Simone badly, breaking her rib in the process. When it emerged that Vanessa had made it up, he assaulted her in turn: in the 40° heat of a Rio summer, she had to walk around for a couple of weeks in a hoody and tracksuit bottoms to disguise the bruises.

Other targets for murder were those who stole from the organisation or disrupted their operations. Andressa and Luana allegedly fell into this category, although as anybody acquainted with the drugs trade in Rio will tell you, no one gets killed for marijuana these days.

It is certainly possible that an ADA member was responsible for the deaths of the two women. But the investigation into the alleged murders reveals so many fundamental lacunae and errors that it is a wonder it was not scotched years ago.

Only a single witness, Andressa's younger sister, Juliana, mentioned Nem. The state is basing most of its case on her testimony. This is deeply problematic.

Juliana gave her statement to the police two weeks after Andressa and Luana were supposedly killed. At the time, she was just thirteen years old. Yet the statement offers meticulous chronological detail in which conversations are reproduced with exact dates and timing. The absence of any hesitation is very atypical of a thirteen-year-old trying to recall the events of a fortnight earlier.

At no point did anyone hear Nem order the death of the two girls. Indeed, it is striking that nobody even recalls seeing him throughout that weekend in Rocinha, although plenty do recall seeing the other suspects. Not a single witness recalled having seen Nem in Rocinha that weekend, whereas sightings of the others allegedly involved were numerous.

When Otávio and Renata pitched up for their final meeting with Nem, the atmosphere had changed. Just before it took place, it had seemed as though everything was back on again and a deal could be struck. The Polinter investigation had collapsed and the arrest warrant against Danúbia had been withdrawn. 'The problem was solved so far as I was concerned,' says Nem, 'because that meant she would be able to look after my daughter if I gave myself up. And then almost immediately, they stuck this murder charge on me.'

Otávio and Renata had been so close, but for Nem, the new accusation was a deal-breaker. He was obviously disconcerted. Before the kidnapping of Foca, and now the case being prepared against him in the matter of the two women, the agents had not noticed any guns visible on the streets of Rocinha. But the course of events had 'made Nem very nervous and it changed things. He disappeared, went into hiding and overnight there were a lot of guns on the streets. A lot of arms.'

At their final meeting, the two spooks were met in Rua Dois by some 50 heavily armed men. It was Feijão, not Nem, who ordered the soldiers to leave the room when the time came for discussions to start. If they hadn't yet understood what was going on, Otávio and Renata were now clear: Nem would no longer be prepared to give himself up. Feijão was winning. In a final gesture of mutual respect, Nem and Otávio swopped mobile numbers as they said their goodbyes. But the chance of an historic surrender appeared to be over.

Something else was happening. While the negotiations on

Nem's surrender were still under way, the incoming chief of the Civil Police informed Detective Lomba that the team was being taken off the case. Over four years, they had built up a rich repository of intelligence, not only about Nem and Rocinha but about ADA and its relations with the other factions as well – an invaluable resource that would soon start gathering dust. Those officers of the Civil Police who took over responsibility for Rocinha did not know the name of a single member of Nem's operation apart from the boss himself. The confusion is evident in the material that the officer in charge of Andressa and Luana's case offered to the public prosecutor.

As pacification drew nearer, Nem continued to wrestle with the dilemma of whether he should hand himself in or not. He could flee, although he realised that by leaving Rocinha, he would be entering a world where he was largely unprotected. He could stay and hide, although his family were against this idea, as they believed that the police would kill him were he discovered. As he became more racked with anxiety, Feijão became steadily more influential, providing Nem with answers that were not necessarily in his best interests.

But few people in Rio at the time were aware of this broader political context regarding Nem's future. Following the events of August 2010 at the Intercontinental Hotel, and with the flight of Red Command from Alemão, Nem was quite simply Rio's Most Wanted, as posters of his face proclaimed across the city and on the Internet. His alleged responsibility for the murders fitted well into a canvas on which all bandits were portrayed as killers who delighted in dispatching innocents in the most gruesome ways imaginable.

Nem may have had nothing to do with the murder of the two women, yet the event posed profound moral problems for him. He had pursued a policy of keeping violence to a minimum, but the philosophy was not apparently shared by all of his followers. Indeed, violence repeatedly took place when he was away from Rocinha. It was as if he were in command of a chariot of tigers: powerful and effective as long as he was controlling them, but as soon as the tigers escaped the reins, there would be carnage.

5

THE ARREST II
3–9 November 2011

The clouds were thickening again above Rocinha. The tropical storms were back, and water spilled from the gutters and drains. The new streams tumbled towards the Atlantic.

Nem was losing control. For some months he had been convinced that Beltrame would not order the occupation of Rocinha until the following year, or even later. Now the signs were proliferating that Rocinha was next on the Secretary for Public Security's agenda. Nem was rarely out of the newspapers. He complained that whenever anything bad happened in Rio, the media immediately speculated that he was responsible. 'There was an explosion in Cinelândia,' he said, talking about a district miles from Rocinha, 'and the next day I was being accused of it even though it was caused by a gas leak!' Too many of his intelligence sources were muttering about Rocinha being next. The invasion was imminent.

It was a year since Complexo do Alemão, the second most important narcotics hub in Rio, had been seized by the state. Beltrame knew that Rocinha was less likely than Alemão to mount an armed resistance. As long as Nem was under lock and key, he believed that the forces at his disposal should encounter no real difficulties in controlling the slum. Nem had been a durable and effective leader of Rocinha; these characteristics had enabled him to build up an omnipotent conglomerate with a decisive role in the political, economic and social life of the favela. He had steered Rocinha away from factionalism and violence. Taking him out entailed a certain risk.

The Secretary felt that it had been worth responding to the feelers that Nem had extended. In the end, however, he dismissed the negotiations regarding the Don's surrender. He had concluded that Nem's various approaches had been little more than a bluff, aimed at trying to discover when Rocinha would be pacified so he could better prepare for it.

Nem, however, was still at large. He was, in Beltrame's words, 'an emblematic figure'. His downfall would be a seismic event. As long as he remained free, he represented a problem for the smooth implementation of pacification.

Nem himself was even more troubled. He found it incredible that the public prosecutor was pursuing him for his alleged role in the murder of Andressa and Luana. He had also become distanced from the one lawyer he had grown to rely on. Saulo was in prison. Lulu was dead. Was there anyone left to whom he could turn for counsel? There was still Feijão.

At about the same time Nem held his final meeting with the detectives, he was put in touch with another lawyer, Luiz Carlos Azenha. Among other areas of expertise, Azenha specialised in defending major drug cartel figures, and as such he had extensive contacts both in the underworld and in Rio's various police forces.

Nem was carefully observing the fate of people in Complexo do Alemão. Thanks to his intelligence network, he knew that a faction of the police force were exploiting their new-found strength inside Alemão to extort former Red Command members and intimidate their families, facts that only became public when allegations were investigated two years later. This heightened his concern for his own safety and above all that of his family.

In October, he had a meeting with Azenha, who by this time had agreed to scrutinise some of the charges the public prosecutor had levelled against him. His greatest worry, Azenha relates, 'was that he was being threatened by police officers'. Nem had received information that there was a price on his head; from his perspective, pacification would present the perfect opportunity for any killers among the various law enforcement agencies involved in the forthcoming invasion to take him out. He was still inclined to hide in Rocinha, but he knew he ought once again to explore the plan to give himself up. He asked Azenha to see if any of his contacts in the police would be receptive.

One morning towards the end of October, Nem woke up feeling unwell. He was sweating and nauseous. A busy day lay ahead, with crucial decisions pending. The demands of his constituents were as consuming as ever.

'It was about a week before it all happened,' recalls Danúbia. 'He was in a bad way and was incredibly nervous.' Nem was struggling to decide what he ought to do. Those close to him, including his wife, were advising him to leave. 'What would I do outside? Where would I go?' he replied to her. '"My love, the minute I try and leave Rocinha, I'll be arrested" – that is what he always said to me. "I just know it," he kept on saying.'

The stress was mounting, and one morning he collapsed. Inside the favela, the rumour went round that he had taken an overdose of ecstasy. This is not, of course, impossible but nobody had ever suggested that he had taken drugs before – not his family, nor his friends, nor indeed his enemies. Whatever the cause, he was rushed to a private clinic, where after a day or so his health stabilised and he was allowed home. Both his family and Feijão were concerned that his ability to manage his complex daily life was deteriorating.

Around this time, he went to see Simone. He started crying, she remembers, 'and said that he wanted to turn back time. He wanted to be that Nem who had no responsibility. "There are so many things going on in my head these days," he told me. "I have to sort out everything here on the Hill and I am just not coping with it all. I am really tired mentally."' Simone looked at him sympathetically and said, 'It's too late now ...'

Simone's account squares with that of most others I spoke to about Nem during the run-up to his arrest. The words 'nervous', 'stressed' and 'worried' crop up repeatedly, although he insists that he was none of these – most likely a case of retrospective bravado, born part of machismo and part to maintain his aura of leadership for posterity.

Whatever the truth about his state of mind, Nem was at this time proving indecisive. He could bring himself neither to flee nor to hand himself in. He was, however, beginning to appreciate that there were drawbacks to remaining, his preferred option. 'If I had stayed,' he reasons, 'then my personal guard may have taken that as a signal to fight. They would have resisted to the death and I had to prevent that from happening.' He also agreed that his chances of being killed would be pretty high.

At the same time as Nem's hospitalisation, Azenha arranged a meeting with a contact in the Civil Police, Inspector Fernando Mussi. The inspector didn't know Azenha well, but still, he reasoned, there could be no harm in having a drink with him. He brought along a colleague who happened to be an adviser to the deputy chief of the Civil Police, a direct line into the higher echelons of Rio's security apparatus.

'Nem wants to hand himself in,' Azenha explained briskly, 'and he wants me to cut the deal.' Mussi looked at the lawyer. The inspector had no inkling that this offer was merely the latest gambit in a long pattern of contacts aimed at securing Nem's surrender. He was surprised, but he and his colleague agreed to contact their boss, the deputy chief of the Civil Police, who also encouraged Azenha to pursue the idea. And then, according to Azenha, the deputy chief told him to pass a message directly to Nem: 'Our information is that you will not survive if you remain in Rocinha.' It was a brutal confirmation of Nem's worst fears – his life and those of his family were under threat.

A week later, he ordered Danúbia to go. As a protective measure, she hacked off her blonde locks and dyed her hair brown before slipping away and heading west through Barra to the upmarket district of Recreio dos Bandeirantes, where Nem had secured a safe flat for her along with her mother and daughter.

The next day, Wednesday 9 November 2011, Nem's right-hand man, Feijão, urged him to consider a different course of action. He should flee Rocinha, Feijão argued, and go into hiding. Feijão had reassured his boss that he would look after the finances when he went underground. Yet Nem was still reluctant to leave the rest of his family, and above all to leave Rocinha. It wasn't just that he felt safe there; his entire identity was bound up with the place. Yes, he had travelled about Brazil a bit. But home was the familiar snake-shaped Estrada da Gávea and the little capillaries that led away from the main road into Rocinha's dense, dark forest of dwellings.

There was one major drawback to staying. If he stayed and was then found by the police, he risked being either killed or humiliated. And even if he avoided the worst, for a Don of the Hill to be arrested in the favela, without putting up armed resistance, would be regarded by the bandido community as a pathetic, shameful sign of weakness.

The world beyond the slum was a foreign country, and one beginning to look unstable and dangerous. Taking flight would undoubtedly entail risks. But so would surrender. For if Nem finally went ahead with the plan to hand himself in so close to pacification, many Rocinhans would conclude that he had been collaborating with the government and Beltrame on a long-term basis. He would be branded an informer, and he knew as well as anyone what happened to informers. As for staying and fighting a last-ditch battle, surely this would make a mockery of everything he had worked for over the last decade?

So what was it to be? Should he go into hiding? Should he flee? Should he surrender? Or should he fight? There was no satisfactory answer. Each was extremely risky. Each might have a disastrous outcome.

That afternoon, Nem invited Azenha to come to Rocinha. And so between 6 and 6.30 p.m., the lawyer arrived in the favela with two colleagues, father and son Demóstenes and André Cruz, in a black Toyota Corolla belonging to Demóstenes's son-in-law.

The scene greeting Azenha when he arrived at Nem's family home was extraordinary. 'I've never seen anything like it,' he remembers. 'Hundreds of people had gathered there in a collective demonstration of friendship and affection. It was one big bawling fest – everyone crying because they thought they might never see him again.'

Before he could do anything, Nem had to wait for his mother to return home to look after the kids. Then, at about 6.50 p.m., the news suddenly broke that four cars had left Rocinha in convoy, only to be stopped by police just a mile further on in Gávea. They were carrying Coelho, the boss of ADA in São Carlos, and his number two, Foca, the man who had been kidnapped from Laboriaux the previous April. Another occupant was a trafficker on release from prison who had neglected to mention to his friends that he was obliged to wear an electronic tag around his ankle. The cops were following his every step.

Live news channels were soon replaying pictures of the dramatic arrests on a loop. When I ask him about the incident, Nem claims that he hardly registered the breaking story blaring from his TV. 'I was a bit upset for the boys,' he says, 'but it didn't bother me that much.' And yet this was the very route he was intending to take later that evening. If he knew of his imminent flight, his apparent indifference is curious. Both Azenha and Feijão had made it plain to him that Rocinha was by now under a full blockade.

Nem asked someone to drop by Simone's place and pick up his daughters, Thayná and Fernanda. After seeing her father, Thayná told her mother later that evening, 'There was something strange about Dad. He really annoyed me because he hugged us and said he was going to have to go away but that he would reappear when we least expected it.'

As Nem went about his preparations, his options continued to revolve in his mind: flight, fight, concealment or surrender. Which was it to be?

To live or to die. This was always part of the equation, whether Nem liked it or not. It was not just a question of his own life and death, but life and death for the people dearest to him; for his enemies; for the innocent and the guilty. He could almost feel death's warm breath on the back of his neck. Death was not a friend he sought, but given the circumstances of his life, it was one he nonetheless had to respect. Even now, he would still prefer to do so at a distance.

If death took him, it might take a lot of other people as well. The possibility lurked at the end of each path leading from this fateful crossroads. So the question for Nem was simple: which path was death least likely to follow?

He couldn't be accused of not taking his decision seriously, packing his agenda with meetings and consultations. His next appointment was with José Junior, the charismatic and highly successful founder of Afroreggae. In 1993, in the wake of the Vigário

Geral massacre,[2] JJ had founded first a newspaper and then a charity that aimed to offer the adolescents in Rio's slums something more than the usual prospects of drugs and unemployment. Afroreggae gained worldwide recognition after the release of a successful film, *Favela Rising*. Its most inspirational programme persuaded adolescents and young men and women who were in danger of being seduced by the world of drugs and violence to embrace instead Brazil's remarkable musical heritage and devote themselves to performing in the most breathtaking ensembles. José Junior attracted sponsorship from some of the biggest companies in Rio, and even from Spain's largest bank. As the money for his favela projects rolled in, he had also developed a close political relationship with the state governor and with José Mariano Beltrame.

When Nem and José Junior had first met a few months earlier, Nem had had the same puzzling effect on JJ as he did on most people. They struggled to see him as a mobster but at the same time they could not shake the knowledge that he swam in the lower depths. I know how José Junior felt. Throughout my conversations with Nem, my strong and abiding impression was that he passionately wanted to do good but that this was impossible to reconcile with being in charge of a large group of armed men and a criminal organisation boasting a huge turnover.

'There are no good traffickers,' JJ avers. 'There are just less bad ones. They are all bad – they all kill. But Nem's a cool guy and I like him. I didn't used to but I came to like him. The guys from Rocinha are more thoughtful than the rest, and Nem is a touch more humble.'

José Junior usually insisted that traffickers wanting his help would have to come to him, not the other way about. But he realised that Nem couldn't leave home on this occasion, so on the evening of 9 November, he went to Rocinha. JJ was yet another emissary hoping to persuade Nem to surrender. Before he left for the favela, he contacted the government, the police and the judge investigating

Nem's case. They were all informed about the impending rendez-vous. It was probably the best advertised of all Nem's clandestine encounters.

Around 8 p.m., Nem's mother turned up to take charge of the children. Soon after this, he received a message telling him that José Junior had also entered the favela.

Outside the tiny apartment where his mother lived and where Nem had grown up, the precarious tall buildings that leaned over the narrow alley darkened in the fading light in preparation for the meeting between the two most influential members of Rio's disadvantaged communities. With his gold hoop earrings, dapper dress sense and closely trimmed facial hair, José Junior was for many the embodiment of political cool. Others criticised him for being too close to Cabral and his government.

The atmosphere was friendly but businesslike. In the middle of the meeting, José Junior spoke by mobile phone to one of his government connections to clarify a couple of issues. But although the exchange was cordial, Nem ultimately was not persuaded by JJ's mediation efforts. Nonetheless, he took down JJ's mobile phone number, and the pair agreed to keep their communication channel open.

Nem's family wanted him to choose the third option and flee. He says they were appalled by his initial plan of going into hiding in Rocinha. His mother and his daughter Eduarda, now twelve years old, pleaded with him to reconsider. Nem explained that he had a refuge in the favela that no policeman would ever find. His family were sceptical. If he were found, he would likely be killed straight away. There were just too many policemen who might want his scalp.

He was still undecided when Feijão arrived. What was it about this man that Nem trusted? Was it his friendship, stretching back to their youth? Or was it that Feijão was both efficient and, as the head of the residents' association, considered acceptable to the outside world? Nem not only trusted him; he relied on him.

Feijão brought more alarming news: the forest surrounding Rocinha was swarming with BOPE officers. He also said that he had received a tip-off that pacification had been brought forward several days and would be launched at 5 a.m. the following day. It was certainly true that the favela was surrounded; the arrest of Coelho and the other ADA leaders confirmed it. But the forest had not yet been occupied, and pacification was still four days away. In retrospect, Feijão very much wanted Nem to go.

Finally, Nem made his decision. He took Azenha aside and said: 'We're going for it.' Azenha called Mussi and warned the Civil Police that the surrender was going to happen. But even at this moment when Nem has apparently committed at long last to a decision, when he has chosen which road to take from the crossroads he has been stuck at for so long, everything may not be as it seems. Has he definitively chosen surrender? Or is this another instance of his talent for keeping the maximum number of options open, even as they diminish? Are Azenha and Feijão now in control of his destiny? None of this is clear. What is clear is that he is about to leave Rocinha, the place he has made his own and where he has made his name.

As he was making his final farewells to his mother and children, Nem received a text from Otávio. The intelligence agent had been following the arrest of Nem's partners in Gávea earlier that day. *My friend*, the text read, *you still have time*. Otávio was hoping that Nem would make the sensible move and give himself up. *My brother*, Nem replied, *thank you for everything. The Lord understands what you have tried to do. May He shine his light on you and your family*. It was a touching exchange between two men on either side of the law who had developed a genuine respect for each other.

When he got the return text, Otávio muttered under his breath,

'The fool. Doesn't he realise he's cornered?' But Otávio may have made the wrong call. Nem understood all too well that he was cornered. He could not stay. Yet if he did surrender, it would again give rise to the suspicion that he had been collaborating. Perhaps he had another option?

Portão Vermelho lies high up Rocinha, where the favela borders a patch of the Atlantic rainforest. At night, the poor illumination and thick foliage turn this peaceful, shady corner into a place of darkness, even malevolence.

Nem arrived there on the back of a motorcycle taxi sometime after 10 p.m., but he and Feijão found it hard to pick out the silhouette of the large black Toyota Corolla. Azenha, along with Demóstenes and André Cruz, stepped forward from the shadows. Nem moved to get in the rear door of the car.

'Uh-uh,' said Feijão, stopping him. 'You've got to get in the boot.'

Nem froze. He thought he had misheard and looked at Feijão as if his most trusted counsellor had taken leave of his senses. All his instincts kicked in. If you enter the boot of a car, he thought, that usually only means one thing. Even if it's your lawyer's car. Especially if it's your lawyer's car.

Feijão held his ground. 'It's for your own good. If anyone sees you – Rio's most wanted – in the back of the car, the first thing they'll do is machine-gun the whole fucking lot of you.' This was actually a very plausible observation, and after a brief conference, everyone agreed it was the right idea.

Nem climbed into the boot. Feijão placed the holdall stuffed with cash – €50,050 and R$ 55,000 – on the back seat next to André Cruz. The money was payment owing to the three lawyers. Swaddled in a tarpaulin in the womb of the car, Nem was rapidly computing the possible consequences of this dramatic move. What will the favela say? Will my kids be okay? What about the money? Who can I trust?

More than ever, the issue of trust was preying on his mind. Nem had spent a decade knowing more than anyone else. Information had been critical to his success. To his survival. In the boot of the car, however, he was cut off. And as he left the favela, perhaps for the last time, he felt as if he no longer knew what was going on. He began to sweat. Was it a trap? 'I thought that it might even be an attempt to kidnap me, and if it was, I would probably not come out of it alive,' he tells me.

The tension mounted as Azenha tried desperately to put in a call to alert Inspector Mussi that the parade was about to begin. Azenha finally had everything in place, but, to his fury, no network signal. 'This was the fatal lapse on my part and on the part of Demóstenes and André,' he later admitted. 'We should have waited a little for the signal and only left once Mussi was in place with his team. It was a real error on our part.'

Slowly the Toyota moved up the hill towards the peak of Estrada da Gávea.

But instead of rendezvousing with Mussi and his colleagues from the Civil Police, Azenha and his two friends ran directly into the roadblock erected by the Military Police. André Cruz told the first officer that he was the honorary consul of the Democratic Republic of Congo in Rio and therefore enjoyed diplomatic immunity, as did his vehicle. The policeman would not be granted access to the car boot.

The officer called in his superior, Disraeli Gomes, a 32-year-old lieutenant who was in overall charge of this and fifteen other roadblocks that had been mounted around Rocinha to monitor everyone entering and exiting the favela. Earlier that evening he had told his men in a pep talk that it would make no difference if the President of Brazil drove out of Rocinha in his official car that night: the vehicle would still be subjected to a thorough search.

As Gomes arrived, Azenha noticed that at last he had a phone signal. He immediately called Mussi. The lawyer considered it vital to hand Nem over to the team from the Civil Police, because it was a faction inside the Military Police who were hunting him as a trophy. He simply could not afford for the boot to be opened.

What followed is contested, and still subject to court proceedings. Gomes claims that when he and Azenha walked away from the rest of the group, Azenha told him that the boot was stuffed full of cash. It was an extraordinary story – the team had just been at a function in Rocinha raising money for an NGO in the Congo, and they were transporting the funds out of the favela in preparation to send them abroad. He then remarked, according to Gomes, that there was over one million in there in dollars, euros and reals. Gomes explained that he took this to be an attempt to bribe him, and he promptly arrested Azenha.

Azenha denies ever having said any such thing. Instead he says he tried to explain to Gomes that they were en route to the 15th Precinct for a prearranged meeting with officers of the Civil Police, then offered the Military Policeman his phone so that he might talk to Mussi on the other end of the line. Azenha later asked why, if he had been arrested, as Gomes claimed, did the lieutenant allow him back into the Toyota? And why did he allow him to keep talking on the phone? Gomes responded by saying he was still worried that if the consul was who he said he was, he might fall foul of a diplomatic incident and shoulder the blame for everything.

At this point, one of Gomes's colleagues whispered to the lieutenant that although the three men had got out of the Toyota, the back end of the car was still sitting low. 'There's something heavy in there,' he concluded.

Gomes then announced that everyone would make their way to

the station. Azenha and the Cruzes were quite happy with this, as they assumed Gomes meant they would be heading for the 15th Precinct of the Civil Police, which was much the nearest station, in the middle of Gávea. Gomes had decided, however, he later explained, that because the incident involved a diplomat, and cash that was to be exported from the country, the whole affair was a matter for the Federal Police.

Both the Mussi and the Gomes versions were going up the chain of the respective Civil and Military Police commands. And both were reaching the Deputy Chiefs of the two forces who were in Berlin together with the Secretary for Public Security. Beltrame, at least, must have known much if not all of what was going on.

As so often happens in Brazil with controversial matters, the case of the black Toyota quickly degenerated into a proxy battle between the Civil and Military Police. When the Toyota made an unexpected right turn after the convoy had set off, it did so on the assumption that everyone was going not to the federal head-quarters but to the 15th Precinct. Azenha's decision to stop at the Naval Club was in order to wait for the support of the Civil Police. That help arrived, although the senior officer from the PC failed to win the argument about whose arrest Nem was. If procedure had been properly followed, this would have been a Civil Police case, as the warrant out for Nem's arrest had been issued by Rio state, not by the federal government. It was truly a farce – a specifically Brazilian farce.

So what really happened? Was Nem trying to escape? Or did he want to hand himself in? For over two years I had been exam-ining the events of that day from as many angles as possible. Nem knows more than he is telling me, but it is almost as though he wants to see whether I can work it out. One critical witness, Feijão, is dead. Who knows which if any of the others are telling the truth?

I asked several people close to Nem what they believed his plan was.

His first lawyer believes that Nem had been set up by Feijão and that the 'escape' plan may have ended in him being kidnapped at Feijão's behest had it not been luckily derailed by the roadblock. Certain aspects of Feijão's behaviour suggested that he was trying to manipulate the situation in his favour. But the theory implies that Mussi and Azenha were somehow in on it, and that makes no sense at all.

Inspector Mussi believes that Nem was trying to escape with the knowledge of Azenha. This is possible but implies an extraordinary risk for Azenha and the Cruzes. Had the plan gone awry (as seems likely given that Rocinha was surrounded) and there was proof that the lawyers were abetting Nem's flight, the three men would have faced a very severe penalty.

Azenha says that Nem never seriously entertained the idea of fleeing and that the plan was always to hand himself in to the Civil Police. This makes a lot of sense, and certainly the actions of the three lawyers and the PC are consistent with this. Had Azenha succeeded in calling Mussi before the Toyota had left Rocinha, then this would be demonstrably true. Because he only called *after* being stopped at the roadblock, there remains an element of doubt.

José Mariano Beltrame, the Secretary for Public Security, dismisses it all as an elaborate bluff, saying that Nem was simply playing for time and that, having miscalculated, he had decided to do a runner. Beltrame's dismissive response does not quite square with his actions. Time and again he approved negotiations between Nem and his officials. Some had been potentially quite dangerous. He was also given a blow-by-blow account by the deputy chief of the Civil Police of the events on the night of 9 November. He later professed not to understand what members of the Civil Police from faraway Maricá were doing at the scene. Yet he knew full well.

Beltrame had good reasons for being sceptical about Nem handing himself in, but he was certainly prepared to give it several tries.

All these people had their own agenda. It almost seemed as if Nem had come to resemble a pawn in his own game. But he wasn't. Whatever the byzantine confusion of his arrest, in his world, right to the end, if anyone was in fact directing everything, it is most likely to have been Nem himself.

Nem insisted to me that he was making a bid for freedom and that he had arranged a rendezvous with somebody who would hide him for a few months, 'until the dust settled'. He would then, he maintained, hand himself in through the offices of José Junior. This is plausible, but I think it would have left him vulnerable to both his enemies inside the police and his enemies among other traffickers. His clearest commitment was to his family, and his children especially. As a dead father, he would be no good to anyone, so this course of action strikes me as just too risky.

There is an answer hovering somewhere, and on occasions I almost feel I can touch it. Then, as I am going back over the dozens of interviews I conducted, something stands out. During the negotiations between Nem and Rivaldo Barbosa, then the sub-secretary for intelligence in Rio's security ministry, Barbosa explained to Nem's lawyer that the ministry would prefer to stage an arrest rather than accept his surrender. The discussions were taking place in the run-up to the 2010 gubernatorial elections, and arresting Nem would be excellent timing for Cabral, who was seeking to serve another term. The lawyer agreed. It was advantageous to Nem. If he was arrested rather than handing himself in, nobody could even remotely accuse him of being a snitch. Indeed, his stock would rise among Rio's bandidos. An arrest was win-win.

Just as my research is coming to an end, I have a conversation with Simone. She is describing Thayná, Nem's adopted daughter, going to say farewell to her father on the evening of his arrest. 'It's only my opinion,' she says, 'but I think he knew the police would get him if he left Rocinha. I don't know, but it's quite possible that he set up the whole thing – his arrest, I mean.'

Later that evening, once word of his arrest spread, Simone went to his mother's apartment, where the clan was gathering. Everyone was crying and lamenting the news of Nem's detention. 'Except, of all people, Dona Irene, who was sitting there perfectly calm sipping a beer,' Simone recalls. 'I imagined she, as his mother, would have been among the most upset of all.' Amidst the hubbub, Simone heard her say quietly, 'Well, it was a little quicker than I thought.'

'Sometimes,' I tell Antônio on my last visit to the jail, 'I can't help thinking that you planned the arrest yourself.' I leave the sentence hanging. He doesn't say anything, but he looks at me and gives me a cheeky smile.

It immediately brings to mind the magical scene in Carol Reed's film *The Third Man* when Orson Welles's Harry Lime appears for the first time. He is standing in a doorway at night. As a light flashes across his face, he gives precisely the same smile to his old friend from high school, Holly Martins.

Antônio never said anything to confirm it, except at the end of the interview, he smiled again and said, 'One day I'll tell you the whole story.' But I am almost certain he wasn't planning to hide, flee, surrender or fight. He was one step ahead of everyone else in this elaborate game. In a typically adroit manoeuvre, he had come up with a fifth option – his own arrest.

He was both the spider and the fly.

EPILOGUE

At 12.45 on Sunday 13 November 2011, the flags of Rio and Brazil were run up a pole positioned just above Rocinha's S-Bend. A choir from the local battalion of the Military Police burst into a rendition of Brazil's jovial national anthem as some 250 residents of the favela clapped and cheered.

'ROCINHA IS OURS!' the newspaper O Globo would trumpet the following day, describing how the three territories of Rocinha, Vidigal and Chácara do Céu no longer belonged to 'armed traffickers who have tyrannised over 100,000 people for decades. They are back in the hands of the state and of all cariocas, with no exceptions.'

In the days before the occupation, the community knew it was coming. 'The prevailing sentiment was fear,' observes Margaret Day, a 40-year-old American who was living in Rocinha. 'People were scared. They were scared because it was a big step into the unknown. They didn't trust the police. They didn't know how long the police were going to stay. And while nobody was particularly enthusiastic about the traffickers' criminal activity, they gave the community a certain stability. If you didn't go looking for trouble, you wouldn't find it.' Indeed, Margaret says that as an African American, she felt safer in Rocinha than in her home city of New York.

The evening before the occupation, frenetic commercial activity had seized Lower Rocinha. Some people were buying supplies in anticipation of being holed up in their homes for a long period. Many crowded around the itinerant salesmen who were flogging off their pirated DVDs, CDs and software for a knockdown R$1 apiece, believing that the new pacification force might want to target their profession in the name of Hollywood and Silicon Valley.

At about 11 p.m., Margaret drifted happily back to the entrance of Lower Rocinha after a night on the Asphalt with some friends. When she had left the favela earlier, Barcelos, Via Ápia, Cowboy Street and Valão were all breathlessly busy. But as she returned to her home turf, Rocinha was empty and almost noiseless. It was Saturday – the social high spot of the weekly calendar, when half Rio would normally descend on the Clube de Emoçoes for the baile funk. Tonight, she thought, was probably the quietest night in Rocinha for over 30 years. The parties, the shops, the hawkers and the moto taxis had all packed up and were leaving as Margaret walked slowly up the hill.

Despite the general sense of foreboding about the impending occupation, felt throughout Rocinha, Nem had indicated that there would be no resistance. If ADA were to put up a fight, he felt that the only possible outcome would be entirely unnecessary bloodletting – and he wanted no part of that. But he was now under arrest in prison. Would his influence hold? Margaret, like the great majority in the favela, had no idea whether the remaining traffickers had resolved to resist or not.

Before returning to her small flat in Cachopa, Margaret stopped at her local store to buy some supplies in case she was stuck at home for a while. She hesitated over what food to choose for such an eventuality. The shopkeeper noticed that she was a tad inebriated and, having got to know her over the six weeks she had been living in the favela, he gave her a stern talking-to. 'You must go home now, and stay home,' he said, clearly and slowly. 'Do NOT leave your apartment until it is clearly safe to do so.'

She wandered upstairs with her shopping, but her mind was a jumble of thoughts. What am I about to experience? she asked herself. Should I try to get some photographs, or will the invasion force end up shooting me? She started tidying her apartment, thinking, rather oddly, 'Well, if BOPE are going to come and search my apartment, I might as well make sure it's looking nice.' After that, she fell into an uncomfortable sleep.

At 2.30 a.m., while Margaret slept, security forces closed off all roads leading in and out of Rocinha, São Conrado and Gávea. They also blocked Avenida Niemayer,[1] which links Leblon with Chácara do Céu and Vidigal. Naturally, the Zuzu Angel Tunnel was shut down completely, and diversions were set up in several parts of the South Zone. Over 1,000 members of the police, military and special forces took up positions in the neighbouring districts, all pumped and ready to go.

Yet inside the favela, the atmosphere remained uncannily still. For a few hours, it seemed a world away from the maelstrom of soldiers, drugs, corruption, police and armoured cars. It was as though Rocinha had been placed under a spell – no music, no spluttering bike engines, no talk, no people. The streets had never been emptier. Now the only sound was that of the cocks crowing.

At exactly 4.09, before dawn had broken, seven armoured personnel carriers started rumbling up São Vicente de Marques, the main road leading from Gávea towards Rocinha. The only resistance they met was in the form of oil, which some of the traffickers had spread across the road – a quixotic gesture against amphibious vehicles with caterpillar tracks.

At the same time, 40 BOPE officers began their stealthy advance from the bottom of Estrada da Gávea. One minute later, the operations against the favelas of Chácara do Céu and Vidigal commenced.

Margaret awoke with a start. The noise of helicopters seemingly right above her apartment was excruciatingly loud. She had not slept enough to be properly hung-over. The lingering alcohol was soon neutralised by the powerful surge of adrenalin rushing through her body.

She could not see the main drag from her apartment, so she texted her friend Leandro, who lived higher up. *It's crazy*, he reported. *There are tanks everywhere.* Suddenly, the dogs that slept on the roof of Margaret's building were barking and squealing, accompanied by a great thumping sound. The father of the family next door clattered down from the roof, leading the dogs down the narrow stairs. It turned out that BOPE officers were running all over the favela roofs. 'It was like in the film *Crouching Tiger, Hidden Dragon*,' someone recalled, 'just so strange.'

At 6.20, Margaret received a text from Leandro. *Are you coming out? Let's go and explore.* At first she was reluctant, knowing that the testosterone-fuelled brigade was running around Rocinha. Leandro pointed out that the TV had announced that pacification had been completed without a shot being fired, and that BOPE and the other security forces were in full control of Rocinha. *I'll meet you at Bob's Hamburgers in five minutes*, he said.

Margaret's friendly next-door family pleaded with her not to go. 'You're crazy – you don't understand how dangerous this is.' But Margaret insisted. She and Leandro gingerly strolled down Estrada da Gávea towards the S-Bend.

Dawn had broken, but the sun had not yet brushed away the night's murk. The emptiness was dreamlike and slightly threatening, as though all the people had simply been removed. Just before the S-Bend, Margaret managed to grab a railing to stop herself from slipping on the oil placed there by the traffickers to prevent, or at least slow down, BOPE's incursion.

Brushing herself down, she saw a BOPE team creeping furtively up Estrada da Gávea with their semi-automatics pointing at her chest and head. Every hair on her body stood on end as the officers made up their minds as to whether she was a potential threat or just somebody really, really dumb who had decided to walk around at this time on this day. They plumped for the latter and walked past her, focusing on the next possible booby trap.

As she got down to the passarella, the pedestrian bridge that marks the beginning of Rocinha, she saw people sleeping in doorways and on the pavement. She remarked to Leandro that she had never seen that in Rocinha. 'Every favela that is pacified,' he explained, 'attracts homeless people because they think there will be a bunch of handouts – food, shelter, perhaps even money.'

Hundreds of favela residents were already queuing for buses, as they did every day. Margaret could not figure out how exactly they had made it to the bus stops: the streets had been deserted. But come rain or shine, come traffickers or BOPE, these people had no choice but to get to their back-breaking work in the middle-class homes of the South Zone. And so they had slunk here down the alleys and lanes, somehow dodging the men with guns.

The pacification of Rocinha was always going to be much easier than its sister operation in Alemão a year earlier. Logistically, there was no comparison. Alemão had 44 entrances, Rocinha just two – one at the top of Estrada da Gávea and one at the bottom. Two days before, BOPE and others had moved into the Atlantic forest surrounding the favela so that it would be impossible for any bandidos to escape that way.

Yet even in the absence of any opposition, the operation was quite a spectacle. Over 1,000 members of the military, civil and Federal Police, plus the marines, assumed control of the three favelas – Rocinha, Chácara do Céu and Vidigal. Another 1,500 were part of the logistical support for Operation Peace Shock, as it was dubbed.

José Beltrame had thought it likely, given the relatively pacific traditions of ADA, that Rocinha would be an easy victory relative to somewhere like Alemão. He suspected that the real challenge would be managing the place afterwards. And here his fears were entirely justified.

Less than three weeks after Nem's arrest, somebody walked into the PC's Gávea station and handed over a DVD. It was accompanied by a note written in capital letters that read:

MESSRS POLICEMEN,
  I HAVE FAITH IN YOU. GANGSTER MUST BE ARRESTED. THE TAPE WAS RECORDED BY ME. I HAD HAD ENOUGH OF SEEING SUCH LIES. NEM AND WILLIAM DA ROCINHA CELEBRATING AT THE SMOKE SHOP AND SELLING ARMS. THE POLICE HERE IS ON THE TAKE AND DOES NOTHING. WILLIAM GETS SUPPORT AND MONEY FROM TRAFFICKING. I BELIEVE THAT WITH THE TAPE IN THIS ENVELOPE THESE SHAMELESS MEN SHOULD BE ARRESTED. LET PEACE BE WITH EVERYONE. AMEN

The contents of the DVD were explosive. It showed Nem meeting William da Rocinha, the former president of the residents' association, who had been wrongly imprisoned in 2005 for his alleged links to traffickers. Nem could be seen handing over a large sum of money to William, who appeared to give him guns in return. A semi-automatic weapon was all too prominent in the video clip, which was uncharacteristic, as Nem always sought to avoid any public identification with guns.

As a result of the DVD, William received a four-year prison sentence for arms trafficking – a charge that was also piled on to Nem's growing list of alleged offences. It looked very bad for both of them. Sitting in jail without access to television or newspapers, only weekly magazines, Nem had minimal contact with the outside world.

But one thing he did know was that the person who had filmed him meeting William was Feijão, his confidant and current president of the residents' association. When he saw the video, Nem must have realised, as did William, that the footage had been doctored to make their exchange seem more sinister than it actually was. They had both been set up. When forensic examination proved that the DVD had been tampered with, the courts declared both William and Nem innocent.

It is hard to imagine who else might have arranged for the DVD to be handed in. From Feijão's perspective, it killed two birds with one stone. Since Nem's arrest, William had been gaining popularity in the polls, and Feijão's position as boss of the residents' association was under threat. The DVD ensured that William would be eliminated as a political rival; indeed, support for him ebbed quickly once he had been charged.

It also threatened a still longer prison term for Nem. Feijão was Nem's money man. He also claimed to remaining members of ADA in the favela that he was his hand-picked successor. It appeared that he was trying to unify political and trafficking power in one person – himself.

Around 3 p.m. on 26 March 2012, Feijão was strolling down a narrow alley linking Via Ápia with Cowboy Street. About halfway down, a motorcyclist whizzed by and fired six bullets. Three of them hit Feijão in the back; the remaining three missed their target. Feijão, it seems, had fatally overplayed his hand. His was the sixth violent death in Rocinha since Nem's arrest and the favela's pacification. It had easily the most far-reaching consequences.

After several months, a computer forensics expert engaged by William's support campaign was finally able to prove what had been obvious to Nem all along: the video had been Photoshopped. Yes, the two men had met, and Nem had offered William money for his campaign. William had felt threatened and decided it was wisest not to resist the offer on this occasion. But there had been no hand-over of guns. Investigators even managed to track down the man who had tampered with the digital evidence, who confessed that Feijão was behind it.

Who killed Feijão? Not long after his death, FM, one of Nem's former employees, was arrested by Rivaldo Barbosa, Beltrame's former intelligence chief, who had since been appointed head of Rio's homicide unit. Feijão had had many enemies inside ADA, especially once Nem was in prison; whether FM was acting on his own, or whether he was carrying out orders, nobody knows.

Between the occupation of a favela designated for pacification and the installation of a fully operational pacification unit, the Secretary for Public Security deploys a tough transitional force that aims to neutralise the influence of any remaining traffickers. Once Alemão was under government control, part of that temporary force engaged in exactly the type of behaviour that Beltrame wished to avoid at all costs: they started extorting the residents. Civil Police officers nicknamed Alemão and the surrounding favelas Serra Pelada, a reference to the garimpo that had attracted so many young Brazilian men in the 1980s.[2] It was a territory where they could simply help themselves to money, weapons and drugs, often left behind by the traffickers who had escaped. One of the chief culprits was Inspector Leonardo Torres, the Thunder, on whom Governor Cabral had lavished praise as a model officer during the incursions into Alemão in 2007 and 2008.[3] The cheroot-smoking Rambo-style figure had been bullying and threatening his way through the area of Ramos, right next to Alemão. Today he is in jail, convicted and disgraced.

Ironically, the corrupt officers counted as their allies some of the leading drug traffickers in Rio. The Federal Police investigation that eventually uncovered this web of extortion had begun when they intercepted a message from a Civil Police officer sent to one of Nem's colleagues from ADA who had sought refuge in Rocinha in 2009. *Tomorrow you will have a BOPE operation there*, the message began. *They are already in the forest.* Naturally, had the PC been dealing with Nem himself, it would have been harder for the Federal Police to pick the message up because of Nem's telecoms security arrangements.

The corrupt officers had been working with both ADA and Red Command, each officer receiving some 50,000 reals a month for their efforts. These included selling weapons to the cartels.

As details came to light of Serra Pelada and Operation Guillotine, the investigation into it mounted by the Federal Police, Beltrame was initially quick to defend the chief of Rio's Civil Police, Allan Turnowski, who resolutely denied any knowledge of extortion. Three days later, he was fired after it appeared that he had tipped off one of the most senior PC officers involved in Serra Pelada that the feds were tracking him.

Serra Pelada had inflicted considerable damage on pacification in Alemão. Governor Cabral and Beltrame needed to avoid a repeat in Rocinha. This they managed, but they couldn't prevent something even worse from happening.

By the middle of July 2013, the Police Unit of Pacification (UPP) was an established presence in Rocinha, comprising some 700 officers whose function was to maintain law and order, support the residents in going about their daily business, encourage support for the UPP, the Military Police and other public forces, and seek out and confiscate illegal weapons. One Sunday, its chief, Major Edson dos Santos, held a meeting with his officers and handed out the names of several dozen people who, he said, continued to work with ADA and were suspected of hiding the organisation's guns.

Later that afternoon, Amarildo de Souza, a 43-year-old brick-layer, was walking from his home to buy some limes when a UPP officer called out to him, 'Hey, Bull!' Due to his profession, Amarildo was well built, and he had a reputation for eating like a bull too. 'I'm going to have to take you in for questioning.'

That was the last anyone outside the UPP saw of Amarildo. The headquarters of the UPP was located in Portão Vermelho, the spot where Nem had entered the boot of the Toyota Corolla two years previously. The station was made from several seagoing containers, and despite its makeshift look, it was a very busy office.

Inside, the officers made it plain to the Bull that they believed he knew where ADA's weapons store was located. In fact they had mistaken his identity – there was another Amarildo in Rocinha who *had* been a member of ADA. The Amarildo now in captivity had, of course, no idea. To persuade him to give up the information he didn't have, officers subjected him to what is known as 'the subma-rine'. According to the police investigation into his death, they placed a plastic bag over his head. When he was close to asphyxi-ation, they quickly removed the bag and plunged his head into a bucket of cold water. As he breathed in instinctively, his lungs filled with water.

One of the many things the officers didn't know that day was that this Amarildo was an epileptic. Before long, he died. Conveniently and mysteriously, the two security cameras at the door of their headquarters stopped working for a couple of hours. However, a year after his death, *Jornal Nacional*, Brazil's main nightly news programme, broadcast astonishing footage from the gates of the compound in which two BOPE vehicles are seen entering and exiting the UPP headquarters on the evening of Amarildo's death. The forensic experts called in to comment demonstrated the chilling possibility that they were removing a body from the compound. No body, no crime. Who needs bandidos when you've got the police?

The limited trust that the police and Beltrame had built up in the year and a half since the occupation of Rocinha evaporated overnight after news of Amarildo's death was made public. In time-honoured fashion, the Rocinhans blocked the Zuzu Angel Tunnel as the nascent cooperation with the UPP collapsed.

Amarildo's death coincided with a much greater security head-ache that was troubling the authorities not just in Rio, but across Brazil. The summer of 2013 had seen a huge wave of anti-government demonstrations sweep the country. It had begun in São Paolo at the beginning of June, when a small group protesting against another rise in local transport fares was broken up by the Military Police using bully-boy tactics usually reserved for the favelas. These demonstrators, however, were good middle-class children, and before long they had a phalanx of lawyers asking questions of the authorities on their behalf. At the same time, the fate of the protes-tors, and the much larger group of demonstrators who took to the streets after the initial event, was being monitored and broadcast by a remarkable new phenomenon: Media Ninja.

This group of young journalists began streaming the demon-strations live over social media. Initially ignored by the two most influential papers, *Folha de São Paulo* and *O Globo*, as well as by the television networks, Media Ninja gained a huge following as it broad-cast frightening examples of police brutality in real time.

Before long, demonstrations had broken out in more than 100 cities, just at the time when the Confederations Cup was kicking off. This is FIFA's curtain-raiser for the World Cup, held by the host nation in the preceding year to demonstrate how well prepared it is for the world's biggest sporting event twelve months later.

In Brazil, the Confederations Cup was a huge embarrassment, as supporters from countries across the globe had to make their way through thousands of angry protestors. Lula's hand-picked successor as president, Dilma Rousseff, against whom much of the protestors' ire was directed, faced boos and derisive whistling when she opened proceedings in Brasília. The growing stench of mega-corruption had begun to waft around her party, which was embroiled in a huge scandal known as Mensalão, the Monthly Payoff. Nor was Sepp Blatter, the president of FIFA, exempt. Indeed, one of the popular slogans during the protests that summer was 'Fuck Off FIFA', suggesting that the corrupt business deals handed out during the construction of new stadia for the World Cup was putting even Brazilians off the event.

The demonstrations reached their most violent intensity in Rio. Before they erupted, Governor Cabral had boasted approval ratings of between 55 and 60 per cent. Within a six-week period to the middle of July 2013, these had fallen to just 13 per cent. Suddenly he and his government were looking vulnerable.

And then Amarildo was killed. His death threatened pacification, the one policy that had widespread public backing in Rio as a whole, and which had, in important respects, started to pay real dividends. However, it was an uneven picture. The reduction in the number of armed members of drug gangs on the streets meant that homicides in the pacified favelas were down by as much as 75 per cent, as were deaths attributed to police in encounters with traffickers. But it also meant that the policing function of the gangs ceased too. As a consequence, domestic violence had increased four-fold, while rape was three times more common and burglary twice as likely.[4]

While most of the bandidos melted into the background, they and their guns didn't disappear. In Rocinha, the pacification police controlled the main areas and Estrada da Gávea. But two years after pacification, I was taking a stroll around the back of Rua Um when the alley I was walking down opened out into a bar area, with furniture fashioned from stone. Sitting around drinking coffee and looking indifferent were nine heavily armed young men, who stared at me and my guide with the dead eyes of the gunman. Fortunately, an apparently responsible man with a paunch was in charge. In his late thirties, he shook my hand amicably, and as soon as the gang members recognised my guide, any tension evaporated. Four days later, the man with the paunch was shot dead on a Saturday afternoon during a confrontation with a UPP patrol.

Traditionally, presidents Lula and Rousseff, along with their Workers' Party, received powerful backing from the favelas, especially since the implementation of the PAC, the Programme of Accelerated Growth, which had been running for several years. In Rio, another party, the PMDB, to which Governor Cabral belonged, were the local allies of the Workers' Party. The favelas had not joined the mass demonstrations that were shaking Rio at the time, and which were more a manifestation of the Asphalt's frustration with the corrupt practices and chicanery associated with both the federal government and Cabral's administration in Rio state.

However, Amarildo's death threatened to bring out if not all favelas, then certainly Rocinha – which would have been regarded as an enormous symbolic blow to Cabral. When asked what he was going to do about it, he tried to shift responsibility for the problem. 'I'm not the police,' he told reporters. 'I have the Secretary of State for that. Go ask Beltrame!' The Secretary of State was under pressure to get results in Rocinha. He had one card up his sleeve: he called in Officer Orlando Zaccone of the Civil Police.

Zaccone is a remarkable character. A Buddhist, he is often minded to quote in conversation both the French philosopher Michel Foucault and the American writer Mike Davis, author of *Planet of Slums*, a book that is highly influential in radical circles in Brazil. Davis, he says, demonstrates that some form of military control in slums was probably established by the ruling class in order to ensure that their inhabitants did not develop political or revolutionary aspirations. Zaccone has a doctorate, which examines the hugely contentious question of so-called *auto resistência* deaths – when police kill people for apparently resisting arrest.

The detective had previously worked with Major Edson, the chief of the UPP. He knew Rocinha well and it didn't take him long to work out what had been going on. Like almost all UPP bosses, Major Edson was a former BOPE commander. He had integrated into the UPP team a number of ex-BOPE officers, who formed the nucleus of a team of extortionists operating on a grand scale. He had turned the UPP into a militia. Everyone had to pay – the gas distributors, the moto taxi drivers and the electricity providers. Perhaps even more disturbing, the traffickers were paying too. The investigation that had resulted in Amarildo's death was called Operation Armed Peace – its target was hidden weapons, not drugs. These had continued to be sold from Rocinha, and according to Zaccone, Edson and his militia team were taking a cut from the profits.

The result of Zaccone's investigation was the arrest of dozens of UPP members, ten of whom were eventually put on trial – including, of course, Major Edson dos Santos. He and his crew were convicted and now face a long spell of imprisonment.

Aside from the legal issues, however, the Amarildo case suggested how difficult it was to sustain the pacification programme. Beltrame was responsible for the security regime, which itself required an immense organisational effort. But he was already complaining that the rest of the government showed precious little inclination to engage with the critical second part of the UPP. This involved the provision of services, and a clear demonstration that the state was not solely interested in getting rid of the weapons but was also concerned with the well-being of residents.

The World Cup in 2014 would be a dry run, but there would be even greater pressure in the run-up to the 2016 Olympics. Unlike the World Cup, which took place all over Brazil, the Olympic Games were being hosted exclusively in Rio de Janeiro. The city and its government could not afford a renewal of violence in the favelas. So they could not afford another Amarildo if they were to start persuading the inhabitants that pacification was worth it.

Although the popularity of President Rousseff's government was draining away, the massive demonstrations during the winter of 2013 were not repeated during football's most prestigious competition a year later, even when, in the first semi-final, Brazil were defeated 7–1 by Germany in one of the greatest shocks in sporting history.

Notwithstanding this ignominy, and despite the embryo of another mega-scandal taking shape at the giant parastatal company Petrobras, President Rousseff secured her re-election for another four years in October 2014.

But her government was running into trouble. After the golden years of presidents Cardoso and Lula, the economy was beginning to falter. The eyelids of Brazil's great sleeping monster, inflation, appeared to flicker as the economy seemed to be heading into recession. Then the astonishing extent of the corruption scandal at Petrobras started spilling out. The public prosecutor estimated that over one billion dollars had been embezzled in a vast scheme keeping happy the most notorious sectors of Brazil's economy and society: political parties, the construction industry and the extractive industry.

As the mood in the country slumped, the grip of the UPPs, especially in the two biggest favelas – Rocinha and Complexo do Alemão – began to slacken. Shootouts between the remaining members of ADA and Red Command on the one hand and the officers of the UPP on the other proliferated.

The costs of the pacification programme were mounting, not merely in terms of cash but in lives as well. In 2012, five UPP police officers died while nine were injured in shootouts. In 2013, three died and 24 were injured, but in 2014, eight died and 84 were injured. The numbers of injuries to traffickers and civilians also reached double figures.

Pacification remains one of the boldest experiments in urban security, but the massive resources it requires have still been deployed in only 37 of some 900 favelas around Rio de Janeiro. As the crisis in Brazil's government deepens, the Petrobras scandal threatens to sweep away both Sergio Cabral and his successor as governor of Rio state, Luiz Fernando Pezão. Who knows whether pacification will survive this challenge. The fundamental issues associated with guns, prohibition and poverty will certainly remain for years to come.

Before he was arrested, Antônio Francisco Bonfim Lopes, Nem of Rocinha, expressed support for Beltrame and his programme of pacification. Since then, he has come to believe that its implementation has been weak and that the policy contains serious risks. From inside the maximum security federal penitentiary in Campo Grande, some 400 kilometres from the spot where Paraguay, Bolivia and Brazil meet, Antônio continues to care deeply about Rocinha and its community. Within the obvious constraints of running a drugs cartel, he worked hard to keep the favela stable in difficult times. The media and some politicians regularly claim that he continues to run ADA and its drug operation from his cell. Significantly, investigators hoped at first to charge him with the crime of issuing orders to the cartel from prison, but these efforts have been dropped because they have been unable to find any concrete evidence. His wife, Danúbia, is also in prison at the time of writing, for alleged involvement in trafficking. Nem expresses no fear about having to spend a long time in jail as long as he is permitted to see his children. He clearly still has money stored away, because he takes financial responsibility for all seven of his offspring. But he is not saying how much he has or where it is.

Nem is no paragon nor is he the devil. He is an intelligent and bright man now approaching his forties. Had he received a decent education, there is no doubt in my mind that he would have been a successful businessman with no criminal profile whatsoever.

Eduarda Lopes, once the little baby whose terrible illness led her father into the drugs trade, is now a vivacious, smart sixteen-year-old. She does well at school and is fully able to comprehend what has happened to her community, her family and her parents. She is a credit to them all and an inspiration for the future. Antônio Francisco Bonfim Lopes sits in a lonely jail but faces his fate with apparent equanimity. 'As long as my children's future is secured, what happens to me is not so important.'

APPENDIX
Main police forces in Rio de Janeiro

There are three main police forces operating in Rio de Janeiro. Two, the civil police (Polícia Civil or PC) and the Military Police (Polícia Militar or PM), are under the jurisdiction of the state of Rio de Janeiro and its governor. The third is the Federal Police (Polícia Federal or PF), controlled by the federal Ministry of Justice in Brasília.

The primary function of the Civil Police is to investigate alleged crimes committed anywhere in the state of Rio de Janeiro. Its work involves a great deal of intelligence- and evidence-gathering. It is also tasked with processing any alleged crimes brought to its attention by the other state-level force, the Military Police. Once officers from the Civil Police have prepared the evidence relating to an alleged crime, they then pass this on to the public prosecutor (Ministério Publico), who will weigh it up and decide whether to launch court proceedings.

The investigative character of the Civil Police does not mean that it is merely desk-bound. If sanctioned by a judge, it has the right to mount raids against private homes or businesses that it suspects of harbouring evidence of criminal activity.

The Civil Police also has a special forces battalion, usually identified by the acronym CORE (Coordenadoria de Recursos Especias – Coordination of Special Resources), which was formed in 1969 during the 21-year-long military dictatorship. This elite squad is deployed when there is a danger of serious armed confrontation. The Civil Police also has a helicopter unit, which is frequently mobilised during operations or unrest in Rio's favelas.

The Secretary for Public Security of Rio state is the minister responsible for both the Civil Police and the Military Police.

The Military Police is Rio state's operational police force, deployed on the streets with the task of maintaining public order. While in theory an auxiliary unit of the Brazilian military, reflected in the structure and designation of rank, the Military Police is under civilian control.

The Military Police has the right to arrest citizens suspected of engaging in criminal activity, but it is obliged to hand over the investigation of alleged crimes to the Civil Police. The rivalry and animus between the two forces is well documented, and is regarded as one of the chief causes of dysfunction in the policing of the state. José Mariano Beltrame, Secretary of State at the time of writing, identified this as a priority on taking office. Certain progress in coordinating the activities of the two forces has been made, but there is still a long way to go.

The Military Police of Rio has a mixed reputation. Although it is proud of its origins as the country's oldest force, tracing its history back to the royal guard of the early nineteenth century, nowadays salaries are low, making many members susceptible to bribery and corruption. A culture of violence and, in some instances, arbitrary killings has led to elevated levels of tension between the force and the residents of favelas in particular. In 2012, the United Nations Committee on Human Rights demanded the dismantling of the Military Police across Brazil in order to counter what some members deemed unacceptable levels of 'extra-judicial killings'.

Among the most controversial aspects of the Military Police are the role and methods of its elite squad, BOPE (Batalhão de Operações

Policiais Especiais – Battalion of Police Special Operations), which, like its counterpart in the Civil Police, was created during the dictatorship. The Military Police also boasts specialist motorcycle, dog and riot squads.

The Federal Police has its headquarters in Brasília and answers to the Ministry of Justice in the federal government. Its primary function is to investigate high-level criminality transcending the borders of Brazil's 26 states and one federal district (Brasília and environs). This means that drug trafficking is a key area of investigation for the Federal Police. Recently it has also been cracking down on large-scale political and economic corruption.

It is harder to pass the exams to be accepted into the Federal Police than it is to enter the state-level police forces. Pay is higher across the board. The Federal Police, which has a similar function to that of the FBI in the United States, also traces its origins to the early nineteenth century, when the Portuguese king and court moved to Rio de Janeiro to escape Napoleon's assault on Lisbon. It was founded in its most recent incarnation in 1944 under the corporatist dictatorship of Getúlio Vargas.

GLOSSARY

alemão	enemy
asfalto	asphalt
assistencialismo	handouts
auto resistência	death while resisting arrest
baile funk	funk ball, rave
balsa	raft housing pumping equipment
bandeirante	pioneer
bandido	gangster
bolsa família	family purse, grant
braço direito	right arm (senior counsellor to the Don)
branco	white
camarote	VIP marquee
cangaceiro	bandit from north-eastern Brazil (hist.)
carioca	native of Rio de Janeiro
churrasco	barbecue
coronelismo	political system based on strong man and patronage
cracolândia	arcas where crack is smoked
cupola	ruling council (pertaining to mafia and other organised crime groups)
currutela	mining settlement, also temporary brothel in settlement
disque denúncia	anonymous tip-off hotline
Dono do Morro	Don of the Hill
endolaçao	retail drug packaging
estica	stretch point, outpost
favela	slum
fiel	loyalist (senior counsellor to the Don; see also *braço direito*)
forró	dance party

garimpeiro	member of mining community
garimpo	open-cast mine
gaúcho	resident of the South American pampas
jeitinho	form of everyday corruption
laje	flat concrete terrace
loló	chloroform-based narcotic
maconha	marijuana
matuto	freelance drug mule
morro	hill
nordestino	native of the north-east of Brazil
olheiro	lookout
pacificação	pacification
pasta base	coca paste
pastel	Brazilian pasty
paulista	native of São Paulo
pó	cocaine powder
preto	black
saudade	nostalgic longing
senhor	sir
sertão	semi-desert area of north-eastern Brazil
telenovela	soap opera
vagabundo	someone involved in the drug trade/gangster
vapores	delivery men
vinho da Jurema	hallucinogenic drink

LIST OF ILLUSTRATIONS

Rocinha from Pedra da Gávea © Ivan Gouveia
Rocinha from the Barra Lagoa highway © Ivan Gouveia
The S-bend © Ivan Gouveia
Antônio as a child, reproduced courtesy of the family
Dona Irene, reproduced courtesy of the family
Gerardo Citó Lopes, reproduced courtesy of the family
Antônio and Danubia, reproduced courtesy of the family
Eduarda and Vanessa, reproduced courtesy of the family
Antônio and Fernandinha, reproduced courtesy of the family
Simone and Antônio with their children, reproduced courtesy of the
    family
The wanted poster of ADA
Dênis of Rocinha, divulgação/24.06.1995, from O Globo
Rocinha bandidos © Mirian Fichtner/Arquivo O Globo
The funeral of Lulu © Ricardo Leoni/15.04.2004/Arquivo O Globo
The arrest of Joca © O Globo
The trial of Dudu © Michel Filho/19.01.2005/Arquivo O Globo
The funeral of Bem-te-vi © Ricardo Leoni/29.10.2005/Arquivo O
    Globo
The storming of the Hotel Intercontinental, photos provided courtesy
    of the Polícia Civil, Rio de Janeiro

The hostage-takers © Cléber Jünior/21.08.2010/Agência O Globo

Bárbara Lomba, Reinaldo Leal and Alexandre Estalita © Ivan Gouveia

José Mariano Beltrame and BOPE © Fernando Lemos/VejaRio/Abril Comunicações S/A

Wanted poster of Nem

The Maximum Security Federal Penitentiary at Campo Grande © Simon Nogueira/Campo Grande News

ACKNOWLEDGEMENTS

t is impossible to write a book like this without relying on the assistance and support of many people. In addition, there are several people whom I would like to thank but who would prefer not to be mentioned here.

First and foremost, I wish to offer my sincere gratitude to Antônio Francisco Bonfim Lopes, Nem of Rocinha. This book could not have been written without his cooperation. I must stress, however, that although he allowed me to interview him for a total of 28 hours in prison, he requested almost no control over the information he offered me. All my interviews with him were transcribed and he only required that any direct quotes from him be checked. At no point did he attempt to influence who else I might interview for this book and he was aware that I would be talking to his friends, family, enemies, to the police, senior politicians and journalists. He made it clear that there was information which he was obliged to hold back because he is still awaiting trial for some of the offences with which he is charged. Wherever I was able, I checked Antônio's assertions against documentary evidence and other witnesses to the events he was describing.

Antônio's family has been equally accommodating from the very beginning of this project. Thanks in particular go to Dona Irene,

Vanessa dos Santos Benevides, Antônio Carlos Moreira da Silva, Simone da Silva and Eduarda Benevides Lopes.

The other interviewees I wish to thank personally are Bárbara Lomba, Alexandre Estelita and Reinaldo Leal whose patience and charm are only matched by their exceptional ability as police officers and their deep understanding of Rocinha and its drugs economy. Equally I would like to thank Otávio and Renata for sharing their unique insights and experience with me. Unless indicated in the text as coming from another source, all the quotes in the book come from interviews undertaken by myself.

Emily Sasson Cohen has been engaged with the research from the start of the project and has demonstrated infinite patience in managing my endless demands. She has had a profound influence on the substance of this book and has been an invaluable support.

The same should be said for Cecília Olliveira who joined the project halfway through and who has demonstrated an unrivalled acquaintance with Rio's underground and police cultures.

Robert Muggah and Ilona Carvalho Szabó offered me food, shelter and emotional support beyond what anyone might reasonably expect. I cannot imagine having completed this book without their help.

Pedro Henrique de Cristo was the first to introduce me to Complexo do Alemão and Vidigal, affording me a quick and effective lesson in negotiating the favelas. I am most grateful to him.

I felt I could not write about any aspect of Brazil without at least having made a stab at learning Portuguese. I have to thank two people in particular for all the effort they put in as I struggled with this deceptively difficult language. In New York, Patrícia Vitorazzi put up with my initial efforts with considerable humour and has been a great help ever since. In Rio, Ana de Andrada conferred much-needed rigour on my attempts to grasp the intricacies of the subjunctive mood.

Notwithstanding their help, at times I needed the guidance of two terrific interpreters, Paulo Eduardo Leite and Ivan Gouveia, who also provided excellent company.

Ana Pas played a crucial role by transcribing almost all the interviews I recorded. She did so swiftly, accurately and at times offering important cultural context.

Without the assistance of Gil Alessi and Clara Dias, this book could never have happened in the first place. They opened the door – thank you.

I would also like to thank the many people I got to know in Rocinha and offer special thanks to Dona Neusa and Obi of the Rocinha Guest House for the hospitality they showed me during my extended stay in the community.

The Director and staff at the Federal Penitentiary in Campo Grande were exemplary in the assistance they afforded me and in that context I would also like to thank Luiz Battaglin for his help in arranging my visits there.

My conversation with Professor Peter Beverley at Oxford University was especially important in verifying all the facts about Langerhans Cell Histiocytosis.

I also wish to thank Katherine Ailes, Ignacio Cano, Emmeline Francis, Paddy Glenny, Elena Lazarou, Beth McLoughlin, Kai Laufen, Julia Michaels, Felipe Milanez, Thomas Milz, Renato Pereira, João Moreira Salles, Paula Sandrin, Regine Schönenberg, Tony Smith, Rane Souza, Branca Vianna, Kelly Wachowicz, Richard Wallstein and Lee Weingast for their important assistance and friendship.

I have been blessed with editors of the highest quality in writing this book and I wish to offer particular thanks to Stuart Williams at The Bodley Head in London. As ever Dan Frank at Knopf in New York and Sarah MacLachlan at Anansi in Toronto have offered critical advice and support at every stage. My thanks also to Michael Carlisle in New York.

ACKNOWLEDGEMENTS

My relationship with my Brazilian publishers, Companhia das Letras, has been crucial from the outset of this project. Many thanks to Luiz Schwarcz, Otávio Marques da Costa and Flávio Mauro.

Clare Conville has gone far beyond her role as my agent. Time and again, when I felt as though I might not be able to see this book through to the end, she has been there to ensure I didn't fall.

This was never more the case than halfway through researching this book, when I lost my daughter, Sasha. Completing the task under these circumstances proved especially difficult. I was able to thanks in the largest part to my family, especially my sons Miljan and Callum and their cousin, Millie Radovic. Above all, I need to thank my wife and greatest support, Kirsty, who was able to shine a light when I fell into the darkest place.

NOTES

I PROTAGONIST

1. His full name is actually Antônio Carlos, but to avoid confusion with Antônio (Francisco) I will simply call him Carlos. To make matters even more confusing, they also have an uncle called Antônio.
2. *Os Sertões* was later adapted into another novel, *The War at the End of the World*, by the Peruvian novelista Maria Vargas Llosa.
3. In the song 'Estação Derradeira'.
4. It was later renamed the Zuzu Angel Tunnel, in honour of the Brazilian-American fashion designer, whose son was murdered under the dictatorship. Many believe that her death in a car crash in 1976 was no coincidence, as she had been very effective in the US in highlighting the crimes of the dictatorship.
5. Carlos Costa, *Rocinha Em Off* (São Paulo, 2012), p.17.
6. *Angu com bofe.*
7. One of the most famous open-cast garimpos, Serra Pelada, in the Amazonian state of Para, developed in the 1980s. Sebastião Salgado's photographs reflect the Dantesque atmosphere, which was later reimagined in riveting detail by the director Heitor Dhalia in an eponymous film from 2013. The film includes a fabulously vivid re-creation of a currutela during the gold rush.
8. Quoted in Christian Geffray, 'Social, Economic and Political Impacts of Drug Trafficking in the State of Rondônia, in the Brazilian Amazon', in *Globalisation, Drugs and Criminalisation*, ed. Christian Geffray, Guilhem Fabre and Michel Schiray (Paris, 2003), p.34.
9. See Part 2, Chapter 4.
10. See Part 2, Chapter 4.

11. João Trajano Sento-Sé, Ignácio Cano and Andreia Marinho, *Efeitos humanitários dos conflitos entre facções do tráfico de drogas numa comunidade do Rio de Janeiro* (Rio de Janeiro, 2006), pp.5–6.
12. William da Silva Lima, *Quatrocentos contra Um* (São Paulo, 1989), p.39.
13. In favela graffiti it is sometimes referred to as CV-RL, the RL standing for Rogério Lemgruber, a man revered as CV's founder.
14. In the 1820s, during the early years of Brazil's independence, the royal government appointed Justices of the Peace, elected by a narrow franchise, as the primary political arbiters of a region. Many quickly used their power to establish corrupt fiefdoms in their territory. Later that century, the strong men were permitted to purchase a military rank, the most senior being colonel, or *coronel*.
15. Interview with Carlos Costa, 14 April 2014.
16. Carlos Costa, *Rocinha Em Off* (São Paulo, 2012), p.30.
17. *O Globo*, 19 July 1987, p.26.
18. Michael Reid, *Brazil: The Troubled Rise of a Global Power* (London, 2014), p.118.
19. Eliza Ackerman, 'Guns R Us', *The Miami New Times*, 7 September 1995.
20. Interview with Regine Schönenberg.
21. Alba Zaluar, 'Crime, medo e política', in *Um século de Favela*, ed. Alba Zaluar and Marcos Alvito (Rio de Janeiro, 1998), p.213. The figures for the city of Rio look positively encouraging when set against those for its urban hinterland, Baixada Fluminense, where the number of deaths in 1990 reached almost 100 per 100,000 inhabitants.
22. Patrick S. Rivero, 'O Mercado Ilegal de Armas de Fogo na Cidade do Rio de Janeiro', in *Brasil: As Armas e as vítimas*, ed. Rubem César Fernandes (Rio, 2005), p.202.

II HUBRIS

1. Quoted in *Violência x Violência: Violações aos Direitos Humanos e Criminalidade no Rio de Janeiro* (Washington/Rio, 1996), p.1: http://www.dhnet.org.br/dados/relatorios/dh/br/hrw/hrwrio.htm
2. A Gol. The Brazilian-manufactured VW looks like a cross between a Golf and a Polo, but with fewer frills.
3. These events are described in fascinating detail in Zuenir Ventura's seminal book about Vigário Geral and its aftermath, *Cidade Partida*,

The Broken City (São Paolo, 1994). The most important NGO to emerge after Vigário Geral, Viva Rio, continues to do outstanding work not just in Rio but in several other parts of the world.

4. Among the most remarkable examples is Pastor Jonny, whose story is told in *Dancing with the* Devil (2009), Jon Blair's exceptionally illuminating documentary about trafficking, which focuses on a favela controlled by the Pure Third Command (for details of this organisation, see later in this chapter).

5. Or Orlando the Footballer; real name Orlando da Conceição.

6. Real name Ernaldo Pinto de Medeiros.

7. Interview with Marina Magessi, November 2014. The superb film *Elite Squad* includes a scene depicting a microwave.

8. Julio Jacobo Waiselfisz, *Mapa da Violência 2012: Os novos padrões da violência homicida no Brasil* (São Paulo, 2013), p.183.

9. Flag-bearers.

10. See Part I, Chapter 3.

11. Interview with the author, 1 June 2014.

12. *Istoé*, 21 April 2004. The think tank was the Getúlio Vargas Foundation.

13. Her name has been changed at her request.

14. See Part I, Chapter 3.

15. Interview with Carlos Costa, May 2014.

16. Much later, those responsible, including the state governor, would apologise for having branded the innocent boys drug dealers.

17. In 2002, there was a coup within the Third Command and a new leadership emerged, renaming the cartel the Pure Third Command. The Third Command ceased to exist.

18. A *Cidade Partida* (*The Divided City*) was the title of a book by Zuenir Ventura, one of Brazil's finest journalists, which examined perhaps the most notorious massacre of favela residents by the police in the early 1990s.

19. In Brazilian Portuguese, the word *bandido* does not carry quite the same pejorative weight as 'gangster' does in English. Its function is sometimes but not always more descriptive than disapproving.

20. The word *alemão*, literally 'German', came to mean 'enemy' during the final three years of WWII, when Brazil became the only South American country to contribute troops to the Allied cause. The usage has stuck in the argot of drug traffickers in Rio's favelas.

21. Rio has four football teams: Flamengo, Fluminense, Botafogo and Vasco.

22. Sebastião José Filho, then president of the Barcelos residents' association, in *Correio do Brasil*, 29 October 2005.

23. This is not the soldier's real name. He requested that his identity remain undisclosed.

III NEMESIS

1. The respective capitals of Pernambuco, Fortaleza and Alagoas states.

2. The use of first names or nicknames (and in Cardoso's case his initials), even for those in the most august positions, is endemic in Brazil, and is never regarded as a sign of disrespect.

3. Mac Margolis, 'Soaps Clean Up', in *Latin Trade* 5, no. 4 (Miami, 1997).

4. Literally a funk ball, the closest equivalent would probably be a rave in Western Europe or Asia, although Brazilian partying has an entirely unique tropical atmosphere.

5. Indicating Rua Um, Joca's fiefdom.

6. The little way.

7. A chloroform-based narcotic that is inhaled.

8. Orkut was Google's forerunner of Facebook, a social media network that became immensely popular in Brazil. With so many subscribers migrating to Facebook, Google closed Orkut in 2014, but during the first decade of this century, it reigned supreme in Brazil.

9. Joca left Rocinha just two months after Operation Service Provider began, and so Estelita and Leal were able to follow the events leading to his expulsion by listening to the discussions of Nem's senior management, above all Beiço and Juca Terror.

10. José Mariano Beltrame, *Todo Dia É Segunda-Feira* (Rio de Janeiro, 2014), p.55. Most of the information about Beltrame comes from his autobiography or from the two interviews I conducted with him in 2013 and 2014.

11. Ibid., p.48.

12. Ibid., p.49.

13. BBC report, 28 December 2006: http://news.bbc.co.uk/1/hi/world/americas/6214299.stm

14. Ironically, levels of violence were steadily falling. Perception was the key.

15. Instituto de Seguranca Pública, Rio de Janerio, 2007.
16. Master, one of his most popular nicknames.
17. See Part II, Chapter 4.
18. Elected as Cabral's successor as governor in October 2014.
19. The same raid during which the PC removed Danúbia's photo album, which then mysteriously found its way to Leslie Leitão.

IV CATHARSIS

1. I interviewed the two agents at length but on the strict condition of anonymity. Nem also confirmed that these meetings took place.
2. See Part II, Chapter 1.

EPILOGUE

1. Named not after the world-famous architect of Brasília's government district but after a military engineer from the early twentieth century.
2. See Part II, Chapter 3.
3. Part of Torres's story is told in Jon Blair's excellent documentary movie, Dancing with the Devil (2009).
4. Ignácio Cano, Doriam Borges and Eduardo Ribeiro, Os Donos do Morro: Uma avaliação exploratória do impacto das Unidades de Polícia Pacificadora (UPPs) no Rio de Janeiro (Rio, 2012), p.35.

INDEX